Beloved:

My friend and colleague Dr. Therman Evans once told me, "If you behaved yourself into a situation, you must behave yourself out of it!" A devotion is a behaviour in service to love, truth, and God that will create powerful changes in the circumstances of your life that have held you down and back *until today!*

Whatever has been going on in your mind, your life, or your heart can stop – *right now*, if that is *truly* what you desire. However, you must be willing to "do a new thing." You must spend a little time, each day, in *devotion* to the truth about yourself and the truth about life. You must *make a conscious approach* to what you think and how you feel about what you do. Devotion will clear up misconceptions that may have obscured your vision of life *until today!*

A *devotion* is a divine action. Its profound dedication demonstrates the desire to be in service to God. Since it is God's desire for you to be happy, any time spent in devotion will be beneficial. Your devotion, as a demonstration of your willingness to embrace new concepts, will ultimately result in your happiness. When you are actively, willingly devoted to seeking a "good thing," the Divine Intelligence of life will guide, support, and reward you. I am excited! It is exciting to be alive in a time when people are actively, willingly, and devotedly seeking ways to be of greater service and create more love in our collective experience.

I can hardly wait to see the good, the joy, and the peace that we can create. I am so grateful to be in support of and of service to you as you undertake this journey. Because I know that "where two or more are gathered" the Spirit of good is present, I believe that the things upon which we focus our hearts and minds will reap bountiful results. So here's to your personal strength and your peace of mind, through the elimination of all things that hindered or denied our collective power and greatness – *Until Today!*

Be Blessed!   *Iyanla*

Other books by Iyanla Vanzant

Acts of Faith

The Value in the Valley

Faith in the Valley

One Day My Soul Just Opened Up

In the Meantime

Don't Give It Away!

Yesterday, I Cried

Until Today!

DAILY DEVOTIONS FOR

SPIRITUAL GROWTH AND

PEACE OF MIND

Iyanla Vanzant

POCKET
BOOKS

LONDON • SYDNEY • NEW YORK • TOKYO • SINGAPORE • TORONTO

First published in the USA by Simon & Schuster Inc, 2000
First published in Great Britain by Simon & Schuster UK Ltd, 2001
This edition first published by Pocket, 2001
An imprint of Simon & Schuster UK Ltd
A Viacom Company

1 3 5 7 9 10 8 6 4 2

Simon & Schuster UK Ltd
Africa House
64-78 Kingsway
London WC2B 6AH

Simon & Schuster Australia
Sydney

A CIP catalogue record for this book is available from the British Library

ISBN 0-671-03766-8

Printed and bound in Great Britain by
Omnia Books Limited, Glasgow

ACKNOWLEDGMENTS

I am humbly grateful that I have been entrusted with and assigned the awesome task of *re-minding* God's children of how divine we are. I have learned, step-by-step, how to stop expecting the worst; to stop trying to live up to the expectations of others; to listen to my heart; and most of all, that I really am okay right now. I admit, I have not always been a good student. Many times, I did not do my homework, tried to cheat on a test, copied from someone else's life or showed up late or unprepared—sometimes, both! I acknowledge that, more often than not, I learned my lessons kicking and screaming, denying and resisting. Many days, I had to sit in the corner. Many times, I have had to repeat a class. I will be the first to admit that my blessings, brilliance and good fortune rest squarely on the shoulders of my teachers. To each of you, for your patience, faith and refusal to give up on me, I am humbly grateful:

To my Children and Wisdom Council, Damon, Alex, Gemmia and Nisa, I want to be a better listener!

To my grandchildren, Oluwa, Niamoja, Adesola and Asole, you are my sunshine!

My husband and best friend, Adeyemi Bandele, just five more miles! You drive!

My best friend and spiritual sister, Shaheerah Stephens, ain't no mountain high enough!

My prayer partners who continually hold me in the light, Raina Bundy, Sarah Porter, Rev. Chester Berryhill and Vivian Berryhill, I just can't tell it all!

The Little People: Simone, Devon, Damali, you always have the kisses when I need them!

My big brothers, Rev. Jeremiah Wright and Rev. Willie Wilson, your genius is showing!

My ever-ready assistant, Bernadette Griggs, I owe you!

My patient editor, Trish Todd, I'm not making any more promises!

My very own Maestro, Kenneth L. Browning, just an old-fashioned love song!

To *Miss Daisy*, Erika Conner, for her persistent diligence toward stepping into her "Bigness."

And to all those whose work and spirit have taught me how to *Be*:

Oprah Winfrey, Susan Taylor, Paul Ferinni, Marianne Williamson, John Roger, Andrew Weil, Neale Donald Walsh, Norm Frye, Ron Hulnick, Mary Hulnick, Sharon Heyward, Patti Webster, Donald Lawrence, L. Barrett Tyson, Louis and Kevin Hutt, Vivian and Ray Chew, the family at Harmony Records, the students of the University of Santa Monica, Rev. Floyd Flake, Rev. June Juliette Gatlin, the *Angels of Inner Visions*: Almasi, Adara, Ahmed, Candance, Cochise, Danni, Doyle, Ebun, James, Janet, Judith, Rev. John, Larcenia, LaTonya, LaQuita, Lucille, Lydia, Maia, Maxine, Muhsinah, Sherman, Viviana, Yawfah and to all the others who have sent prayers and blessings my way. Finally, a very special thank you to my sister-mother, friend and prayer warrior, Helen Jones, *for you know what!*

This book is dedicated to my big sister
Her Royal Highness Leola Iyalu Oredola Opeodu; and
Edna Hassell and Grady Owens,
whose spirits live in my heart forever.
And to:
Those on the journey to truth and wholeness;
those who started the journey
but found a reason to stop;
those who want to begin the journey but
don't know how to start;
those who have questions about the journey
that they are afraid to ask;
those whose spirits are willing to take the journey
but whose flesh has *issues;*
those who have taken the journey
and are willing to do it again.
To us all, may our paths be lit with God's love.

CONTENTS

INTRODUCTION:
There's Always More!

If by chance no one has told you that they love you today, I would be honored to be the first to say, I love you today! I love you because you are and have been so willing to grow. And my how you have grown! You've grown from struggling to searching. From trying to do to learning how to do. You've grown from fear to having faith, to demonstrating your courage. You have grown in many ways, consistently demonstrating your willingness and courage to take the next step—the step toward the profound and divine wisdom buried within yourself. The step toward knowing more about yourself. This is exactly why I love you—you are so profoundly divine.

Growth is a very profound experience. It can be beautiful and ugly, empowering and confining, thought-provoking and mind-boggling, pleasant and unpleasant, all at the same time. Just when you think you've got it, life seems to say, "Well, now take this!" And you do. Then, the minute you are ready to throw your hands up, give up or beat up on yourself for doing the same thing in the same way and ending up in the same place again, you realize you haven't done so badly after all. You know you have grown when you can meet a challenge, an obstacle or a difficulty without totally losing it. Somehow, someway in the growth process, you have come upon the understanding that the more you grow, the more you know, the more you are encouraged to grow and know.

There is more of you waiting to unfold. There is more about the world you desire to understand. There are more people coming into your life, and you are gaining more knowledge about yourself through your experiences with them. There is so much more, so much new information coming your way that you are continually being reminded that you owe it to yourself to do all you can to prepare yourself to receive these new insights. There is also so much more wealth, well-being, peace and joy waiting for you, and, because I love you, I want the very best for you. Offering you this book is a demonstration of my support as you prepare for the work and blessings that are to come.

I want to tell you a story. You know I always have to tell at least one story, and this is it. In preparing for an upcoming event, I gave my team what I thought was a simple assignment. You see, you cannot teach what you have not experienced. I asked each person, each potential teacher, to write a five-hundred-word description of themselves, using the first person, in the present tense. I had faith that these powerful and loving individuals, with whom I have worked for over seven years, would take the task in stride. What we learned in the process was profoundly healing for us all.

As we sat to review each response, my team members shared with me the overwhelming feelings, even fears, they had experienced while completing the assignment. I know from experience that examining yourself, what you do and how you feel, can be one of the most challenging and frightening things you will ever face in life. To then share that information with others is the stuff that fried brain matter is made of. Yet my team members understood that the journey into self-acceptance and self-love must begin with self-examination. We all also understood that until you take the journey of self-reflection, it is almost impossible to grow or learn in life.

Each response we shared that evening was deeply moving and radically honest. More important, we all heard a bit of ourselves in each response. One response stood out. It captured what we all knew but lacked the requisite courage or insight to say. I share that response with you and pray that it will prepare you, as it has prepared us, to really examine how we do, what we do.

The Landscape of Myself

As I pondered my own response to this assignment, I came to the realization that there are three very different aspects of myself that I could describe. The question then became which aspect do I describe? Which part and how much of myself do I choose to reveal? Life is so wonderful! It is always offering to us the opportunity to get it together. So I decided to come clean and, as honestly as possible, describe all three "selves" that I have now come to know. These selves make up the landscape of me that I am working to transform. That I am devoted to transforming.

The landscape of me varies in its appearance depending on who you are, where you stand in my life and how I choose to present myself. First, there is the self that usually appears in discussions like these. The self that I want others to see. This is the self of majestic mountain peaks and verdant meadows. This is the self of strength and power. This is the self of educational and career accomplishments, leadership skills and the demonstrated commitment to service. This is the public self, the one I struggle to hold on to.

Then there is the self that does not want to be revealed. It wants to hide. This is the landscape of weaknesses. There are many valleys and few peaks in this self. This self encompasses my secret thoughts and beliefs about who I am. This is the self that I do not share with others. This is the self I travel with in times of darkness, times of fear, through experiences of worthlessness and hopelessness. Yet I have come to recognize that this self guides me to the places of the truest teachings, learning and growth.

In the landscape of this self, the topography includes places like the "swamp of self-deception," overflowing with the waters of dishonesty, steaming with the fog of selfishness and reeking with the stench of egotism. Venomous snakes of procrastination, laziness and lack of self-discipline breed here freely. Quite often they threaten to eat me alive.

Nearby lies the "valley of self-doubt." This valley is littered with huge boulders of fear, formed from anxiety about failing, held in place by the pebbles of insecurity. The ground is dry and parched from long droughts of shame and guilt. Nothing grows in this valley. It is littered with weeds of limitation and lack.

The desert of anger surrounds the valley of self-doubt. It is heated by the unrelenting sun of self-hatred and resentment that give rise to the hot winds of resistance, disobedience, competitiveness and arrogance. These winds create sandstorms of jealousy, meanness and envy.

There are places in this landscape that cannot be seen by the viewer. These are the underground caverns and caves of "not good enough" and "not worthy of good" that run beneath the swamps and the valleys and the desert. These caverns underlie all of the self-destructive, nonproductive scenes. It is only recently that I discovered just how deeply these caverns and caves extend into my life. It is on this foundation I have stood most of my life. Until today!

During this process, I found it extremely interesting that while I am able to identify the weaknesses in such great detail, I am challenged in identifying the strengths. There is, however, a third realm in the landscape of self. It is not new, but it is a place I am just beginning to know and accept. This third landscape is a place of beautiful, inspiring scenery, scenes of dreams and aspirations. It feels new to me because I have wallowed in the swamp of self-deception for far too long, visited the cave of not good enough too often—so often, in fact, that I lost sight of my right to dream dreams and aspire to the goals that I had created for myself.

I now stand boldly in this new land, dreaming joy-filled dreams and devoted to their realization. I now see lush, sunlit hillside terraces of hope; sandy white beaches of confidence; floral gardens of self-love and mountains of faith in my ability to have it all. In this new place of dreams, I am singing and dancing with delight; visiting breath-taking sites of peace, as I walk on the abundantly wealthy earth, talking to God in the silence. I now see myself learning new things, teaching new things, creating objects of beauty, loving others and being loved passionately. Most of all I see myself in a landscape of happiness. I am just as I am, and as I become, I am.

In the landscape of dreams there is the horizon of aspiration. The aspirations are becoming clearer in this new third self. I see myself as a teacher not of the former self, but of a new, true Self. I am a teacher willing to support others in their quest to connect with God. As I learn and teach myself, I will share with others. I will teach the process that is written in the curriculum guide of the heart, as I have learned it by walking through the desert, the swamp, the cave, coming to a place of rest on the beach of devotion, in the gardens of dreams.

Isn't it amazing that we go to so many dark places to find the light we've always had? I ran from myself only to find myself through seeking to help others. I see myself with more clarity now, and I am devoted to use what God gave me in order to achieve what I desire and offer myself to the greater good of the planet. To this I am devoted.

Devotion as a Way of Life

Time spent in devotion offers divine revelations. Through this assignment, we all learned that our devotion to doing a specific thing is not about making things happen the way we want them to happen. Devotion requires a *willingness, openness* and *readiness* to embrace the truth. It is a process of opening yourself to receive what already is. God's goodness and love already exist. God's love leads us to the truth. The minute we believe that we know it all, have it all figured out, or that something about life does not apply to us, we cannot know the truth. When we devote time to knowing the truth, all else that we need has a way of finding us.

Devotion, as offered in this book, is not a New Age trick through which you can impose your will on God, the universe, or those around you. Devotion is the reverent, personal act of surrendering your will to Divine will. The devotions in this book will help you open your mind and spirit and become one with all the good that God has in store for you. We often work so hard trying *to get* the things we want that we miss the fact that it is the landscape of our inner world that stands between us and true happiness. When we become devoted to healing our inner world, loving and honoring ourselves and using that love as the standard by which we interact with others, all the riches of this life will fall into our laps. That is what the journey of this book is about: learning to love and honor yourself from the inside to the outside. More than this, our Creator has not asked of us.

How to Use This Book

Until Today! is divided into twelve sections. Each section, representing one month of devotion, focuses on a spiritual principle that will support you in examining, exploring and healing the landscape of your inner thoughts and feelings. These principles are universal concepts. They are presented in an order that will guide you, step-by-step, to a deeper level of awareness of yourself and the process of life.

Each day you will read a passage. At the end of each day's passage, an old way of thinking is presented. It is presented as the *Until Today!* statement. This statement represents the old sentiments, resentments, beliefs, decisions, agreements, judgments and ideas that may have become habitual. Often, these are the very things that prevent us from moving into a greater experience of life and a fuller expression of our true Self.

Following the *Until Today!* statement will be a prescription for a new approach, a new way of thinking. It is presented as the *Just for today* statement. Your task on this journey is to *remember the new way* and commit yourself to the practice of it throughout the day. The practice of a new way of being will be your devotion.

Some devotions require only a thought. Thoughts become the experiences you live. Releasing old thought patterns clears the way for new patterns of living. Hold the *Just for today* thought in your mind, and support it by repeating the affirmation offered at the bottom of each page as often as you can during the day. As simple as it may sound, just one day of pure devotion is enough to set a pattern in motion.

Other daily devotions will require action. You will be asked to do a particular thing in a particular way as a means of putting the new thought into action. A dear friend and colleague of mine, Dr. Therman Evans, teaches us, "If you behaved yourself into a situation, you must behave yourself out of it!" Daily devotions announce to the universe your clear intention to do better, be better and experience the better things in life. One day at a time, your devotions will liberate you. Just imagine! One day at a time, one step at a time, you can take your walk of faith to the heights of your greatest potential. And you know what? Regardless of where you are, or what your current experience may be, there is always more. I can hardly wait to hear about all the good things that you will experience as a result of daily devotions.

Let me be very clear, I am in no way saying that these devotions should replace your daily devotions to God. As a matter of fact, since every devotion in this book is based on a spiritual principle, you can incorporate the work you will do through this book with whatever your religious or spiritual practices may be. This book is a companion, a signpost. It is not meant to convert you to anything you do not choose to be. You will also find that I use the words God, Spirit and Universe, interchangeably. That is because I want everyone to feel comfortable. You are, as always, free to substitute the word representing whatever sacred Being you are comfortable calling upon. Whatever you choose for yourself, if you are devoted to it, you will be blessed.

You are such a blessing to me! Yes! You are the blessing! The love, support and enthusiasm with which you have received all of my work has given me a renewed sense of purpose. You have shared with me. You have trusted me. You have encouraged me to dig a little deeper, come up with a little more, give what I find with a new, fresh insight. You keep me on my toes, and for this I am so very grateful. On this leg of our journey, I want to return the favor. I want you to dig a little deeper. I want you to study a little harder. I want you to devote a little more time to the life assignment of discovering your true Self, your God Self, celebrating life and doing what brings you joy. I pray that *Until Today!* will bless you with the information, principles and guidance you need to such a degree that it surpasses your wildest imaginings. *In the meantime,* while you are growing, know that I walk this path with you, not as a leader, but as a companion and friend.

I thank you!

I salute you!

I honor your greatness!

Iyanla

JANUARY

LIFE

If there is a day you have eaten until
you were full;
if there is a time of joy you can recall;
if you have escaped even once the
clutches of death;
if you can remember one or all of the above,
then you have something to be grateful for.

JANUARY 1

Life will work for me when I realize . . .
I must put first things first!

The *Law of First Things* is a mandate for all of our lives. This principle encourages us to acknowledge, accept and embrace God first in all things that we do. First, inquire of God. Then, listen to God. When you hear God, respond. Then, trust God to lead and guide you. If and when we do these things, the *Law of First Things* ensures that God will reward us ten times over.

When you breathe, that's God. When you move, that's God. When you think about where you need to be and what you need to do, that's God giving you the power to take the thought and translate it into action. When you speak, that's God. When you eat, it's God. For without God's love, God's mercy and grace, nothing you consider important would be possible. The truth of the matter is, God *is* first. The *Law of First Things* simply asks that we acknowledge it.

When you take your first breath in the morning, remember it's God who is making it possible. When you swing your feet over the side of the bed, acknowledge God for moving through you as the source of your life. Before you do one thing in the day for yourself or anyone else, thank God for every ability, talent, gift and opportunity that lies within you or before you. As you move through each day, keep God informed about what you are doing and ask that you be guided toward right thought and right action. And don't forget to invite God to participate in all of your activities. As your activities begin to bring you rewards, thank God first. If you make an earnest effort to follow the *Law of First Things,* you will never have to worry about being left out of God's good.

Until today, you may have believed that you needed to go someplace special to find the power, strength and love of your Creator. Just for today, be devoted to remembering, acknowledging, trusting and expressing gratitude to God for being present right where you are.

Today I am devoted to putting God first in all things!

JANUARY 2

Life will work for me when I realize . . . I must make
myself available to life.

The highest form of service you can offer to yourself and God
is to spend time each day in silence. This is time to spend
with your true Self. It is time spent being available to the
Source of your life and the Force behind your life. Time spent
in silence is time spent in contemplation of your purpose in life. It is time
spent to gain clarity and build confidence. It is time spent strengthening
your mind, clearing your heart and fortifying your spirit. Time spent in
silence each day serves the greater *You* and is therefore, time well spent.

The highest form of love you can offer to yourself, to God and to
those you love is to spend time each day calling on the presence of God,
the name of God and the light of God. Time spent calling on God's presence strengthens you. It is time spent in recognition of your dependence
on the Creator and giver of life. Time spent calling on God's name opens
your soul to be filled with the essence, the energy of God. Time spent
calling on the light of God cleanses you. It gives you access to the sweetness of life without the struggle and drama we humans are accustomed
to experiencing.

The highest form of praise you can offer to yourself, to God and to
the world is to spend time each day expressing gratitude. It says to God
that you are aware and appreciative of grace. It says to life that you are
acknowledging its awesome presence in you. It says to yourself that you
are worth the time it takes to be healed. Time spent in silence, contemplation and gratitude is time spent in devotion to a higher calling and a
more loving state of being.

Until today, you may have been trying to squeeze God into the rest
of your daily activities. Just for today, give God a full ten minutes of your
time when you silently call upon God's love, God's name, God's light
and God's presence in your life.

Today I am devoted to spending quality time with God.

JANUARY 3

Life will work for me when I realize . . . I have the
power to walk right! The power to talk right!
And the power to live right!

What is your spiritual plan? Do you have a clear vision about
where you are headed spiritually? Do you know where you
want to be? Do you know how to get there? Do you know
how to achieve the spiritual stamina required to move ahead
in the world? You cannot have one without the other, you know. You
cannot achieve success without spiritual strength. What is spiritual
strength? How do you achieve it? Maintain it? When was the last time
you asked yourself any of these questions? How can you make a spiritual
plan without the answers to these questions?

A spiritual plan is a statement of clear intention about what you desire to experience within yourself and a clear definition of what you must
do to make it happen. A spiritual plan is not only about prayer and meditation, it is about action—what you will and will not do, what you can
and cannot do, in order to achieve your spiritual goal. A spiritual plan
requires you to take an in-depth and honest look at where you are and
make an accurate assessment of how you arrived there. Then you must
determine if this is where you want to be, and if not, what you must
eliminate, or incorporate, in order to move forward. These examina-
tions and resolutions must be made by yourself, with yourself and for
yourself. And if you are serious, you will write it all down.

Until today, you may have believed that your spirit was strong
enough to get you through everything. Just for today be devoted to examining what you are going through and planning how you want to go
through it. Your spirit cannot show you the way until you are clear about
the direction you want to travel. If you want to make your travel worthwhile, you must have a plan.

*Today I am devoted to examining and planning how my
inner world will impact and affect my outer world.*

JANUARY 4

Life will work for me when I realize . . .
trying to prove something to someone is never a valid
reason for doing anything.

Have you ever wondered why, when you are about to do something of great magnitude, people will say, "Break a leg!"? It is a term used in the theater to convey good luck. However, as a student of empowerment, I also know the power of words. Words become conditions you experience on a very real level. Very recently, I heard something that made me a bit more comfortable when someone wishes that I "break a leg."

A line in a song declares, "I've got power shut up in my bones!" "Break a leg" means let your power loose! Stand firmly in your power and do what you have come to do. As a forty-something woman, facing a natural calcium depletion, I had to ask myself, "Are my bones healthy?" For that matter, is my body healthy?

At least once a fiscal quarter, I promise myself that I am going to exercise regularly. Yet when I have the option of taking an elevator or walking up a few flights of the stairs, I admit, I take the ride. I join the gym, but I'm usually too busy or too tired to go. Why should I bend over when the grandchildren are closer to the ground? Why should I lift weights when they are heavy? And why shouldn't my power, my energy, my genius stay shut up in my bones?

If you want to enjoy your power in life, you must have a plan for your physical body. More important, you must follow the plan. There is divine power in our bones that flows with greater effectiveness when the tissues and muscles surrounding the bones are fine-tuned.

Until today, you may have had a great deal of power lying dormant in your bones. Just for today, become devoted to strengthening your physical self. It is the most important step you can take toward realizing the full potential of your divine self.

*Today I am devoted to making and committing to a plan
that will strengthen my physical body.*

JANUARY 5

Life will work for me when I realize . . . every decision
I make is based on every other decision I have made,
which is based on everything that has ever
happened in my life.

Are you paying attention? Are you aware of what you do? Are
you paying attention to the results you get? Are you paying
attention to what you feel? When was the last time you took
stock of what is really going on around you? Are you paying
attention to what you do, or are you just doing what comes naturally?
Habitually?

Are you paying attention to what you say? What you mean? And to
what you expect once you have spoken your mind? Are you paying attention to how you feel when you wake up? What you expect to feel as
you move through the day? Are you paying attention to what happens
based on what you expect? And are you aware of how what you expect
makes you feel? Or how it motivates what you do?

Are you paying attention to how much you smile in any given day?
Or to how long you have been holding back tears? Are you paying attention to whom and what you give your attention? What you expect to
get? And what you actually do get in return for the attention you give?
Are you paying attention to what life is saying to you? Are you paying attention to what your living feels like? Or are you living mindlessly, missing the details of who you are, what you do and how it all makes you
feel?

Until today, you may not have been paying attention to the details
in the moment-by-moment experience of life. Just for today, pay very
close attention to what you are doing and how you are feeling. Write
down every little detail of what you discover. Then you will know to
what and whom you have been giving most of your attention. Then you
will have all that is required to make the necessary changes.

*Today I am devoted to paying attention
to every little detail of my life.*

JANUARY 6

Life will work for me when I realize . . . I will continue
feeling bad until my attitude improves!

Are you having a hard time getting through life or facing a
challenging situation? Are you trying your best, only to find
there is usually something or someone in your way? Perhaps
you should consider these words: "Your external world is an
accurate reflection of your internal state of being." Believe it or not, your
inner life is the cause and the source of everything that manifests around
you. Consequently, your life will always let you know when there is
something "in" you that requires your attention.

There is a life *within you* that requires tender loving care and attention. Your inner life must be cleansed, strengthened and well ordered
(which, by the way, is your "soul" responsibility in life). You are responsible for being the things you desire. For being the way you desire others
to be. It is your responsibility to take the necessary steps to ensure that
what is going on inside of you is in perfect harmony, because everything
you desire will happen through you, not to you!

Be peace! Be joy! Be strength! Be wisdom! Be creative! Be inspiration! Be a delight! Be a helping hand! Be a smile! Be a hug! Be a success!
Be gentle! Be kind! Be hope! Be faith! Be truth! Be trust! Be honor! Be
forgiving! Be patient! Be calm! Be encouragement! Be discipline! Be obedience! Be fun! Be freedom! Be wealth! Be respect! Be fearless! Be a
friend! Be prayer! Be love! Be the miracle! Be the possibility! Be the opportunity! Be the purpose! Be the mission! *Be*-gin within and allow all
the things you know how to be blossom into the truth of who you are.

Until today, you may have been waiting for something to happen
before you could experience something better in your life. Just for today,
be devoted to being all the things you say you want. Do it in faith,
knowing that like draws like!

Today I am devoted to being what I am,
which is all that I want to be!

JANUARY 7

Life will work for me when I realize . . . within me
is the essence of everything I am!

Life produces plants that are exactly like the seeds. The
essence of the seed will always be duplicated in the plant.
The seed from which we have grown is the essence of God.
God is Spirit. You are Spirit. God is good. You are good. At
every twist of life, we doubt, question and, in some cases, deny the
essence of God that does, without any doubt, exist within our being.

The life within you is the very same essence that *is* God. In that
essence, you have the same power, the same wisdom and the same love
that God has. It is the presence of this God essence that is the truth and
the essence of who you are. You also have a body. Chances are, you complain about it. If you consider for just a moment how you feel about and
care for the part of you that you can see, what does that mean about the
part of you that you cannot see? In other words, how much care do you
give to your God Self? How much grooming do you do for your essence?

Your God-essence must be groomed. Not because God needs it, because you do! You must bathe your God-essence in the spiritual waters
of seeing and serving the God-essence in everyone else. You must wrap
your God-essence in a blanket of self-love. Your must sweeten your
God-essence with the perfume of forgiveness. You must feed your God-
essence with hearty helpings of prayer. Every now and then you must
give your God-essence a treat—silence. You must rest your God-essence
on a bed of faith. If you dress your God-essence in spiritual clothing designed by kindness, compassion and humility, it will quickly outgrow all
the limitations of being covered by your humanness.

Until today, you may have focused your energy on changing your
physical being. Just for today, be devoted to the care of your essence. If
you do, something really wonderful and powerful will grow right where
you are standing.

*Today I am devoted to nurturing the seeds of
God's essence in me!*

JANUARY 8

Life will work for me when I realize . . . the "right now" problem could be a "happened long ago" story.

Shhhh! Don't tell that story again! Do not talk about how you were done so wrong by so many bad people. Do not talk about him, her or them unless it will make you feel better right now. Hush! Don't utter another syllable about the pain, the losses that have left you broken, unless you are ready to recover right now. Stop it! Stop dragging yourself back there, reminding yourself of how bad it was for you then unless it has some relevance to what you are doing right now. Each time you think about, talk about, or remember then, you put that energy squarely in the middle of your life right now.

Of course you must acknowledge how you feel about all the things you have experienced. You must not, however, tell the story in a manner that makes you feel bad right now. Tell what you learned! Tell how you have healed! If you look at your story, there is probably a great deal you can use right now to move forward. When, however, you find yourself stuck on the details that break your heart, you are telling the story in the wrong way, for the wrong reasons.

Yes, you must inspect the details of your life in order to accept your share of the responsibility. In fact, each time you tell your story you discover new levels of understanding and forgiveness. When you approach the sordid details of your life from this perspective, you will propel yourself into a higher state of being. When, however, you are telling the story and it makes you feel bad, do not tell that story! Tell a story, any story, that will take into account the wonderful opportunity you have before you to write a new story.

Until today, you may have been telling the story of how bad it used to be. Just for today, rethink your conclusions, pray for understanding, then write a new story that begins where you are right now.

Today I am devoted to laying down the old story and writing a new script that begins with right now!

JANUARY 9

Life will work for me when I realize . . .
the only walls, locked doors and prisons in my life
are the ones that I have built.

Let today be the day that you develop a plan to clear your mind of clutter, congestion and conflict. It is called a *mental health plan*. Free your mind of unproductive, nonessential, potentially hazardous thoughts about yourself, others and your life. This is called *mental health refinement*. Clear out all grudges, lay down all burdens, heal all wounds and settle all debts. This is called *mental health freedom*. You can use this day to abandon the anger, defy the defeat, forgo the fear, get rid of the guilt, shatter the shame that may be clogging your mind. This is called *mental health development*.

Once the channels are cleared you may find that you have more energy to celebrate your creativity, declare your divinity, embrace excellence, validate your own value and become aware of all of your blessings. A clear mind will help you make required changes in your life. A clear mind will change how you see things and people. A clear mind is more valuable than a map. It is like a fine-tuned instrument that leads you to exactly what you are looking for.

You must have a plan to develop and fine-tune your mental health. This plan will help you choose to whom and to what you give your life's energy. You must take the time to think about what you are thinking about. You must filter through the layers of your mind on a daily basis just to make sure that you are not lost in the fog of yesterday. A mental health plan will keep you from getting stuck. A plan gives you direction.

Until today, you may not have had a mental health plan; a plan for the freedom, development and refinement of your mental faculties. Just for today, be devoted to planning how you will open, free and fine-tune your mind to bigger and better things.

Today I am devoted to developing a mental health plan!

JANUARY 10

Life will work for me when I realize . . .
the experience of my faith keeps my faith alive.

You must have faith and experience in order to live life fully. You must have faith that all of the things you expect from life are possible for you. You must have faith that no matter what life brings you, you will be able to handle it. You must have faith that your faith will eventually lead to good experiences.

Experience teaches you that your faith is paying off. Once you have had an experience, *you know* that *you know*. When you know, you become more faithful. Once you have an experience, it makes you want better or different experiences. The difference between faith and experience is this: One you must work on. The other one works on you.

You must work to keep your faith alive. When you are working on faith, it may feel as if you are going against the grain. There may be no evidence that what you believe has any validity. Still, you must move forward faithfully, until you have the experience that will lead you to *knowing*. An experience leaves a mark on your consciousness. An experience will guide your thoughts and your actions. An experience can open your heart to new horizons or close your heart in fear. In the midst of an experience, you must have faith that you will ultimately reap some benefit from what you now know to be true.

It is important to know what experiences to put your faith in. If you have an unpleasant experience, have faith that you will learn something new, useful or productive. When you have a pleasant or productive experience, have faith that you can duplicate the experience and make it better. Have faith that your mind and heart will always be open to bigger, better experiences than those you have already had.

Until today, you may not have realized that your faith and your experiences work hand in hand. Just for today, use your faith to create better experiences. Use your experiences to activate a deeper sense of faith.

Today I am devoted to faithfully seeking to broaden my experiences and to experiencing a deeper faith!

JANUARY 11

Life will work for me when I realize . . .
I have everything I need within me to create everything
I want out there!

What is the difference between joy and happiness? What is the difference between knowing and believing? What is the difference between love and pleasure? Joy, knowing and love are what you feel. Happiness, believing and pleasure are ways you think. The former are all internal experiences. The latter are responses to external events. The former are things over which you have control through the power of your mind. The latter are experiences through which you can be controlled by events and people!

If you are waiting for something to happen that will make you happy, chances are you are killing off your joy. Joy comes through you. Happiness comes to you! If you seek your joy within, you will be happy, no matter what is going on around you. When you know you will be protected, guided and blessed, it is easy to believe in more than what you can see. If you only believe what you can see around you, you may miss the blessings that are right under your nose. If you have and hold love in your heart, you will always know what to do and what to say. If you measure out how much love to give, you will undoubtedly meet people and situations who have a reflective measure of love for you. *Nothing can happen for you in the outside world until you create the energy to attract it to and through your inside world.*

Until today, you may have missed the little differences that could make a big difference in your life. Just for today, be devoted to developing a strong inner life that can create a better outer life. In prayer and meditation ask to experience joy, knowing and love, knowing that once you ask, you will receive!

*Today I am devoted to experiencing joy,
knowing and love!*

JANUARY 12

Life will work for me when I realize . . . when I've done
all I can do, and I cannot regret what I did not do!

If you want a lesson in patience, go stand in a long line in a
small bank—on a Friday, at noon! It is here that you come
face to face with the realization that you cannot make your
life move faster than it is moving. No matter how urgent
your situation may seem to be, things are going to happen when they
happen, not a minute sooner. It does not matter how many times you
roll your eyes, suck your teeth, huff or puff, you cannot make your life
happen any faster than it is happening right now. In a long line, in a
small bank, when it seems like people are not moving as fast as they
could, remember that the process is in motion and that things will get
done when they get done.

Patience is a choice. It is the conscious choice to be reliant on the un-
ceasing movement of life. Patience is an ability. It is the mental ability to
remember that once the wheels start turning and the movement has
begun, the destination will surely be reached—eventually. Patience is a
skill. It is the emotional skill of *knowing* that what you expect, intend
and desire will happen exactly when it needs to happen. Patience is a science. It is the spiritual science of using your mental and emotional skills
of creation to such an exacting degree that the outcome is assured at the
beginning. It is the science of knowing that what you set in motion with
your mind, what you believe in your heart, what you praise in your soul
must happen—at just the right time, in just the right way.

It may be challenging to practice patience while on a long line, in a
small bank, on a Friday, at noon. However, if you can master patience
there, you can practice it everywhere. Until today, you may have experienced bouts of impatience. Just for today, be devoted to mastering the
art and science of being patient. Be patient with yourself. Be patient
with others. Be patient with life. Patience always pays off!

*Today I am patiently mastering the art and science of
patience with myself, others and life!*

JANUARY 13

Life will work for me when I realize . . .
I cannot fail in life!

The Spirit of life cannot fail! It may not always get an A, but it cannot fail! You are the Spirit of life, which means *you cannot fail!* You can pass with a grade of B or C or even D. You can repeat a class or skip a class, but under no circumstances that really matter in life can you ever fail. You may stumble. You may fall. You may meet up with many things that push you into dark and scary places—face first! It's a spiritual thing, don't worry about it!

You may break an arm, a leg, or a foot. You may lose sight. You may become hard of hearing. You may lose touch. It's okay! You are building stamina. Spirit is always trying to see just how much you will take and how much you can do, under as many circumstances as possible. Spirit knows that you cannot fail, and it will try every way possible to convince you of the same thing. Get convinced! You simply cannot fail!

You may get lost. You may lose some things. You may have some things you really think you really need taken away from you at a time you believe you cannot do without them. Regardless of what happens, when it happens or how it happens, remember that the one thing you cannot do, under any circumstances is fail! The moment you realize this, and stop trying to get an A from life, you will quickly move to the head of the class.

Until today, you may have been sitting around, afraid to move, afraid to fail. Just for today, be devoted to seeing yourself and your life as a function of spiritual truth. Remind yourself that you cannot fail! Remind yourself that you don't need an A! Allow yourself to move through every experience and situation with grace and ease, supported by the Spirit of life, which knows that your success is assured.

Today I am devoted to remembering and accepting that
I cannot fail! I cannot fail!
I simply cannot fail at life!

JANUARY 14

Life will work for me when I realize . . .
the only problem I have is the belief that I am not
doing the right thing.

I've got a question for you. How can you evaluate the process
when you don't really know what the process is or how it
works? Many of us believe that we are not doing life right,
or that things are going wrong in our lives, when we have absolutely no idea what the process is or how it really works. Yes, we all
have some basic ideas of what to do and what not to do. Many of us
know what we want. Some of us even believe that we know how we can
get what we want. What few of us know with an absolute certainty is
whether or not what we believe about the process is the truth about the
process.

The process of life is ever unfolding, guiding you, pushing you,
preparing you for the next part of the process. Life often takes a twist, or
makes a turn that is frightening or confusing. Difficult challenges, bad
days, upset feelings, moments of confusion are part of life's process. Perhaps these things are there to keep us alert, to make us stronger, or to test
our resolve to keep moving forward. Perhaps they are not a sign that we
are wrong, that we are failing or that our life is about to fall apart. The
only way we can know for sure is to be willing to walk through every part
of the process. The good and the not so good. The easy part and the hard
parts. Perhaps if we stopped trying to figure out the process, the process
would proceed exactly as it should.

Until today, you may have believed that you were doing something
wrong in life, or that something was wrong with the process of life. Just
for today, be devoted to embracing the process of life without fear by reminding yourself that you really don't know what the process is, but you
are equipped to handle whatever shows up.

*Today I am in the process of learning more about
the process of living!*

JANUARY 15

Life will work for me when I realize . . . when I tell
myself the truth, I can trust myself!

If your life is a mess, here are a few things you may want to
consider cleaning up:

1. Are you keeping your agreements? Are you doing
what you say you will do? Or are you telling little fibs to get
out of the things you agreed to do?

When you do not keep your agreements then lie to cover them up,
you create little messes all over your life. In addition, when you do not
keep your agreements, you learn that you cannot be trusted. If you can't
trust you, who can you trust?!

2. Are you overcommitted? Are you agreeing to do more than you
can, or need to do, because you are trying to get people to like you? Are
you making commitments so that other people won't be mad at you?

When you are overcommitted, it is a sign that there is a deficit of
self-value, self-worth, self-esteem. When you don't feel good about you,
you will continue to do things that will maintain the status quo of *not
feeling good*. When you do not feel good, you make a mess in and of your
life.

3. Are you telling the truth about what you feel? What you know?
Who you are? Or, are you sugar coating the truth to yourself and others
to avoid hurting their feelings and putting yourself on the spot?

When you do not tell the truth, you are enslaved by a lie. The lie
controls your life. The lie determines what you do, how you do it and
what you receive as a result. When you are a slave to a lie, you eventually
become the very one who keeps the "master" alive.

Until today, you may not have realized how the mess in your life got
started or how to clean it up. Just for today, be devoted to examining, acknowledging and cleaning up the little things that create such a mess in
your mind and your life.

Today I am devoted to cleaning up the mess!

Life will work for me when I realize . . . I must be open
to receive and willing to accept the goodness of life!

Everybody knows somebody who has a "goodness allergy."
Whenever things get too good in their lives, they find something wrong, some reason to reject the good. A person with
a goodness allergy will focus on what happened yesterday, in
order not to focus upon the good they are experiencing today. When a
person is allergic to good, they don't expect good. They can't expect
good. Instead they make up stories about why nothing good can or will
happen to them. If by chance it does, they rub their eyes in disbelief.

When you are allergic to good, you rely on the past. You stay mad
about what happened back then. You pick fights and keep arguments
going. When your goodness allergy really flares up, you find something
wrong with how the good came or who brought the good to you. You
question why *you* are receiving the good and how much it is going to
cost you.

A goodness allergy is grounded in fear. Fear that you will get hurt.
Fear that you will lose what you have. Fear that you don't deserve good.
You are in fear that if you open your heart and mind to receive good, you
will have nothing to whine and complain about. There will be nothing
wrong. At the heart of a goodness allergy is the fear that if nothing is
wrong, then you too must be all right. And that would be too good to
believe.

Until today, you may have been suffering from a goodness allergy.
You may have lived in fear that you were not good enough to receive
good. Just for today, spend some time identifying all of the good things
that have happened to you, for you and through you. Write them down
and ask yourself how you really feel about all the good that you have received and the good you have done.

Today I am opening myself to see and receive more
goodness in my life!

JANUARY 17

Life will work for me when I realize . . .
I cannot break through until I have a breakdown!

Each of us must face a moment in our lives called "the breakdown moment." This is the time when you must stand toe to toe, eyeball to eyeball, with the very thing you have tried desperately to avoid. In that moment, you will want to find a way around, over, under or out of having to do what you are faced with doing. You will do anything, say anything to avoid having to go through what is facing you. You will want to run and hide. You will get weak, almost faint. You will believe you are going to be sick. You won't be! What you will be is on your way to greatness.

In the breakdown moment, the very thing you have feared, resisted, denied will stand before you, shaking its finger in your face and sticking its tongue out at you. It will show you things about yourself that you refused to see or acknowledge. It will tease you, taunt you, push you, pull you to the verge of breaking down. In fact, that is its purpose. In the breakdown moment, your defenses break down. Your fantasies shatter. Your excuses fail. Your resistance erodes. In that moment, when there is nothing standing between you and the thing you fear the most, you will be forced to step into your greatness, because that is what life is demanding of you.

Until today, you may not have realized that you are totally able, perfectly prepared, fully capable of doing the very thing you have convinced yourself you could not do. Just for today, be devoted to doing just one thing that will help to convince you.

Today I am devoted to stepping into my greatness!

JANUARY 18

Life will work for me when I realize . . .
I am the light of the world!

Please be advised that there will be situations where you do and give your best, your all, with the best intentions, and what you get in return is crap! Pure dung! At first you will get angry. You will be angry with yourself and then angry with everyone else. You will be angry because other people do not understand or appreciate you or why you are angry.

Eventually, the anger will give way to confusion. This will be the "what did I do wrong?" kind of confusion. The kind that eats away at your heart, mind and spirit. The kind that makes you feel stupid and valueless and worthless. You will stay confused until doubt sets in. When that happens, you will question your motives for trying to be a decent human being! Then you will get numb. You will numb yourself to the anger, confusion, the self-doubt and self-judgment. At this point you will probably swear that you will never be hurt or disappointed again. Of course, you won't mean it. You can't mean it because—*You are the light of the world!*

When you are the light, you cannot complain about the darkness. The only thing you can do is shine. You must shine brightly, in everything you do, in everyplace you go. That is your job. When you are the light, you must realize that without the darkness you would have no meaning. You must also understand that just because there is darkness does not mean you are not doing what you are supposed to do.

Until today, you may have believed that light must come to you. You may have complained about the darkness around you and how it seems that you are the only one trying to make the darkness brighter. Just for today, be devoted to being the light. Give of yourself without the expectation of receiving light or recognition or rewards in return.

Today I am devoted to shining my light without complaining about the darkness!

Life will work for me when I remember . . .
there is more to life than meets the eye!

Never allow what you look like to determine what you can or cannot do. Never allow what you are looking at to determine what you believe. Never allow what you can see with your eyes to lure you into the belief that there is nothing more. Always allow your spiritual eyes to take you beneath the surface. It is there that you will see and know the truth. Until you can see yourself, your life and everyone around you with spiritual vision, you will be confused by the appearances of lack and disorder.

Everything you see in the outer world has an inner meaning. In the midst of every fact is a hidden and invisible cause. At the heart of every experience, every situation, every circumstance, there is an invisible truth. For every single thing, no matter how unsightly, unpleasant, or disconcerting, there is a true, hidden meaning that represents the activity of Spirit. This also applies to you. There is a truth about you that may have gone undetected. There is a cause which you live to fulfill. There is meaning beneath your physical exterior that represents spiritual activity. In order to see this activity, we must develop spiritual vision. Until we do, we can always be fooled by appearances! To see the spiritual presence in all things is to know the true nature of God. To know the nature of God is to know yourself.

Until today, you may have been caught up, put off, confused by the way things appear to be. You may have been fooled by the appearances of things and people around you. Just for today, be devoted to asking for and receiving spiritual insight into yourself and about all things.

Today I am devoted to developing my spiritual vision!

JANUARY 20

Life will work for me when I realize . . .
I can take my own advice!

If I had a little girl, I would tell her all the things I think she would need to know to be fully prepared for life. I would tell her that there will be good days and bad days, and that she should be grateful for them all. I would tell her that she is always protected, and no matter what she does, she will always be loved.

I would tell my little girl that life is full of wonder and excitement, and that it is all available to her. I would tell her to focus on one thing at a time. Enjoy it, taking the most pleasant memories of it into the next experience. I would tell her to be kind to all people, even when they are not kind in return. I would tell my little girl to find something to appreciate about everything and everyone. When you are appreciative, you get more to appreciate.

I would tell my little girl that she did not have to rely on people for her good, that she could withdraw all that she needs from Heaven. I would tell her to always tell the truth in the way she would want to hear it; always give her best and never doubt that it was good enough; always remember where she came from and the people who helped her along the way.

I would tell my little girl that the best things in life are not things. They are people. I would tell my little girl that it is important for her to honor what she feels. I would tell her that a well-ordered mind will never lead her astray, and that if her mind and life are to be in order, she must put God first. The most important thing I would want my little girl to know is that she should never be afraid of making a mistake, because mistakes, when evaluated, make masters.

Until today, you may have found it easier to provide others with guidance in their time of need than to help yourself. You may not have realized how truly wise you are. Just for today, listen to and heed your own advice. Anything you can tell anyone else probably applies to you too!

Today I will talk to myself, listen to myself and heed my own advice!

JANUARY 21

Life will work for me when I realize . . .
I can always re-create what I believe!

If I had a little boy, I would tell him all the things he would need to know to be a peace-filled man. I would let him know that if a man cannot follow, he will never be able to lead. I would tell him that commitment, determination, endurance, patience and faith are much more powerful than speed, force and physical strength. I would tell him that people may not remember everything you do, however, they will always remember how you do it. I would tell him to always strive to make people feel worthy and important for whatever they can contribute.

I would tell my little boy that the omission of information is the same as a lie. I would tell him that when you try to meet life on your own terms, you may be forced to renegotiate those terms. I would tell him that each day is a blessing, and what you do with your blessings determines how you will be blessed.

I would tell my little boy to be willing rather than willful; to listen rather than being the first to speak; to be open to correction rather than unwilling to hear another point of view; and that the accumulation of material possessions is not the measure of success. I would tell my little boy that a man who cannot laugh at himself is a danger to himself and others. A man who does not trust himself is a man who cannot be trusted, and a man who cannot be trusted is a man who cannot love.

I would tell my little boy that a man is what he thinks, and that what he thinks is a reflection of what he holds in his heart. Most important, I would want my little boy to know that it is okay to be vulnerable, because when you are vulnerable you are innocent. I would tell my little boy that innocence is our gift from God.

Until today, you may not have realized that all men start out as little boys who need information. Just for today, be devoted to rethinking what you believe about men, manhood and your understanding of both.

Today I am willing to re-create my beliefs about manhood.

JANUARY 22

Life will work for me when I realize . . .
I am loved by life!

Listen carefully, as if someone were whispering into your soul. There is something you must know. It is very important, no, it is imperative that you receive these words into the deepest core of your being. These words are essential to your very existence. They will feed, nurture and nourish you. They will support, assist and guide you. When all else fails, these words will give you the strength and courage you need to weather the storm and walk through the fire. These are simple words, yet they are very powerful. If you can accept them in the spirit in which they are given, you will be blessed. Receive these words—*Life loves you!*

Life loves you enough to live as you, to breathe through you, to express itself as you. Life loves you so much, it does everything in its power to stay in you, to be with you and to allow you to depend on it. Life is, at this very moment, totally and absolutely in love with you! Life wants to look like you, be like you, live as you because it respects and honors all that you are.

When life sees you coming, it gets excited! It can hardly contain itself! Life is ready to fill you up, spill over through you and experience the best it has to offer you, as you. If you were to ask life what it is about you that makes you so loveable, the answer would be simple. You are alive! That is all it takes to make you loved, loving, and loveable. Now isn't it good to know that you are loved?

Until today, you may not have realized just how much life loves you. You may have believed that life was not on your side. Just for today, be devoted to honoring, cherishing and enjoying life's love for you. Sit silently and ask life to fill you with its love.

Today I am devoted to allowing life to love me!

JANUARY 23

Life will work for me when I realize . . . I am
in a different part of the same boat as everyone else.

Life doesn't always go the way you want or plan that it will
go. It hardly ever looks the way you first envisioned that it
would look. It rarely feels comfortable or as if you have it
under control, and quite often there are things that you cannot control! That's life! Life is usually what happens just when you are
planning something else.

It moves at its own pace, which is usually faster or slower than you
would like it to. It moves in its own direction, which is often not the direction in which you are going. It opens up when you least expect it and
shuts itself down at the most inopportune moments. It gives for no reason and takes the same way. It starts abruptly and stops just short of the
goal. It changes. Then it refuses to change. It runs smoothly, then hits a
bump. It feels good for days, weeks or months at a time. Then, all of a
sudden, it makes you sick. It loves you. Then it leaves you high and dry.
It will help you out when you need it most, then knock you down and
roll right over you. It will present you with an answer. Then it will present you with questions that do not match the answer you have been
given. It is good for a while. Then it sucks all of the goodness out of you.
That's life!

Until today, you may have spent a great deal of time focused on
making life move around you. Just for today, be devoted to allowing the
life within you to flow in its own way, at its own pace.

Today I am moving in the flow of life!
I am living the life that flows!

JANUARY 24

Life will work for me when I realize . . .
Life is always accommodating my requests!

Life will accommodate you in any way that you choose. Life is always listening to the silent requests of your heart and mind. Life is always surveying the landscape of your heart, gathering the bits and pieces of the emotions buried there. Life is always monitoring the activity of your tongue, checking for ruins and sacred elements. Life knows that your mind, heart and mouth will produce the requests of your consciousness even when you are not aware of it.

Life can be an open book through which you can learn about great mysteries and wonders. Or life can be a mysterious and frightening pit through which you fear to tread. Or life can be an open basket into which you can place your treasures, in which you can carry abundant blessings. Or life can be a locked trunk from which you can retrieve or receive nothing. Life can be a journey or a struggle. A paradise or a prison. A calm sea or a turbulent ocean. It's all up to you. Life will accommodate whatever you choose, exactly the way you choose. And, whether or not you believe it, what you have in your life right now is a function of your own requests! Some of those requests you made openly. Others you made silently. Doesn't matter! Life is very accommodating, and the minute your requests change, your life will follow suit.

Until today, you may not have realized that life is answering your requests. You may not have believed that you have the power and the right to ask life for more than you already have right now. Just for today, be devoted to creating a list of positive, joyful requests. Create them first in your mind. Next, create them in your heart. Then speak them into existence. Be sure to remember what you have created. If it does not show up, check your counterrequests.

Today I am devoted to creating and requesting what I truly desire to experience in life.

Life will work for me when I realize . . .
I must learn how to wait!

Waiting on the Lord is a good thing. However, there are times when we must know *how* to wait. Sometimes we wait in fear, wringing our hands and checking over our shoulders. Sometimes we wait in arrogance, patting our feet with our hands on our hips. We may wait in indifference, picking our teeth and shrugging our shoulders. At times we wait in anger, huffing, puffing and pounding our fists on the table. Then there are the times we wait helplessly, hopelessly, with our heads bowed and hands in our pockets. How we wait is just as important as what we are waiting for.

Waiting does not mean sitting around in a fantasy land, anticipating that something good will fall down on us from the sky and hit us on the head. That is not waiting at all. That is fooling yourself into not taking responsibility for your vision, your dreams and your desires. Waiting is the realization that God knows what God has done, will do and can do. While waiting, your job is to put your faith in that realization.

Waiting requires joy accompanied by the belief that what you need or request will be provided by God. Waiting is knowing and accepting that if it is good for you, if it will bless you and others, then what you request must happen! Waiting is having enthusiasm and excitement about where you are and what you have right now. Waiting is clarity about the how come's and "what for's" of yesterday that have prepared you for "your goodness" tomorrow. Yes, waiting is good! However, if you cannot wait peacefully, faithfully, confidently, joyfully, gratefully and lovingly, then you are waiting in vain!

Until today, you may have believed that just waiting to be blessed or inspired or guided or discovered was all that you had to do. You may not have been aware of how you are waiting and what you are really expecting. Just for today, be devoted to examining how you are waiting and be willing to make any necessary changes.

Today I am devoted to not waiting in vain!

JANUARY 26

Life will work for me when I realize . . .
goodness and mercy do follow me.

Wrap a rubber band around your finger. Notice how dark the finger becomes. If you leave the rubber band on long enough, you will also notice that the neighboring finger will begin to get dark. Eventually, your entire hand will be affected. The pain you experience in the rubber-banded finger demonstrates what happens in your life when you become tense or uptight about something or someone. Sooner or later, your entire life will be affected.

There is no way you can be angry at one person without having that anger filter into every other relationship in your life. When you become tense, anxious, worried about one thing, everything in your life will become dark, stiff and painful. Worry, fear and desperation about the thing you are uptight about will not help matters; instead, what you feel, what you tell yourself, will charge the atmosphere of your life with more of the very thing that you do not want.

There will come a moment in which you must simply make the choice to let go in order to get on with your life. Letting go means making a decision not to be angry, not to be upset, not to hold on to thoughts of unfairness and revenge. Letting go means opening your heart and mind to an explanation that you do not now recognize, may never recognize, but choose to live in recognition of. You will know that there is a rubber band tightening itself somewhere in your life the moment you see darkness, experience tightness or pain. In that moment, you must make the choice to simply let go.

Until today, you may have been holding on to something that was cutting you off from life. Just for today, be devoted to hanging loose, being free and going with the flow. When you feel your body becoming tense, drop your hands to your sides, take a deep breath and relax. If it does not work the first time, do it again and again until it does work.

Today I am devoted to relaxing, releasing and letting go!

JANUARY 27

Life will work for me when I realize . . .
I am totally, completely and fully responsible
for what goes on in my life!

One of the greatest challenges in creating a joyful, peaceful and abundant life is taking responsibility for what you do and how you do it! As long as you can blame someone else, be angry with someone else, point the finger at someone or something else, you are not taking responsibility for your life. Sure, things happen! It is absolutely true that there are situations, circumstances, social constructs and common elements that can and do affect you. It is your responsibility, however, to determine *how* and *how long* they affect you.

It is easy to find reasons not to be responsible. In fact, many of us are not aware of how we do it or that we do it at all. Not taking responsibility for your life means blaming, finding causes, excuses and reasons for what is going on in your life as if they had nothing to do with you. Not taking responsibility means crying or complaining about the good that is not happening, while making very few efforts to determine that *it will* happen. Not taking responsibility means asking someone to do for you the things you must do for yourself, and being angry when they don't do it. It cannot be said loud enough, or enough times—your life is your responsibility! Think of it this way, if you cannot be responsible for your life, how can you expect to be responsible for the good things you want to receive?

Until today, you may have held others responsible or blamed external situations and circumstances for the condition of your life. Just for today, be devoted to surveying your life. Identify the areas that are dysfunctional, challenged or simply not as you would have them be. Make a list of all the things you can do to create the needed change. Make a plan to execute the things that you have put on the list.

Today I am devoted to taking full responsibility for
everything that is going on in my life.

JANUARY 28

Life will work for me when I realize . . . I cannot change
what I believe as long as I believe it!

At the center of every problem, the answer is present. In the
midst of every challenge there is comfort, guidance and relief. In the midst of illness there is healing. At the brink of
disaster there is salvation. God is the answer! God is the comfort you seek, the guidance that you need, the healing you have prayed
for and the saving grace in all situations. If, however, you have problems
believing in God, you will be challenged to find the answer, feel the
comfort, receive the healing or be saved from disaster.

God is the essence of life. Always present. Always knowing. Forever
giving us exactly what we need, exactly when we need it. Unfortunately,
far too many of us believe that God only provides for the *good* people,
because God likes them for being good. And, if we believe that we have
not always been good, chances are we also believe that God is not always
blessing us. Nothing could be further from the truth!

God is the grace in which we live. God does hold us accountable for
the things we have done but does not see our actions as reason for pun-
ishing or abandoning us. God expects us to learn from and grow
through our erroneous beliefs and actions. He expects us to rely on and
turn to him/her when our way does not work. When we believe that
God requires a certain thing to be done in a certain way, at a certain
time, and we know we have not done it, we will have difficulty feeling
the presence of God when we need it most.

Until today, you may have told yourself that you were not worthy of
being in God's presence. Just for today, be devoted to believing in and receiving the presence of God in you heart, mind and life. Stand before a
mirror. Look deeply into your own eyes. Ask the question. Turn over the
illness. Present the challenge. Request the comfort. Express heartfelt
gratitude by believing that God is present with you right now.

Today I am devoted to believing in the presence of God!

JANUARY 29

Life will work for me when I realize . . . I have a Father
who has always loved and will always love me!

It is quite common these days to hear people say, "I never
knew my father!" "He left when I was young!" (No he
didn't!) "He died." (He can't die!) "He went to jail." (No
such thing!) "My mother never told me who he was." (She
didn't have to!) You see, somehow we have confused the seed from which
we were conceived with the source from which we come. Yes, we all have
a human father whose seed contributed to our being, but we also have a
divine Father whose life gives us life.

Then there are those of us who knew our fathers but did not like
them. We didn't feel loved, accepted or respected by the father we knew.
Perhaps he drank too much, spoke too little, rarely if ever came home.
Maybe he criticized or ridiculed us in ways that wounded us. Perhaps
there was some physical or verbal abuse that damaged us in some way.
Many of us believe our relationship with our father was challenged, and
of course, it was all his fault!

The truth is your Father has never mistreated you, abandoned you,
harmed you or denied you. He knows exactly what you need and he provides it the only way he can—in love, because of his unyielding love for
you. Your Father has always been there, guiding you, protecting you,
providing for you. Your Father is as alive and well today as he was the day
you were born. It may be that your *father* was not around, or that he was
difficult to deal with. It is also true, however, that you could be confused
about just who your *Father* is!

Until today, you may have held the man who *contributed* to your life
responsible for your life. Just for today, be devoted to knowing who your
real Father is. Ask him to help you understand yourself, your life and the
role he plays in them both. Ask him what he knows about you and what
he sees for you and your life. Then ask your Father to teach you how to
forgive the man he used to bring you into this life.

Today I am devoted to getting to know my Father better!

JANUARY 30

Life will work for me when I realize . . . I must know the elements of success if I plan to be successful!

How do you spell success? P-R-A-I-S-E! Give thanks for all that you are, all that you have. Praise and gratitude are the tickets you need if you want to experience victory in all things.

How do you spell peace? P-R-A-Y-E-R! Anything you believe you need is available to you through prayer. We are not talking here about a magic formula of proper and distinct words. Oh no! We are talking about opening your heart and your mouth, saying what's on your mind, knowing that once you do, the answer will be revealed.

How do you spell joy? S-U-R-R-E-N-D-E-R! When you can give up your mental and emotional attachments to what has to be, how it has to be, when it has to be, why it has to be, you open the door to the Holy Spirit. When that energy, the energy of life, light and love enters your world, your life becomes more than you ever dared ask for.

How do you spell life? T-R-U-S-T! At some point in the midst of praise, prayer and surrender, you will learn to trust. You will realize that the only thing that stands between you and your success, your peace, your joy is your bad memory. You simply *forgot* to praise, pray and surrender! You forgot that you can trust the Holy Spirit of life to open doors, show you the way and bring you all the help that you need.

Until today, you may have been trying to find success, peace and joy. You may have made plans and executed them, only to meet with failure and disappointment. Just for today, devote yourself to praise—giving thanks for everything and everyone in your life; to prayer—asking for what you need, believing that you can have it; and to surrender—detaching yourself from a specific outcome. I trust that these activities alone will put your life and your mind on its divine course.

Today I am devoted to practicing the elements of success!

JANUARY 31

Life will work for me when I realize . . .
trouble comes to pass, not to stay.

Somehow, in the midst of what seems to be the worst possible thing that could happen, you must find the strength that you need to persevere. You must develop the courage that will be required to take the next step. You must face the challenge eyeball-to-eyeball in order to realize that challenge comes to *make you, not break you.*

Losing a job, home, loved one can be a devastating experience. Your challenge may be a child or family member who has gone astray. You could be faced with an unexpected change like a divorce or an illness. Whatever your challenge may be, it can rock you to the core. Somehow, you must remember that you are up for the task. Remember that you do have the strength. Remember that you can trust life to give you the courage that is required to do anything or face anything. As painful or frightening as the difficulty may be, you will do what needs to be done because you have no other choice. *Giving up is not an option!*

Give yourself a moment to take a breath. Allow everything that you are feeling and thinking to move through your body. The moment that you feel that you can't take it or won't make it, reach down into the essence of your being. From that place pull out a scream. Then pull on your power, your strength, the divinity of life within you. Tell yourself, *"This is going to make me stronger! This is going to make me wiser!"* This challenge, no matter what it is, has come to make you bigger, brighter, stronger, more loving and compassionate. *It will not break you!* Trust yourself. Trust life. You will make it through this!

Until today, you may have been feeling as if you were about to break down. Just for today, call forth the strength, courage, wisdom, insight, power and love of the spirit of life. Ask that you be guided through the next minute, hour or day to a place of peace.

Today, I am devoted to calling forth whatever I need to make it through difficult and challenging experiences!

F E B R U A R Y

LOVE

Love is the greatest, most enduring power
in the universe.

Then again, there is no other power.

God is love and life and you and me.

FEBRUARY 1

I will know love when I realize . . .
love is not what I say. Love is who I am and what I do.

How do we take love and ideas about love out of the clouds and anchor love's presence right here on earth? Here are a few things you may want to consider.

Love is who you are. How you see yourself, how you treat yourself, how you express yourself is a direct reflection of your true beliefs about love. When you can be gentle and compassionate with yourself, you will feel love. When you can be nonjudgmental about yourself, you will experience love. When you can trust yourself and tell yourself the truth, you will express love. When you can see and celebrate your worth, value and your beauty as a divine expression of life, you will be love.

Love is what you have come into life to give. Treat everyone, regardless of who they are, what they do or how they do it, the same way you treat yourself. See the good about everyone and in everyone, even when they make mistakes you feel they should not make. Speak to people in a way that will open their hearts, allowing them to feel welcome and worthy. Give others the same benefit of the doubt that you give to yourself. Are these not the things you need to feel loved?

Love is the cooperative, harmonizing, accepting, forgiving, essence of your soul. Love does not give up. Love does not demand what it does not have. Love doesn't force itself on others in order to feel better about itself. Love doesn't attack to avenge itself. Love does not withhold itself. When we learn to see ourselves as love and to be present with others in loving ways, love will be anchored in our consciousness and on the planet.

Until today, you may have been trying to figure out what love is and how to find it in your life. Just for today, be aware of and accept yourself as the expression and example of the love you are seeking.

Today I am devoted to knowing myself, expressing myself and experiencing myself as love!

FEBRUARY 2

I will know love when I realize . . . I have the power to
call a thing that is not as if it is so that it will be!

Today is a very special day for you! Today you are having a naming ceremony. Today you are going to step into your true identity! You see, your *name is your nature.* What you are called is a reminder to your Spirit of what you have come to life to do. As of this day, your name is, *Beloved!* That's right! You are now known as the *Beloved* of life. The entire world must know that you are God's *Beloved child!* You are the heart of God's heart! You are the one God is depending on to express goodness and *God-ness* on the face of the earth! So you see, this is more than just a name. It is a command to you from God.

Be-love! Be-love in everything you think, because your thoughts express the core of your identity. Be-love each time you open your mouth, because you have the naming power! Be-love in everything you do, because that is your nature. Be-love when you are tired and weary. Be-love to those who feel rejected and abandoned. Be-love in the midst of anger and hatred. Be-love when everything else you have tried seems to be failing. Be-love because no matter what is going on, love is the one thing every living soul needs. In other words, *they need you!*

Be-love! Be-love when you think you have made a mistake that cannot or will not be forgiven. Be-love when you suffer material loss or experience material gain. Be-love when you are afraid that who you are is not enough. Be-love when those you have trusted seem to be abandoning you. Be-love when you are falsely accused. Be-love when the world does not give you the credit you think you deserve. Be-love because when everything else fails, the power in the name of love will lift you up.

Until today, you may have been known by a name that was less than a true expression of your identity. Just for today, try on a new name. Be the love that God created you to be, to know, to experience and express.

Today I am devoted to being the love that is
my true nature and identity!

FEBRUARY 3

I will know love when I realize . . .
God wants to love me!

God wants to love you. God has so much love for you and God wants to give you more love than you have ever dared ask for. It is God's desire to guide you, protect you, provide for you and shower you with love-filled goodness. It is also God's desire that you be happy, healthy and loved. God wants you to be filled with peace and to have peaceful, joy-filled experiences. Because God cherishes you as the loved one, God desires that you live in the lap of abundance, that you experience total well-being. The question is, can you stop trying to convince God that you do not deserve the love that God wants you to have?

Very often we hold on to thoughts of unworthiness and hopelessness because of experiences we have encountered. Or we look at the absence of certain experiences in our lives as evidence that we are being punished or forgotten by God. Of course you want to do better and be better than you are right now. God will take you exactly as you are, because God knows exactly who you are. You may be concerned about what you are going to do next in your life, or what you have done in the past. God knows that no matter what you have done, things go better when God is on your side.

God wants you! Not because God wants or needs anything from you, but because God wants you to realize the fullest potential of the goodness that is already in you. That goodness is God's love.

Until today, you may have believed that there was something you needed to do to render yourself more pleasing to God. Just for today, spend time allowing God to know you just as you are. God, as the peace, joy, strength, power and abundance you desire in your life, is yours for the asking. Let today be the day you ask for and receive it.

Today I am devoted to knowing, experiencing and receiving God's love for me.

FEBRUARY 4

I will know love when I realize . . . there are times when I
allow fear to stand between me and those I love.

How do you withhold your love? We all do it at one time or
another. We shut down, shut people out, refuse to budge
from our opinions or demands. We hold people hostage,
knowing that they care about us, because we are angry or
upset with them. Sometimes we make ourselves busy. So busy in fact
that we don't have time to address the issues, the feelings or the incidents
that first led us to withhold our love.

When you refuse to share what you are feeling and how the other
person has contributed to those feelings, you are withholding your love.
When you don't provide the other person with valuable information
that could make your relationship with them better, you are withholding your love. When you allow the fear of being hurt, the fear of being
rejected, the fear of looking dumb make you act like you just don't care,
you are withholding your love. Whenever you are not offering the truth
of your experience to those who share the experience, you are withholding your love.

Whatever is not an expression of love is an expression of fear. Withholding love for any reason is a sign that we are crying out in fear. Fear of
being hurt. Fear that our love will not be reciprocated. When you find
yourself backing up, pulling back, withdrawing from another person,
ask yourself, "Why am I withholding my love?" What you are likely to
discover is that there is a hidden fear forcing you to do something you
would not like to have done to you.

Until today, you may not been aware of the ways and the reason you
withhold your love. Just for today, stand in truth! Do what is loving!
When you feel afraid, acknowledge and admit it. Then love yourself
through it.

*Today I am devoted to loving and being loved
without being afraid!*

FEBRUARY 5

*I will know love when I realize . . . I can love people
even when I believe they are not nice!*

It would be very nice if all people were nice, loving people.
Unfortunately, they are not. It would be wonderful if, while
you are on the path to spiritual enlightenment, every person you met would wish you well, or join you on the journey.
Unfortunately, they will not. There are many people who are in a great
deal of pain, and on certain days these people will, consciously or unconsciously, inflict their pain on you.

People will speak ill of you for no good reason. People will return
your good deeds with unkind, unloving words and deeds. People will lie
to you, betray your confidence, selfishly hoard your property, and if they
are really hurting, they may physically strike out at you. The human tendency is to offer insult for insult, hurt for hurt, ill deed for ill deed. The
spiritual imperative is to offer love for insult, love for hurt, love to everyone regardless of the ill they may offer you. The human perspective is to
hate those who hate you, take from those who have taken from you,
harm those who have harmed you. The spiritual perspective is to recognize that the more unlovingly a person behaves, the greater is their need
for love and healing.

If you should encounter angry words or unkind actions on this day,
take a deep breath, reach deep within yourself and greet the lack of love
with love. Until today, you may have responded to human unkindness
with human unkindness. Just for today, be devoted to greeting everything and everyone with the gentle kindness of love.

*Today I am devoted to giving love to everyone and
everything no matter what is said or done.*

FEBRUARY 6

I will know love when I realize . . . the only way
I can challenge fear is to do the very thing I am afraid
to do in the moment that I feel afraid.

Here is a recipe for living and loving that will yield satisfaction and success:

1 Mind full of positive vision
1 Moment of openness
1 Second of willingness
2 Drops of readiness
1 Dash of love

Mix the above ingredients with trust and faith. Roll the mixture into a ball of clear intention. Knead the ball into a thin layer of belief. Smooth out any lumps and cover all holes with prayer. Gently place the layer of expected intent in a dish of great expectation.

Preheat your mind with warm loving thoughts about yourself. Allow the layer of belief to rise in words of praise and thanksgiving. Patiently wait for the intention and expectation to be divinely fulfilled.

Until today, you may have experienced many failed or fallen dreams. Just for today, try a new recipe for loving yourself into a new vision for yourself and for your life. Be devoted to focusing your energy and love on just one thing.

*Today I am devoted to using all the right ingredients
for a life full of love!*

FEBRUARY 7

I will know love when I realize . . .
the world as I know it begins and ends with love!

Books have been written about it. Many have dreams about it. Some chase it. Others find it. At some point in our lives, we all experience what we believe is the loss of it. When it's gone, we want some more. We have some basic ideas and beliefs about what it is, or what it should be, and we *know* what we believe is right. When, however, what we believe doesn't quite work, we change our minds, find a new approach, write more books and head off down the new paths we create. We change, but *it* does not. Love never changes. It remains constant and available in an unlimited supply.

Close your eyes for just a moment. Think about the face of a newborn baby—pure, innocent, defenseless and at rest. That is love. Imagine the touch, the smell, the embrace, the sight of a face, or a place that has warmed your heart, brought a smile to your face and caused all of your fears and worries to vanish. That's love. What color is it? What is the sound of it? Imagine yourself surrounded by it, embraced and protected by it, free from all harm for just a moment. When your defenses fall away and your heart opens, you've got it. Love is right where you are, wherever you are, in this moment—love is. Love is available to you right now. Will you be available to love? Can you be? Are you open to receive it?

Until today, you may have believed you had to *find* love. Just for today, hold thoughts and images of love in your mind. When you can be love, move in love and see love in all things, you are living the truth of your soul. What could be more fulfilling?

Today I am devoted to thinking loving thoughts, seeing love in all and giving love to all.

FEBRUARY 8

*I will know love when I realize . . . my life is
the sacred and holy ground of love!*

It is not loving to stay in a place or an experience where you are happy sometimes, sad most of the time. It is not loving to convince yourself that it is okay to stay in a place where you are not loved, honored and valued the way your heart tells you you deserve to be. It is not self-loving, nor is it loving to others involved, to allow yourself to be mentally, emotionally or physically abused in hope that things can, or will, get better. When you participate in actions and activities that are not loving toward you, you are helping them do things that hurt you, and that is not a loving thing to do.

It is easy to convince yourself that you must stay where you are because you have no place else to go; or because you know things could be worse, or because you know things could get better. It is easy to overlook things that eat away at your sense of self, your sense of value, your sense of well-being. As easy as it may be to blame someone else, to try to ignore what you feel, to call your pain a sacrifice for love, you are not being loving or wise to do so. Eventually, you will be held responsible for everything you experience and how you have responded to it.

Love does not ask us to lose ourselves, harm ourselves or sacrifice ourselves for its sake. Love offers itself to us, measure for measure, what we offer it. If you are being dishonored, disrespected, physically harmed for the love you give, you must ask yourself, "Am I really giving love, or am I simply afraid to leave?"

Until today, you may have participated in being unloving toward yourself. Just for today, allow yourself to stand in the truth, honor and peace of love. Ask yourself, "Am I receiving all that I am giving?" If not, ask yourself, "Why not?"

*Today I am devoted to loving myself, honoring myself
and removing myself from unloving experiences.*

FEBRUARY 9

*I will know love when I realize . . . there are times
when the right road takes a wrong turn!*

When you do not stand fully in the truth of what you know, what you feel and who you are, you are withholding your love. To stand means to express, to share and to honor. Standing is the way we demonstrate self-support, self-love and self-respect. In doing this for ourselves, we do it for others. Often we withhold our truth, and our love, because we do not want to hurt or upset people. Sometimes we simply are not aware of what we are doing. When, however, we consciously choose not to express what we feel, not to share what we know, not to be honest about who we are, we are in fact, withholding our love.

At the core of your being, there is love. Love is your spiritual identity. Every experience, every encounter, every lesson learned is life's way of training you to be a greater expression of love. The only way you can express love is to stand in the truth of your identity. Love is a force. Very often it is the force that shakes us awake, slaps us into reality, moves us out of fear or forces us to do the very thing we convinced ourselves that we could not do. For all you know, you may be the only expression of love that another person comes in contact with on any given day. When you withhold what you think may hurt them, you may be withholding the very thing that could save, help or heal them.

Until today, you may have believed that the people in your life could not handle the truth you know and feel. Just for today, be devoted to loving and trusting people enough to share with them the truth about you. Express what you know in a loving way. Share what you know from a place of love and concern. Be who you honestly are, as a demonstration of your understanding that love harmonizes all things, and all people.

*Today I am devoted to telling the truth to those I love, and
I am trusting that they can handle it!*

FEBRUARY 10

I will know love when I realize . . . I am a sexual being,
and I am okay!

Love and sex are not the same thing! So many people think
they know the difference. Yet, when you come right down
to the truth, it is easy to mistake one for the other.

Love is a natural instinct. Love makes you feel warm and
fuzzy, protected and secure, bigger than life and welcomed in life. When
we are loving and being loved a sense of well-being permeates our entire
existence. Love makes us feel totally accepted, totally fulfilled. Love allows us to experience one another at the deepest level of our identity.
When we experience love in its fullest and truest form, we want to experience it again and again. In fact, this is what we look for in and expect
from our sexual encounters.

Sexual activity is a perfectly natural and normal expression of who
we are as human beings. We need not make excuses about our desire to
experience ourselves sexually. Our sexual experiences are opportunities
to abandon ourselves, our coverings and masks. A sexual encounter is a
powerful experience in which bodies can share pleasure, with or without
the benefit of intimacy. Because sex feels good, we often mistake our sexual experiences for true giving and receiving of love. We tell ourselves we
were in love, that is why we "did it!"

In love, there is a total acceptance of self, and a willingness to give of
self without an expectation of receiving anything in return. When you
love, you are not afraid to share the truth of who you are, and you accept
the truth of others without judgment. Love feels good because it is good,
not because of what you do, but because of who you are.

Until today, you may have thought your sexual experiences were
true expressions of love. Just for today, devote yourself to giving and receiving the intimacy of love, without physical contact.

*Today I am devoted to expressing the love of my soul
in sexual and non-sexual ways.*

FEBRUARY 11

*I will know love when I realize . . . people will come
into my life for a reason, a season or a lifetime!*

Leaving just isn't easy! It is unfortunate and it happens.
When it does, we fight it because leaving someone you have
spent time living with and loving is no easy task. In every relationship, regardless of how it started or how it is ending,
there are so many good things you have convinced yourself could and
should keep you together. They do, until the day you wake up and realize the things that once worked no longer do.

You know you've changed. You've grown. The little things that once
brought a smile to your face are now a burden in your heart. You know
what you have to do. You just don't know how to do it. You don't want
anyone, especially you, to get hurt. You know that if you could just say
what you feel, if you could just move beyond the fear, the guilt, the anticipation of anger, you could close this door. It wouldn't be easy, but
you could move on. You know you have done the best you could do. You
know you have given all that you have to give. Yet for some reason you
keep on trying to make it work. Well, here is something that you may
not know . . .

When you have learned all you can learn in a relationship, its season
will end. When you have healed what you came into the relationship to
heal, its purpose has been fulfilled. When a relationship is over, it is over!
Hanging on will only make the days ahead darker!

Until today, you may have thought that ending a relationship was a
difficult, challenging or unnecessary experience. Just for today, be devoted to acknowledging and accepting all that you have learned and all
that you have healed. When you can be grateful for those things, it will
be easier to let go.

*Today I am devoted to acknowledging lessons learned,
blessings earned and wounds that have been healed!*

FEBRUARY 12

I will know love when I realize . . . I cannot hide
what I think, what I feel or who I am!

You cannot be fully present in your loving if you are happy
sometimes and sad most of the time, if you are afraid to
leave while you are wondering if you are going to get left.
You cannot be fully present in your loving if you are wondering why you should stay or how you can go without hurting and being
hurt. You are not present in love if you are afraid to tell the absolute
truth about who you are, what you need and what you want. Under
these circumstances, you are not present in love. You are in hiding!

Love does not hide anyone! Love stands tall in the truth of what it is
for everyone to see and receive it. Love does not tell half the story, some
of the time. Nor does love avoid telling its story just to save time and
feelings. Love is respectful, honorable, noble and honest. Love is gentle,
compassionate, willing to share and able to comfort. Love speaks boldly
yet softly. It reaches far without losing ground. You know that love is
present when in the midst of the storm you can find something, some
one thing, to laugh about, smile about and hold on to.

You are not fully present in your loving if you are blaming and not
accepting your share of responsibility, if you are not acknowledging your
part in whatever is going on or your pain about it. You are not and cannot be fully present in your loving if you are not expressing gratitude for
all you have received, if you are not supporting or sharing your vision for
yourself. You cannot be fully present in your loving of another if you are
still making excuses for not being present because you are probably in a
great deal of pain!

Until today, you may have made excuses for not being fully present
in your loving relationships. Just for today, be devoted to being fully
present in all of your relationships. Share the truth of your thoughts and
feelings. Share the truth about yourself.

*Today I am devoted to finding the courage to be fully
present in my relationships!*

FEBRUARY 13

I will know love when I realize . . .
relationships never die. They change!

Some people stay in unsatisfying relationships just to be able to say they stayed. At times we stay simply because we are tired of walking away. Or we may stay for the "bragging rights," to be able to say, "I did my best! I tried really hard! I gave all I had to give!" Or we may stay hoping against hope that things will get better, that we will one day get what we believe we have given. Sometimes we stay just to prove we can stay. The question is, what are you really proving?

As children, we learn how to take a spanking. We learn how to run. How to hide. How to duck, dodge and cover the various parts of our bodies to avoid the pain of a spanking. If we are lucky, we eventually master just what to do and how to do it to lessen the blows. The question is, what do you say about yourself when you show that you know how to take a beating?

In relationships, it is quite possible to stay long after it is healthy or wise to do so. But you can only duck and dodge for so long. You can only take so much. You can only master what you know is coming, which leaves you completely unprepared for new developments. To stay for the sake of staying could hurt you or get you hurt. Beyond the physical, mental, and emotional pain, there is the damage that is done to your spirit. When that damage happens, there is no way to duck, run or hide from the pain.

Until today, you may have considered yourself brave for staying in a relationship or other situation because you knew *how* to stay. Just for today, be devoted to evaluating why you stay, what you must do to stay and whether or not staying is causing you spiritual pain.

Today I am devoted to the examination of my motives and methods for staying in a situation where I could possibly get hurt!

FEBRUARY 14

I will know love when I realize . . . if I am hurting,
I am not loving!

Love is simple. We make it hard with our trappings, expectations and demands. We make loving difficult, painful, hurtful and regrettable because we keep trying to figure out how to do love, give love and get loved right. We place limits, restrictions and conditions on our loving and those we love. Sometimes it works. Usually it does not. Then, when we don't get the right kind of love, we feel hurt. We blame love.

Love does not hurt! Falling into the traps we set to get and keep love makes us hurt ourselves. Love is! It is the experience of joy we have when we have the courage to tell the truth, when we have the courage to be exactly who we are and when we allow those we love to do the same. Love is not what we have been told it is by others who have been hurt. Love is not what we have seen in pictures. Love is not a tool or a weapon. Love is the key. It is the key that allows you to see more in yourself, for yourself and about yourself than you would ever dare to show to the world.

Love is simple! You simply give love for the sake of love, or you don't! You simply know love and share love, or you don't! You simply are love without demands and expectations or you will continue to fall into traps and hurt yourself because you fail to acknowledge *yourself* as the love you keep trying to get right!

Until today, you may have believed that there were things you had to do to get love. You may have demanded that others do things to prove their love for you. Just for today, be devoted to evaluating beliefs you hold about love. Take this opportunity to ask yourself whether or not you believe that you are loved, loving and loveable!

*Today I am devoted to identifying the ways I place
demands and expectations on love!*

FEBRUARY 15

I will know love when I realize . . . the goodness of love is its presence!

The voice of love is always calling out to you. It is whispering gently into your heart, reminding you, "I am here for you! I love you just as you are!" Love offers you everything you need and desire. Love wants to give those things and more because love recognizes the jewel that you are. Do you recognize the jewel that love is and offers?

Love wants to hold you, comfort and lift you. Love knows you! It knows what you have to offer life. More important, you don't have to work to get love! The only work love requires of you is the work you must do on yourself. Work on your heart, your mind, your behavior, your false notions about love that have caused the pain, confusion and despair you believe have something to do with love. While you are working on yourself, love wants you to be aware! Keep your eyes open because there are many things masquerading as love that are not at all loving.

Love will not leave you, nor will it ever dishonor you. Love will not rush you. Love will not come to take anything from you. Love gives to you! Love protects you! Love is the voice of God whispering to you from within yourself. The voice of love tells you that God loves you right now! No matter where you are or what you have done. The voice of love is asking you to tell love where you hurt, tell love why you hurt, tell love how you got hurt. Love wants you to know that it doesn't matter who hurt you, why they hurt you or how long you have been hurting. Love wants you to know that just a little bit of God will heal you!

Until today, you may not have realized that the voice of love is God's voice calling out to you. You may have been so busy trying to find love that you were not available to hear its call. Just for today, listen closely for the voice of love. Be diligent in remembering that love is always available to care for you and heal whatever is ailing you.

Today I am devoted to identifying the voice of love when it speaks to me!

FEBRUARY 16

*I will know love when I realize . . . truth is a powerful
and meaningful expression of love!*

You have to really love someone to tell them the truth. Because
you love them, you want them to have all the information
available to help them be the best they can be. You tell them
the truth because you want them to be able to make choices
and decisions. You want them to have everything they need to fully weigh
their options. More important, when you really love someone, you want
to tell them the truth as a sign of your respect for them. You not only love
them, you respect that they are capable of handling the truth!

It is not a sign of loving someone to withhold information you think
will disturb them. It is understandable that you want spare their feelings.
However, it is not loving! It is not a sign of loving someone to do things
you know will cause them grief and lie to them about what you have
done. When you love someone, you conduct yourself in ways that not
only honor them, but in ways that honor you! When you love yourself,
you honor yourself. When you honor yourself, you can honor others
with the truth.

It is not a sign of loving someone to watch them engage in conduct
that is potentially dangerous and to say nothing. You may not know
what to say or how to say it, but if you love someone, you will figure out
a way. You will figure out a way to let them know you cherish and honor
them, but that you do not support their behavior. When you love someone, it is okay not to like their behavior. It is also okay to let them know.
When you love someone enough to tell them the truth, chances are you
are giving them exactly what they need in order to realize just how much
you really do love them.

Until today, you may have been withholding the truth, censoring
the truth or deciding just how much truth a loved one can handle. Just
for today, be devoted to finding loving ways to let others know the truth
about themselves that you already know. Whatever you have to say,
begin with "I love you so much!"

Today I am devoted to expressing truth as a sign of love!

FEBRUARY 17

I will know love when I realize . . . love equally given
and equally received is love equally shared.

Love can only exist between equals. If one person is trying to
get something from the other, if one person believes they
have something that the other one lacks, if one person believes that the other person makes them something that they
are not, the union is not grounded in love. It is an invitation to disaster!

When a relationship is not between equals, it quickly disintegrates
into the "I-You" scenario. *I give. You take. I need. You give. I know. You accept.* Under these conditions, one partner is bound to feel more powerful than the other. When a relationship is not between equals, it quickly
disintegrates into a bargain-hunters delight! *I have this. What will you
give me for it? I did this. What will you do in return? I need this. What must
I do to get it from you? I want this. What can you do to help me get it?*

You will know you are in a loving relationship with an equal when
you are willing to see a person exactly as they are and hold no grievances
against them. You will be willing to accept that there are differences between you and not be afraid to allow the differences to exist. You will be
open to making choices and decisions for yourself and allowing your
partner to do the same. You will be able to ask for and receive support
and constructive criticism. More important, you will know that you are
loving an equal when you know within your heart of hearts that everything you have and can do, your partner already has and can do for him
or herself. If you are not loving an equal, chances are you have some issues with control.

Until today, you may have believed it was your responsibility to give
your partner what they do not have, or to be for your partner what you
believe they are not. Just for today, be devoted to seeing your partner and
your friends, as peers, as equals. Be available to assist and support them,
but be aware of the ways in which you try to do things for them.

*Today I am devoted to seeing myself and
those whom I love as equals!*

FEBRUARY 18

I will know love when I realize . . . I have to see
the love that is present right now!

Have you confused loving someone with wanting to be in a
loving relationship with them? Have you confused caring
about someone with wanting to be around them all of the
time? Have you confused having needs and desires with
needing to have those desires fulfilled? Chances are if you have confused
any of these things, you may not know it.

It is perfectly natural and normal for a human being to want the
companionship of another human being. We want to be held and heard,
honored and respected, cherished and valued by someone. You can have
these things in your life, in one form or another, but if they are not tied
up in the bow of an intimate, loving relationship, you may wonder why
nobody wants to be in a relationship with you.

We get confused about what a relationship is and what it says about
us. We confuse the need for loving care and concern with our desire to
be in an intimate union. We also confuse a good, loving, platonic relationship with some form of rejection. *To be in a relationship is a choice!*
Human beings have a right to choose to be or not to be in a relationship.
What they choose may have nothing to do with you.

People can love you and care about you without experiencing you in
an intimate, loving relationship.

I know this may be a little hard for you to swallow. It may also be
confusing. I offer you this: Cool out on the demand to be in an intimate,
loving relationship! Open your eyes to the love in the relationships you
have right now!

Until today, you may have been confused about the people who
chose not to have an intimate relationship with you. Just for today, be
devoted to embracing the love, support and comfort you receive in the
relationships you have with family, friends and coworkers.

*Today I am devoted to embracing and acknowledging
the love I receive in all of my relationships!*

FEBRUARY 19

I will know love when I realize . . . I must open my heart
if I want to feel love!

No words can bring back what you believe was taken from
you or fix what you believe to be broken in your heart. No
matter what is said, or how it is said, words cannot heal or
open a heart that has been closed by pain. When your heart
has been closed in anger or fear, only the power of love can open it.

There is absolutely *no-thing* anyone can say or do to make you trust
them once they have betrayed you. You will not depend on someone
once they have let you down. No matter how hard they may try, no one
can find the words that will make you forgive them once you have decided you cannot. In either of these states, you are not open to love. You
are holding on to grievances, judgments, expectations or demands. You
seek punishment or revenge. And no matter what anyone may say or do,
you will not feel fulfilled. In this state, you are not open to love. Instead,
you are intent on the punishment of yourself and others.

Many of us have had the experience of shutting our hearts down. We
do it unconsciously to protect ourselves. We do it in response to the pain
of losing love. We do it to ward off the desperation of unrequited love.
You see, when a heart goes into shutdown, the love that is required cannot come from someone else. It is a love you must bring forth from
within yourself. This is the love required to heal, and it cannot get in or
get out as long as you are holding on to grievances, judgments, expectations or demands.

Until today, you may have closed your heart to protect yourself. Just
for today, open the doors of your heart. Release all grievances you are
holding against others. Allow one person to do something nice for you,
say something nice to you. If your heart does not open just a little bit
today, try it again tomorrow.

Today I am devoted to opening my heart
to express and experience love.

FEBRUARY 20

I will know love when I realize . . . I cannot do unloving things for the sake of love.

When you love someone, you must be willing to share certain things you believe will save them trouble or grief. That is the nature of this message. It is an attempt to save you grief. So here goes—*don't sleep with other people's partners!* It's not nice! In fact it is dangerous! It really pisses people off, and if you are not careful, you may find out just how pissed off they are! I know you think it's love. I know *you feel* this one is *the one.* You are mistaken. The one who is with someone else cannot be *the one* that is meant for you. Forget what they may say! Forget all the things you tell yourself! It is *never* a loving thing to do to sleep with someone else's partner under any circumstances. So please, don't do it!

This is not an easy thing to share with you. Most people who say they love you simply won't talk about it at all. Some of those same people may even help you do what they know *you should not do.* But I really love you. I want the best for you, and I know that sleeping with someone else's partner is not the best you can do! It is not very spiritual! No matter what the other says to you, if you two are supposed to be together, you will be together—*after the divorce!*

Oh, you didn't know they had someone else? Well, the minute you find out that they do, your duty to yourself is to pack your bag of "reasons why!" You must pick up all the rationales that support you in doing *one of the most unloving things* you could ever do and *get the heck out!* You must take full responsibility for what happens if you choose to stay. One day, when you least expect it, the very thing you have done will be done to you. You can never expect to realize the love you deserve when you insist on doing such an unloving thing as sleeping with someone else's partner!

Until today, you may have convinced yourself that love was the reason you were in a relationship with someone else's partner. Just for today, lay down all of the reasons and excuses. Vow to start packing and get out!

Today I am devoted to ending the dead end in my life!

FEBRUARY 21

I will know love when I realize . . . there are places
in me that only love can heal!

Whether you explain it with the saying, Opposites attract or
Like draws like, there is something mystical about the way
we attract people into our lives, particularly our lovers.
There is a divine setup working that ensures we attract the
people who will cause us to take a deeper look at ourselves. The people
we are attracted to and who are attracted to us are the ones who volun-
teer to help us heal our unseen wounds.

Within each of us are the impressions of every experience we have
had in our lifetime. Some of those impressions are smooth. Some are very
rocky. Some of the imprints are shallow. Others are very deep. The depth
and texture of each one depends on our response, our reaction during an
experience. The smoother, more shallow impression indicates a gentle,
more peaceful experience. The rougher, deeper imprints indicate harsh,
less loving experiences. As we have new experiences, some of the patterns
are repeated, creating mental and emotional responses within us.

As far as relationships are concerned, we attract people whose impressions are similar to our own. The interactions we have with the other
person evoke the responses within us that require healing. By the same
token, our behavior stirs the responses that are imprinted within the
other. The healing takes place when we choose a new response.

The next time your interactions with another person evoke anger,
fear, sadness, or any other painful response, know that you are in the
process of healing. In the precise moment that you feel the need to react,
call on love and thank the other person for showing you things about
yourself that you need to know.

Until today, you may not have understood why you have certain reactions to certain people in certain situations. Just for today, when
someone evokes a negative response in you, remember that they are
helping you heal.

Today I am devoted to healing the wounded spaces in me.

FEBRUARY 22

I will know love when I realize . . .
there is nothing in my heart that God doesn't know,
love and understand.

When it *feels like* there is no one that you can turn to, no one that you can trust, remember there is always God. There is nowhere you can go, no state of mind in which you can dwell that is beyond the reach of God. God knows your heart. God gave it to you, remember? God knows all about those things that you have buried so deeply you may have forgotten they exist. God never forgets.

God knows your shame. God knows the things that have have angered you, frightened you and caused you to doubt the power and purity of love. God knows *all* about *all* of the things that you are so ashamed of you dare not speak them aloud. God *knows* and is still there with you, because shame is not in God's vocabulary. *Forgiveness is!*

God knows your fear. God knows all about those things you have done when you were afraid of losing or afraid of being left. God knows what you have done to be accepted. God knows all of the things you could not do because you were afraid to do them wrong. God even knows about the things you want to do but are afraid to do because you fear you don't really deserve them. God knows what you deserve. God also knows what you have left undone because of anger, hurt, fear and shame. You, like God, know that those are the things that make you feel guilty and, in response, you have closed your heart. God knows every nook and cranny of your heart. What you may not know is, if you are willing to open your heart to God, God will take the old, hurtful, shameful, guilt-ridden things out and put some new, good things in.

Until today, you may have allowed shame, guilt, fear or anger to close your heart. Just for today, find one thing that you are willing to cleanse from your heart. Give it to God in word, thought or writing.

Today I am devoted to opening my heart to God!

FEBRUARY 23

I will know love when I realize . . . there is nothing
I have done that God cannot forgive or understand.

Let's lay our cards out on the table. You have not always done
your best. You have not always lived up to your responsibilities or your own expectations. There have been times when
you have not *shown up* prepared to do what you needed to
do. Even though you really don't like to admit it, there are times when
you feel inadequate, afraid of failing. Is it not also true that to cover up
for all of the things you have difficulty admitting about yourself, you
hide behind a harsh, I-don't-give-a-damn veneer? If you are able to
admit any of these things about yourself, then we are on the right track!
You see, God already knows this about you and loves you just the same.

Let's take this one step further. Would you say that there have been
times when you have chosen to be less than honest in order to get what
you want? How do you respond when you get caught in a lie? Would this
mean that you have said and done things that still haunt you? Have there
been occasions when you have made promises that you knew at the time
they were made you would not keep? How did you get out of doing what
you promised you would do? Don't you hate to be wrong? What do you
do to keep others from knowing when you are? How do you act out your
anger? How do you hide your fear? How do you live with the fact that
there are things you have not done because of fear or anger? Before you
try to answer one or more of these inquires, there is something I want
you to remember: God knows all about you! God cares. God understands. And God loves you anyway.

Until today, you may have been hiding things about yourself. Just
for today, allow yourself to remember, to accept and to acknowledge that
God knows you and loves you.

Today I am devoted to laying all of my cards
on God's table!

FEBRUARY 24

I will know love when I realize . . .
the fibers of a relationship are constructed from
the fibers of my heart.

Are you relationship material? The question is not are you *looking* for a relationship? Nor is it do you *want* a relationship? The question is, *are you a clear example of the stuff a relationship is made of?*

In order to be relationship material you must be able to open your heart to someone, and you must know what to do when they open their heart to you. You must be absolutely okay with every little thing that you know to be true about you. Now here's the kicker. Once you see yourself, you must be willing to allow others to see you exactly as you are! You must be able to stand before another person without fear, without excuses and with all of your defenses down. And if you cannot, you may not be relationship material.

If you are relationship material, you are trusting and trustworthy. If you are relationship material, when your dark hour is upon you, there is a light switch inside of you that you know how to turn on. By the same token, when your partner faces his/her own darkness, you are there. You don't fall apart because he/she seems to be falling apart.

In order to be relationship material, you must take a risk, tell the truth, trust that you will be heard. You must lay down all defenses, expectations and judgments. You must give without taking, grow without overshadowing, bend without feeling broken and know without doubt. Most important of all, you must know exactly what you want and be willing to ask for it, knowing exactly what you are willing to do if you do not get it.

Until today, you may not have realized what it takes to be relationship-ready. Just for today, ask yourself questions in order to discover whether you are ready to have the relationship you are seeking.

*Today I am devoted to getting myself in shape
for a relationship!*

FEBRUARY 25

I will know love when I realize . . .
it doesn't have to be easy to be good!

Relationships are not easy! They are not easy to find, to get in or to stay in. And sometimes, you must answer the question, *Why?* Relationships are wonderful *healing tools.* A relationship can *heal* us of *the fear* of having a relationship. A relationship can heal you of the fear of being seen for who you are. When you pour the kind of love that a relationship requires into the darkness in your own mind, everything comes to light. And that, my dear, is not an easy thing to see!

Relationships are wonderful *teaching tools.* A relationship makes very clear to you and others those things to which you have a tendency to *selfishly cling*—thoughts, feelings, memories and sometimes possessions. A relationship will teach you what you really believe your all is worth. It will point out your need to be *self-full,* as you pursue your goal to be *self-defined* and *self-reliant.* When you are faced with the decision to hold on to or let go of the relationship, everything the relationship has taught you about yourself must be examined. And believe me, that is not an easy examination to make!

Relationships are *God-given.* This means they are a blessing! A relationship blesses you with the opportunity to share who you are with someone else who is willing to see the truth of who you are. A relationship is the home of love, which means it is a palace built by God. Unfortunately, it is not an easy task to keep the place clean!

Until today, you may not have realized the healing effect of your relationships, or you may not have known what you were being taught about yourself. Just for today, look at all of your relationships. Embrace your healing needs. Recognize that there are still some things that you are learning about yourself.

Today I am devoted to the healing and learning
opportunities available to me in all of my relationships.

I will know love when I realize . . . people do not change
just because I want them to change!

If you are looking for a change in your mate and see no signs
of its coming, stop looking! You are with whom you are
with because *you choose* to be with them. Stop looking for
something else and see the love in whom you are with.

If you are listening to hear something from your mate that you
haven't heard, stop listening! If you are waiting for a change, stop! You
chose this person! You chose them because they opened your heart. You
chose them precisely because of who they are and how they sounded.
Stop checking to see if they are going to change because you may have
changed. Stop waiting to see if they are going to change into what *you
knew they were not.* See who this is. Hear what they say. Accept what they
do as the truth of who they are and look for the love in them.

It is not loving to expect someone to change because you want them
to or because you think they should. Love is consistent. Love allows us to
see and hear the best of what we have right now. The love within us
grows when we grow. It shifts as we shift. When how we love grows and
shifts, love gives us the opportunity to choose again, whether or not our
partner changes.

Very often when we change, our needs change. At this point, we can
become very demanding of our mates. By asking your partner to change
to your reality, you are asking that they ignore their own. Looking for,
listening for, checking for or demanding change is not loving. It is controlling! The cure for this type of unloving control is simple. If who you
have and what you have no longer meet your needs, choose again.

Until today, you may have been preoccupied with changes you need
your mate to make. Just for today, look for and embrace the things you
love about who your partner is right now.

*Today I am devoted to putting aside my demands for
change and seeing the truth and love in who my partner is!*

FEBRUARY 27

I will know love when I realize . . . loving myself
helps to resolve the things that make me feel bad.

When you are feeling bad within yourself, anything and
everything outside of you looks better. You may be able to
convince yourself it is better to run away from your feelings.
You will probably think the bad feeling is gone—*for a little
while.*

When you are feeling bad, the feeling is *in* you. You can't get away
from it! You might find someone to blame it on. That will only work for
a while. Sooner or later you will be forced to accept the fact that the bad
feeling is your feeling and it has nothing to do with anyone else.

Most bad feelings are the result of conflict. The conflict may be the
result of not getting what you want or believe you can have. The conflict
could come from the feeling that you are losing control of yourself and
your life. You may have a partner or a parent who wants you to do something, and you are not sure what to do about it. In any case, at the core
of all bad feelings there is an absence of one essential thing—love.

When you are feeling bad about yourself or your life, do something
you love. Make sure that the thing you love to do is good for you. Make
sure that it will not hurt anyone else. Make sure that while you are doing
it, you remind yourself of all the ways you can be more loving, more supportive and more encouraging to yourself. Love is really the only thing
that will help you resolve your internal conflict so that you can feel better indefinitely.

Until today, you may have been blaming someone else when you feel
bad. You may have turned to something or someone that made you feel
good for a little while. Just for today, take the time to resolve the inner
conflicts so that you can be more loving to yourself and to everyone else.

*Today I am devoted to identifying the core of the
conflict that makes me feel bad!*

FEBRUARY 28

I will know love when I realize . . . love may embrace
some of the stuff I do not want to see!

If you are a woman looking for a man to love, stand up. Go
ahead! No one is looking. Stand up! If you are a man looking for a woman to love, stand up. Don't let your ego get in
the way. Stand up. Now look around. Open your heart and
your mind and look. What do you see? Do you see too short? Too tall?
Do you see lack of education? Or too much pride? Do you see fat? Thin?
Do you see black? White? Do you see *another one, just like the other one?*
The one you tried it with before? Do you see too much money? Not
enough money?

If you are looking for a mate, rest assured there is someone, somewhere who is standing up right now looking for you! Perhaps you just
can't see each other because of all the *stuff* you're looking for. Or maybe,
you can't find anyone because of all the *stuff* you refuse to look at!

Until today, you may have been searching for a mate with all of the
right stuff. Just for today, broaden the parameters of your search. Open
your heart and mind to all of the *stuff* that is available, including some of
the stuff you may have refused to look at.

*Today I am devoted to opening my heart and mind
to some new stuff!*

FEBRUARY 29

I will know love when I realize . . . love offers me
many things that I may not always see.

 Living, learning, light, luminosity,
law

Opportunity, oneness, openness

Vastness, versatility, virtue, victory

Enlightenment, eternity,

endurance, endeavor

Until today, you may not have recognized some of the less obvious
elements of love. Just for today, look beyond what you know to the hidden gifts, blessings and beauty of loving yourself and others.

Today I am devoted to going beneath the surface of love!

MARCH

AWARENESS

Open your mind.

Open your eyes.

Open your heart.

*If the eyes of your mind and heart
are not fully opened,*

*there could be some love that you
are not aware is present.*

MARCH 1

I open my heart and mind to be aware . . .
that I am the matter that matters!

Matter is anything that has weight and occupies space. The only thing standing between you and exactly what you want is space. The question is, *are you willing to be the matter that occupies this space?* You can choose to fill the space with what you need. Or you can choose to fill the space with what you lack, fear or you could fill the space with what might not happen or what cannot happen. Or you could find the courage to fill the space with the holy boldness of "I can because I am; I will, because I am!"

In the space that stands between you and exactly what you want, there is the fullness of God. The question is, how do you see the space? Have you placed the matters of others in this space? Do you see your place in the space? Do you see your joy in the space? Do you see God's grace, God's mercy, God's light and God's love in the space? Perhaps you see a risk that you can't take? Do you see what others have done and what you can't do? Or do you see the impossible dream becoming possible with God?

In the space of God's fullness that stands between you and what you want, there is an opportunity. The question is, how are *you going to use* the opportunity? You could use the opportunity to tell yourself what you have always told yourself about why you cannot or must not step into the space. You may believe that the space is too big, too wide, too much for you to handle. Or you just might realize that you have been given a divine opportunity to change the way you see the space and to close up the gap between you and God.

Until today, you may not have realized that the only thing standing between you and what you want is the opportunity to spend more time with God. Just for today, be devoted to closing any gaps between you and what you want.

*Today I am devoted to taking every opportunity
to spend time with God!*

MARCH 2

I open my heart and mind to be aware . . . I must make a
decision about how my day is going to be.

As soon as *you decide* that you are going to be faith filled, joy
filled, peace filled and filled full, you are going to have a
good day. The moment you decide that you are not going to
be beat down or weighed down, put down or run down,
hung up or beat up, upset or set up, pissed off or blown off, you are
going to have a good day. When *you decide* in your own mind that you
are going to get grounded, be centered, stay focused, have a vision, accomplish a goal, complete a mission, pursue a dream, live with purpose,
you are going to have a good day. As soon as *you decide* to accept yourself,
celebrate yourself, correct yourself, authorize yourself, validate yourself,
to be who you are, and to love yourself just the way you are, you are
going to have a good day.

If *you decide* to take just a moment, just a moment to get still, to
clear your mind, to open your heart, to listen to the sacred voice that
guides you, that protects you, that knows you and loves you, you are
going to have a good day. And if you find that you are not having a good
day, it could be that *you have not* made the decision or taken the time to
do what you know you must do to ensure that your day goes the way you
have decided it should.

Until today, you may not have been aware that decisions fuel the
spirit. You may not have realized that *you* have the power to decide the
direction of your day and your life. Just for today, make a decision about
how you want to experience the day. Fuel that decision with a commitment to do whatever it takes to ensure that it happens.

*Today I am devoted to making clear decisions about what
I choose to experience!*

MARCH 3

I open my heart and mind to be aware . . . I cannot judge
my clarity based on someone else's response!

One day, the light bulb is going to go off in your head. You
will become aware of what you are destined to do in life. On
that day, you will feel drawn away from everything you
know into a space of *unknowing*. You may be a bit frightened,
but, at the same time, you will be perfectly fine with what you *don't know*.
You will be willing to give up everything and everyone you now know in
order to pursue your destiny. Rest assured, on that day, should you share
your new awareness, you are going to upset quite a few people!

When the people in your life know who you are, they know how to
push your buttons. Believe it or not, this makes them quite comfortable.
They know just what to expect, and you give it to them. It is easy to understand why people get upset when you get clear. *They get confused!*
When people get confused about you, they may try to convince you that
it is you who are confused. A word of advice: Don't worry about how
people respond to your clarity! Worry will make you confused!

When your light bulb moment comes, sit alone in the light for a few
moments. Give heartfelt thanks for each moment of your new awareness. Write down each of your thoughts. As you feel inspired to act, *act!*
If you feel shaky or uncertain, sit down again. Call on the presence of
Spirit. If at any time during the process you experience a set back, do
not, I repeat, *do not* ask another human being for advice. Remember,
they could be confused. If you are directed by Spirit to ask someone
something, be sure to ask *who* to ask.

Until today, you may have felt the need to have those around you ap-
prove of your ideas and insights. Just for today, turn all new ideas, insights and revelations over to the Holy Spirit. Allow yourself the
privilege of basking in the *Spiritual Light* of your own heart and mind.

*Today I am devoted to becoming aware of the light
of insight within me!*

MARCH 4

I open my heart and mind to be aware . . .
I cannot sit in judgment of anyone else!

You may be looking at some people, observing their actions, trying hard to understand their motives without a clue about why they do what they do. From where you sit, it may seem that certain people *should* know better, they *should* be better and they know they *should* be doing better. The truth is that every time you *should* someone you make a judgment. This means the *wrong* you attribute to them actually belongs to you.

When you make a judgment you make a decision that the way things are is not the way things need to be. Your judgment reflects your belief in right and wrong based on what you may or may not know. Your judgment reveals your attitude of superiority that says you have the right to determine what must be done, how it must be done and who must do it. Your judgment shows that you resist accepting things the way they are. A judgment is a means of control. It is an attempt to get people to do what you need and want them to do in order to feel better about yourself. A judgment is a sign of fear. It is the foundation of discontent. Most important of all, judgment is the way you set yourself up to be judged by others.

People are who they are and do what they do whether or not you like it or agree with them. We each have different lessons to learn. We each take a different path to our lessons. There are times when someone's path will cross your path and cause you to stumble or fall. That does not make them wrong. That does not make you right. The only thing that a judgment does is distract you from what it is that you must do for yourself.

Until today, you may have decided that you knew what others should be doing and how they should be doing it. Just for today, suspend all judgments. Learn to see things and people as they are. Find a way to be okay with yourself and others.

Today I am devoted to living without judgments!
I am devoted to letting things be!

MARCH 5

I open my heart and mind to be aware . . .
everyone who grows up does not become an adult.

There are people who walk around in grown-up bodies who *are not* adults. Often they are people of advanced age and accomplishment. They can be people you trust with your life and worldly possessions. You may leave your children in their care. In fact, if you are not observant, you may find yourself sleeping with one. Because you are unaware, you expect these grown-ups to act in an adult manner. Then, in a moment of dire need, when you least expect it, you discover that this very grown-up person has no concept of what it means to be an adult. The results can be quite mind-boggling!

An adult is a person who is able to accept total responsibility for themselves and their actions. They don't blame other people for what they cannot do. They don't employ excuses to cover what they have done or not done. An adult is a person who is not afraid to say what is on their mind and say it without attacking you. Adults have a sense of clarity that will keep them calm. Adults will give themselves the benefit of the doubt, knowing that they are human. Because adults accept and acknowledge their own humanness, they can accept and acknowledge yours. Adults do not strive for perfection. They see things as they are and accept them. Adults do not fall apart in the face of disappointment. They answer frustration with patience. Adults know how to take care of their physical, mental and emotional needs, and they are able to put their needs aside in order to handle an emergency. An adult is a person whose attention is not totally focused on their wants and needs. God gets some attention, the adult gets some and you can have the rest.

Until today, you may have been confused about the differences between a *grown-up* and an *adult*. Just for today, spend some time examining yourself to ensure you are developing adult qualities and behaviors.

Today I am devoted to growing into adulthood!

MARCH 6

I open my heart and mind to be aware . . .
pain is a warning that something is out of order!

A philosopher once said, "Until a man gets into trouble with his own heart, chances are he will not get out of trouble with God!" In other words, pain is not natural! It is an indication that an *ungodly condition* exists. It is a warning that something is placing a strain on your divine connection. Pain is life's way of getting your attention. It is also God's way of letting you know that you are out of balance, out of order or both!

It is rare that pain will slam you to the ground without a warning. It starts small. If left unattended, the pain becomes a flashing neon sign in the center of your brain. This is not natural. It is natural that you may feel a few pains at the beginning of a new experience. That's just a little fear passing through. The problem is that we have come to accept gnawing, sometimes debilitating pain as a natural way of living. We almost expect it! We believe that pain is a good thing. Nothing could be further from the truth!

There are people who will tell you that it is noble to tolerate pain. "Bite the bullet!" "Grit your teeth!" Pain, they believe, is good for you. In response, you may try to find ways to *deal with* pain. You *expect* to experience pain in your life, and when it strikes, you don't complain about it. Pain is not a godly, natural experience. When it erupts in your life, you must stop doing whatever is causing it, and start doing whatever it will take to eliminate it.

Until today, you may have been making excuses for why you have pain in your life. You may have been afraid to acknowledge what causes you pain. Just for today, be devoted to identifying and eliminating the situations and the people who cause you pain. Oh, sure! The thought of doing it may be painful, but awareness is the first step toward healing! Once you become aware and acknowledge the cause, you will be headed toward a pain-free existence!

Today I am devoted to the elimination of pain in my life!

MARCH 7

I open my heart and mind to be aware . . . God can only
do for me what God can do through me!

God cannot help you unless you allow God to help you! Many of
us could be accused of trying to out-God God. We think we
know more than God. We think we can do more than God.
We actually believe that what we want and how we want it is
better than the way God can bring it to us. In fact, we get so busy doing
what we do the way we do it, there is no opportunity for God to get into
our lives at all!

God is so merciful! God will not fight you. If God did, you would
get beat up *badly! Most of us could use a divine butt whipping.* Instead,
God sits back and waits to be invited into your life. God will let you do
whatever you want to do until you realize that God can do it better.

If you want to run the show, God will let you. If you want to pull all
the strings, that's up to you. If you want to insist that what you are doing
is the way it should be done, even when you are not getting anywhere, go
right ahead. God will let you run yourself ragged, if you choose to do so.
Unfortunately, you may not always be aware that you are in God's way.
You think you are demonstrating your independence. You think that it
is all up to you and that you must do it or it won't get done. God knows
better! God knows that God cannot fail! However, God has no need to
prove to you what God can do.

How do you know when you are in God's way? How do you know
when you are running your program rather than allowing God's divine
plan to unfold? It's very simple! If you are struggling to make things happen and they are not happening, it's you, not God, running the show.

Until today, you may have been directing your own life and attempting to produce your own blessings. Just for today, ask for direction. Open yourself to guidance. Give up your attachments to having
things *your way.* Open yourself to God's way.

*Today I am devoted to allowing God to work
through me and for me!*

MARCH 8

I open my heart and mind to be aware . . .
I am constantly setting standards for how others
will see me and treat me.

As you move into the day, be aware of how you treat yourself.
As you shower or bathe, be aware of how you handle your
body. Are you gentle? Or are you rough? As you eat your
meals today, be aware of how much time, energy and attention you give to nourishing yourself. When it comes to self-nurturing,
are you attentively conscious? Are you unconsciously rushed? Be aware of
what you do to and for yourself, because you set the standard for others.

Be aware of how you handle your mind. When you talk to yourself,
do you yell or scream? When you question yourself, do you accuse? Do
you allow yourself the pleasure of a complete thought, or do you cut
your thoughts off with judgments? Just be aware of how you think what
you think. You don't have to do anything about it right now.

Be aware of how you handle your soul. Do you give yourself permission to ask what you need to know? When you do not keep the commitments you make to yourself, are you understanding? Are you the
merciless rough rider who rarely cuts yourself any slack? How do you
handle yourself in a crisis? Just be aware. It is not necessary to do anything about it right now. However, as you grow in your awareness of
how you treat yourself, you will probably become aware of the example
you have set for others. You may realize that the time has come to set a
new example.

Until today, you may not have been aware of how unkind, impatient, unsupportive, critical, angry, frustrated and rough you can be with
yourself. Just for today, be aware of how you treat yourself. Remember,
awareness is the first step toward change.

*Today I am devoted to becoming more aware
of how I am with myself!*

MARCH 9

I open my heart and mind to be aware . . .
there are some things about me that nothing can change.

 In your deepest, darkest hour, when it seems like all you have ever wanted is about to escape your grasp forever, hold on to these words:

As divine beings we can really do no wrong.
We make choices.
Choices have consequences.
The only way wrong gets in is when we put it on the path, when we judge ourselves and others.
Life is merciful!
Life offers us an endless supply of *do-overs.*
Life always offers you the opportunity to do it over until you receive the desired results of your heart.
This is the key to your righteousness. (right-use-ness)
Ron Hulnick

Until today, you may have regretted your mistakes. You may have felt as though the things you have not done could not be done. Just for today, seize the opportunity to do over some of the things you have already done.

Today I am devoted to viewing mistakes and misfortunes as do-overs!

I open my heart and mind to be aware . . . if I walk in the
footsteps of the Master I will master my true Self.

Jesus the Christ had a goal: to serve God. On that goal he remained focused. He had a purpose: to teach love. On that
purpose he remained focused. He had a mission: to demonstrate to people how to lovingly serve each other while serving God. To that mission alone, he gave all of his energy. In his own
words, he revealed the power of having a purpose when he said, *"But for
this purpose was I born."* In essence, Jesus was saying to us, when your life
is for a purpose, you will rise above all difficulties.

Focus on the goal. Focus on the purpose. Focus on accomplishing
the goal. Each day hundreds of thousands of people get out of bed with
no goal. Going to work is not a goal! It is an activity! Paying bills is not a
purpose! It is an activity! Providing for a family is not a mission! It is an
activity!

Your goal is the *what* of your life. The goal is not the place you begin.
It is the place you end up! Your purpose is the *why* of your life—why you
as an individual are moving toward the goal, the end. Your mission is the
how of your life. Once you are clear about the what, the why and the
how, you have a focus. You have something to live for that moves you
into, through and out of the activities of your life.

We were each born for some purpose. Jesus was clear. He was focused. He mastered his mind and his life with focus. He was kind
enough to leave us instructions on how to do what he did. He said, *"Follow me! For the things I have done, greater things than this shall you do."*

Until today, you may not have been aware that the Master teacher
left you instructions. You may not have realized he said do as I have
done. Stay focused! Just for today, shift your attention from the activities
of your daily life and discover your goal, your purpose and your mission.

*Today I am devoted to following in the footsteps
of the Master teacher!*

I open my heart and mind to be aware . . . the energy
I give to what I do determines if my actions are
healthy or unhealthy.

There is a difference between a goal and an obsession. There
is also a difference between being responsible and being
compulsive. Many people are obsessive doers. They have so
much to do, that the very qualities that drive them toward
success are the qualities that create their tension and frustration.

It is true that anything you desire to have in life, you must work for.
The question is, *do you have to work so hard? Must you always have something to do? Is it possible that you could ease up just a little?* Most people
would say no. Very few of us understand that for every step we take toward our desires, the Universe will take two. If we have to do it all on our
own, there is absolutely nothing left for God to do for us.

One reason we work so hard is that we are afraid. Few people will
admit it, but most of us live in fear that we are not going to achieve our
goals, receive the results we expect or fulfill our heartfelt desires. It is this
fear that causes us to engage in a power struggle with God. If you really
believe that you have to do it all, *what do you think God is doing or can do
for you?*

Strain, struggle, frustration, tension, anxiety, compulsion, obsession
and fear are the results you get when you are pushing too hard. God, the
creative force of the universe, the power over all life, doesn't have to push
to get you what you want. As a matter of fact, if you would just ease up a
little, you might be surprised by what God will do on your behalf.

Until today, you may not have been aware that you can do too
much. In fact, you may have been a stumbling block on your own path.
Just for today, ease up! Relax! Sit back and put your feet up! Give God a
chance to do something for you.

Today I am devoted to not doing what God can do for me!

MARCH 12

I open my heart and mind to be aware . . .
that I can be led into believing things that are not true!

There is a force that uses our fears and insecurities to keep us off track. It is called "the deceptive intelligence" and it is a tricky little bugger! The deceptive intelligence will lead you to believe that all of your prayers have fallen on deaf ears. That all of your faith will prove to be fruitless. At the slightest sign of weakness on your part, the deceptive intelligence will send you off the deep end, to chase shadows in the dark and abandon your dreams.

The deceptive intelligence will use your mouth to say things that you cannot take back. It will use your body to do things that cannot be undone. The deceptive intelligence will keep you up at night! The deceptive intelligence will make you see things that are not there and hear things that are not said. You must be aware of the deceptive intelligence! More important, you must recognize that the deceptive intelligence is not lurking *out there*. Oh, no! It is in you!

If you are afraid of *them,* leery of *this,* doubtful of *that,* thinking of yourself as *unworthy, undeserving* or *out there on your own,* the deceptive intelligence will move into your heart and mind, set up housekeeping and have a banquet on your dreams! There is only one way to save yourself from the influence of the deceptive intelligence. That is to know the truth! The truth is: "No weapon formed against me shall prosper!" The deceptive intelligence may be in you, but you must know that neither inner nor outer enemies will prosper or take over unless you let them.

Until today, you may have been employed by the deceptive intelligence to frighten yourself, confuse yourself or to take yourself off course. Just for today, refuse to be used by the inner voices that will lead you to believe something other than the truth.

Today I am devoted to remembering that
"No weapon formed against me shall prosper!"

MARCH 13

I open my heart and mind to be aware . . . that I may not always be aware of exactly what I am seeing!

Today's message continues yesterday's theme regarding the deceptive intelligence. If you have made a decision about your life, the deceptive intelligence will use *coulda, shoulda, woulda,* to make you doubt yourself. When these thoughts raise their ugly little heads in your mind, it is up to you to blast them out! *Do not* allow the deceptive intelligence to make you believe there is no blessing or lesson in being exactly where you are, doing exactly what you are doing.

If you are in a situation you cannot get out of, or looking at a situation you cannot get into, the deceptive intelligence is going to start singing to you. The songs will sound like this, *"I could if . . ."* Or *"I should have seen . . ."* Or *"I shouldn't have said . . ."* Or *"If only he would / she would / they would, I could . . ."* The minute you hear the first note, start humming your own tune! Something like, "Ain't gonna let nobody turn me around!" Or "This little light of mine!" Or "Ain't no stopping me now!" Start singing any tune that will drown out the deceptive voice that will lead you to believe you cannot get to where you are going.

Be aware! The deceptive intelligence is very smart! It will show you evidence, physical proof. It will use the people you love. Don't be fooled! You can have it! Be it! Do it! As long as you do not get sucked into the web of the deceptive intelligence, which will cause you to abandon your goals based on what you did or did not do yesterday.

Until today, you may not have recognized the songs, games or tools of the deceptive intelligence. Just for today, sing an affirming song to yourself, and stay focused on your goals.

Today I am devoted to affirming, supporting and staying focused on my goals!

MARCH 14

*I open my heart and mind to be aware . . . that I have
the power to take what appears to be bad
until it becomes something better!*

If what you are thinking doesn't make you feel good, change that thought. If what you are feeling doesn't make you feel better, change the feeling. If what you are doing doesn't make you feel worthy, change the deed.

Feeling bad has a way of luring us into complacency. We begin to accept that this is the way it is always going to be, that what is going on is out of our control. This is true, to a point. You can never change what is going on outside of you; however, you can always change what you do in response.

Every experience leaves an imprint on our hearts and minds. That imprint evokes certain feelings and thoughts. When an experience triggers those thoughts and feelings, we have the right to say *no!* Yes that's right, you have to talk to yourself. Talk to your brain. Talk to your heart. Talk to the cloud of funk that is lurking around, waiting to suck you up.

No! You are not going to lure me into feeling bad! No! You are not going to convince me that I have to be angry! I am going to think good thoughts no matter what! I am going to love you and accept you no matter what! And if you don't like it, you can take your negative energy someplace else! Try responding to a negative feeling once or twice in this way and watch how fast it will leave you alone.

Until today, you may have allowed yourself to be sucked into the energy of bad thoughts, bad feelings and bad experiences. Just for today, remind yourself that bad cannot bother you unless you are available.

*Today I am devoted to speaking to the conditions in my life
until they become better!*

MARCH 15

*I open my heart and mind to be aware . . . the power
to change leads to a powerful change!*

Just in case you missed yesterday's message, here is another perspective. No matter what is going on in your life at any given time, there is *only* one thing you can do. No matter how you feel in response to a specific experience, circumstance, situation or memory, there is *always* one thing you can do. In every or any situation, regardless of the mitigating factors, you can always *change your mind!*

If what you are thinking, saying or doing in response to any person or experience is not bringing you peace, *change your mind!* If your mind is flooded with memories and thoughts of a pain-filled past or a not-so-promising future, *change your mind!* You can do it, just like that! When you change your mind, the things you've been thinking about, worrying about, crying over, running from, will look completely different. It may not be that anything in the actual picture changes; however, your changed mind will alter the way you see it.

If you are serious about creating a change in your mind, here are a few tips. Do not insist that people be who you want them to be. Do not insist that you are someone you are not. Do not insist that you can do things you cannot do. Do not insist that you know things that you don't. Do not insist that you will do things that you won't do. Do not insist that everyone is wrong about you. Do not insist that you are right. Whenever you are insistent about something, you create an attachment. Breaking that attachment creates disruption in the mind.

Until today, you may not have realized that you can always change your mind. Just for today, be devoted to changing how you think about things, how you see things and what you tell yourself about everything. Changing your mind about anything or anyone transforms how those things or persons impact your life.

*Today I am devoted to changing my mind
about things and about myself!*

MARCH 16

I open my heart and mind to be aware . . .
there is a difference between constructive criticism
and destructive criticism.

No one, not even you or I, is above criticism. Criticism is constructive input from others that makes us aware of aspects of ourselves where improvement is needed. Criticism, when offered with love, opens our eyes to blind spots, makes us aware of unconscious or habitual responses. Criticism keeps us on track. Criticism, even when we don't want it, did not ask for it or do not like the source from which it comes, is very important feedback.

Criticism is not a license to tell others what you don't like about them. It is not an opportunity to tell people what you think they are doing wrong. Criticism does not make you smarter or better than the one you are criticizing. In fact, the stuff you are critical of in others is the same stuff you don't like about yourself. When you see your insecurities and inadequacies, the things you deny or judge about yourself, showing up in someone else, your first instinct is to get as far away as possible.

When you offer criticism, it must be from the place in you that can see the best in and want the best for someone else. When it is offered in this way, what is commonly called criticism becomes care-frontation and share-frontation, not confrontation. When you use criticism as a way to make someone wrong or to prove you are right, then you, my dear, are out of order!

Until today, you may not have been aware that criticism of others is a reflection of the nonacceptance of self. Just for today, care-front and share-front rather than confront those around you.

*Today I am devoted to sharing observations and
expressing concerns in a loving and caring way—the way
I would want to hear them!*

MARCH 17

I open my heart and mind to be aware . . .
only my inner authority can give me outer authority.

If you think about it, you would become aware that credentialization, certification, authorization and validation share a common definition. Each is a process in which someone else tells you how good you are or are not. There are areas in which people must be well trained and equipped to handle the demands of their craft. However, there are also judgments attached to the words "credential," "certificate," "authority" and "validity." These judgments have a subtle impact on the human psyche. The implication is that something outside of you can make you okay.

You may think that because you don't have the credential or the certificate, you do not have the authority to *be*. Perhaps because you are afraid of not making the grade, not being *okay* in the eyes of someone else, you have convinced yourself that you are not okay. What no one apart from yourself is going to tell you or convince you is that, *with the power of a made-up mind, you are authorized to do anything you choose.*

There is nothing more validating than belief in yourself and your abilities. If you believe you have the power, the power is yours. There is no credential, certificate or authority beyond the power of a made-up mind. There comes a moment when you must decide that you are going to believe in yourself. When that moment comes, you become aware that outside authority is the icing. Your mind is the cake!

Until today, you may have been waiting for someone to tell you something or give you something that would make you feel okay. Just for today, accept that there is a place in you where you are just fine. Make it your business today to tap in to that place.

*Today I am devoted to becoming aware
that I am okay as I am!*

I open my heart and mind to be aware . . .
I have allowed what others believe about me
to become what I believe about myself.

If you tell yourself something long enough, you will believe it. If you fail to take the time to question why you do what you do, you can become convinced that you cannot do anything else. Other people will help you stay convinced. People are in the habit of telling other people who they are. They tell you who they expect you to be, who they need you to be and who they want you to be. If you listen to people about who you are, you may realize you cannot be yourself because *you have been somebody else for so long!*

How can you be yourself and still please your parents? How can you be yourself and meet the demands of the world around you? How much of what you do is what is expected of you? How can you figure out how much of *you* is *them?* Well, needless to say, *it ain't easy!* But there is a way.

When you can be happy with yourself and what you do without feeling guilty about it, your parents will be pleased. When you negotiate the salary you believe you are worthy of having, you will be excited about going to work. When you can resist the tendency to control your children, you will be the parent that every child needs. When you are willing to accept yourself without believing that you have to be right all of the time, everybody will want to marry you. When you open your heart and allow people to see you exactly as you are, you will attract more friends than you will know what to do with. If on the other hand, you are defending the reasons, holding on to the excuses, offering explanations for why you are the way you are, you may never know the truth of your being.

Until today, you may not have been aware of your true identity. You may have accepted the expectations of others as the fabric of your being. Just for today, stand in your true identity without guilt, defenses or apologies.

Today I am devoted to finding out exactly who I am!

I open my heart and mind to be aware . . .
without death there can be no change.

Author John Roger wrote, "We are only born once into life,
but in life we are re-born many times." He was describing
the many "mini-deaths" we experience on our journey
through life. We die to old ways of being to be reborn in our
power. We die to old beliefs to be reborn in the truth. We die to habits of
need, dependency and control to be reborn in reliance on Spirit. We die
to fear of Spirit to be reborn into the Spirit of *fearlessness.*

We are taught that death is the end. It is, we believe, the darkness
into which we plunge, never to return, of which no one can speak. As
long as you are still breathing, death becomes what we commonly call
change.

Until today, you may not have been aware of the many times you
have faced death or the ways in which death can alter your state of being.
Just for today, lay down your notions and fears about death and be willing to change.

*Today I am devoted to accepting that I must accept
death in order to change!*

MARCH 20

I open my heart and mind to be aware . . . when I am listening to myself, I cannot hear other people.

We are taught that communication is a two-way process. Consequently, we are not aware that there are three essential elements. There is talking, there is listening and there is hearing. We talk a great deal because we have much to say. In fact, we talk so much we often miss the point someone else is trying to make. Our talk about our past experience is loaded with perceptions and judgments. When we are listening, what we hear gets filtered through the same. We do talk, and we can listen. What challenges most of us is learning how to hear.

If you really want to *hear* someone when they trust you enough to talk to you, don't listen to the words, hear *how* the words are spoken. All too often, we cannot *hear* the words because we come to the conversation with our own ideas about who people are. At the same time, we are determined not to let them see who we are. In order for effective and valued communication to occur, you must believe that you are safe, and you must offer that same safety to the other person.

If you want to communicate with another person, you must hear their fear and not dismiss it. You must hear a person's pain and not overlook it. It is important to hear a person's guilt and not buy into it. You must be ready to hear a person's anger and not fuel it. Most people need to know that they have been heard. Listen to their body. Listen to their eyes. Listen to colors they are wearing, the way they touch their hair. Listen to the volume. Listen to the tempo. If you really want to hear someone, open your heart and listen to their soul.

Until today, you may not have been able to hear what people are saying to you. Just for today, close your eyes when you are in a conversation. Hear every word that is spoken through the center of your heart.

Today I am devoted to being engaged in effective and valuable communication!

MARCH 21

I open my heart and mind to be aware . . . trust is the foundation I must build my life upon.

You cannot realize the meaningful fruits of a commitment or an agreement if you do not have trust. Trust is the belief that you will do what you say you will do, regardless of what anyone else is doing. This does not mean that you should not expect other people to honor their word. Trust, as the foundation of any relationship, means knowing what you know about yourself, being willing to share that information with the other people involved and believing that what you know about yourself can and will get you through whatever happens. When you don't trust yourself, how can you expect to trust someone else?

If you are not willing to ask for what you want up front, you are not going to get it. When you make an agreement with someone without asking for what you really want, you will undoubtedly become suspicious of them because you know that they don't know everything that you know. When you enter an agreement built on this kind of foundation, you will ultimately become resentful of the other person. It's not them, it's you! You know that they don't know what you really expect them to do.

Many agreements fall apart because the people who enter them are not ready to share the truth about themselves. They are hiding and believe that something is being hidden. They are not being honest and are on the lookout for dishonesty. It is only when you trust yourself to be able to move through whatever happens that you will attract people who can move smoothly with you.

Until today, you may not have been aware of the agreements you made where trust and self-trust were not present. Just for today, work on trusting yourself. And be sure to let yourself off the hook for the agreements you have made that did not work out.

Today I am devoted to building a trusting relationship with myself and other people!

MARCH 22

I open my heart and mind to be aware . . . there is
no need for me to be guilty about what I cannot
or could not do.

An indictment is a statement of charges. We would like to believe that an indictment does not import guilt. The truth of the matter is, once the finger of guilt is placed upon you, it can be quite difficult to shake it off. Nowhere is the presumption of guilt more devastating than when you point the finger at yourself.

Guilt over what you did. Guilt about what you didn't do. A guilty mind or heart is incredibly destructive. Guilt damages your self-worth almost as quickly as it erodes your self-respect. The guilt then flows into your relationships, which makes it difficult for you to give anyone the benefit of the doubt. When you believe that you are guilty, you will re-create situations in which you will be accused.

Guilty people are defensive. Quite often they overcompensate by giving too much and saying too much. When a person feels guilty, it is difficult for them to see anything good in themselves, and so they are compelled to try to do more to prove their innocence. Unfortunately, the more they do, the more guilty they feel.

You are not guilty! You may be right that you could have done things in a better way. This does not mean you must be sentenced to a life term of proving you are good. In order to remove guilt you must acknowledge to yourself what you have done. When possible you must make amends. Once you have done these two things, let yourself off of the hook! Letting yourself off of the hook means that you will not beat yourself up forever, and it gives you the opportunity to make better choices next time.

Until today, you may have been unable to see yourself as guilt free. Just for today, be devoted to reclaiming the innocence of your heart. Acknowledge what you have done or not done, and then let it go.

Today I am devoted to living a guilt-free life!

MARCH 23

I open my heart and mind to be aware . . . the things
I see in others could be the very things they see in me.

Chances are that when you nail someone on their "stuff,"
they are going to get angry. When, in the most innocent
way, you touch upon a person's insecurity, inadequacy, the
place where they are most wounded, they are going to attack
you. When that happens, all of *your* stuff is going to come up! Every little thing you have ever believed was wrong with you is going to rush into
the forefront of your mind, and you will begin to doubt the validity of
what you think and feel.

It is extremely difficult to hold on to a sense of personal power as
long as you believe there is something wrong with who you are. As long
as *you believe* that who you are is wrong, or that what you want and need
is wrong, you will be daunted by every challenge. You will be broken by
every criticism. Most important of all, you will eventually become unable to tell the difference between your stuff and someone else's stuff.
This is not a good thing!

Each of us is aware of those things we could do better. The fact that
something needs improvement does not mean it's wrong. There is nothing wrong with you! A negative response from someone else does not
mean you should doubt yourself. It means that you must always be
aware. *Just because you are defective does not mean you cannot see the defects
around you!* You always have the right to address what you see and feel.

Until today, you may have allowed what you believe is wrong with
you to prevent you from addressing conditions, situations and people
who do or say things that you believe are inappropriate. Just for today,
be determined not to allow feelings of *wrongness* to keep you silent.

*Today I am devoted to moving beyond any feelings
of wrongness to do and say what I believe
is the right thing for me!*

MARCH 24

*I open my heart and mind to be aware . . . people can see
things about me that I cannot see about myself.*

When someone points out to you all the stuff that you have
been ignoring, avoiding or denying, don't get mad! You see,
life uses people as its eyes and as its hands. The person is simply a tool. They are life's tool. They are being used by life to
work on you because you have been resistant to working on your *stuff!*

You can always tell when someone is saying something that you are
resistant to hearing because it hits you in the pit of your stomach. Or it
makes your ears hot. Or it causes your face to flush. Your first reaction
may be to cut them off. Or the moment they finish, you attack! The
moment you find yourself doing this, stop! Ask yourself, *Why is it so
hard for me to hear this? What is it that I am resisting?*

When you feel the need to defend yourself, people are in your stuff.
We are not addressing the situations in which you are being falsely accused, or when you know the person does not have complete information. Nor are we addressing those situations when people dump *their*
stuff on you. We are talking about situations in which someone reveals
to you things about yourself that you have refused to address. Those
things that you have done your darndest to keep other people from
knowing about. If and when that happens, don't get mad! Take it as a
sign that life is onto you. Take it as an opportunity to heal.

Until today, you may have been unaware or reluctant to acknowledge that there are things about you that could stand a little attention. In
fact, you may have overreacted when people pointed them out to you.
Just for today, allow yourself to be aware of your weaknesses when they
are pointed out. Pay particular attention to those things that upset you
or make you angry when they are pointed out. Consider yourself blessed
that the Spirit of life is bringing them to your attention.

*Today I am devoted to allowing life to reveal to me things
I need to know about myself.*

MARCH 25

*I open my heart and mind to be aware . . . I cannot hurt
for someone else more than they hurt for themselves.*

How do you assist a wounded person when they do not realize, or are not willing to admit that they are wounded? We are talking about mental, emotional and spiritual wounds. We are talking about internal wounds that drain the life force and cripple the spirit. We are talking about wounds that you can recognize because they are so much like *your own*. The wounds that you are healing or have healed. The kind of wounds that at one time you were not aware of or were not willing to acknowledge. The wounds that are so fresh in your memory that you recognize them when you see them on the soul of another. You can see their pain. Sometimes you can feel their pain. You can tell that their pain is the result of suppressed anger or imbedded remorse. You know they are suffering but, unfortunately, they do not agree with you or will not admit it to you.

When you see a wounded person, you want to ease their pain. You do everything you know how to do, and you offer to do more. You know they will feel better if they would just open up. If they would lay their burdens down. When you point out their pain, they deny it. When you ask them about their pain, they ignore it. Your awareness of their suffering is causing you to suffer. You want to put an end to the suffering but you just don't know what to do. Here's a suggestion.

Do your very best *not to push* a wounded person beyond where they are willing to go. Honor their boundaries. Honor their choices. It is important to realize that your only responsibility is to trust that when they are ready to be healed, they will be healed.

Until today, you may have believed it was your duty to take other people out of their misery. Just for today, be aware that every living being has the capacity to do what they need to do when they are ready to do it.

*Today I am devoted to seeing everyone as capable of
eliminating their own suffering!*

I open my heart and mind to be aware . . . I have to
establish inner cooperation in order to have outer results.

It is important that you do not send people mixed messages.
A mixed message is one in which you say one thing and do
something else. A mixed message is a sure sign that there is
a part of you that doesn't believe you can have what you
want. It is also a sure sign that you probably won't get what you want.

Mixed messages *confuse the universe,* making it almost impossible for
the forces of good to work on your behalf. If you talk about the actions
or attitudes of people but never request a change, you probably won't see
a change. If you say you want to grow but make no steps to make it happen, it probably will not happen. If you say you really want to change or
to have a particular experience, you must also believe you have the right
to have it. When you do not believe you do, you will send out a mixed
message.

A mixed message is clear evidence that there is a conflict between the
I am unworthy aspect of you and the *I am worthy aspect.* If you are self-
observant you will notice the gap between what you *say you believe* and
what you *actually believe.* Before you can effectively create change in
your life, you must *believe* you are worthy to have, *feel* you have a right to
have a better experience. Most important, you must know that what is
going on outside of you is merely a reflection of the conflict within you.

Until today, you may not have been aware of your own inner conflict
or the mixed message you are sending into the world. Just for today, pay
very close attention to what you say you want and what you believe
about your ability to have it.

*Today I am devoted to eliminating the inner conflict that
broadcasts mixed messages!*

I open my heart and mind to be aware . . .
there are no points in the game of life.
How I play determines if I win.

The goal of a football player is to get the ball over the goal line in order to score a touchdown. The goal of a baseball player is to hit a home run in order to increase the team's score. The goal of a basketball player is to get the ball in the basket and increase the team's points. Each of these players is focused on the goal, clear about the rules and prepared to win the game. This is not always true for those of us who are playing on the field of life. Our goal is not always clear. Our team is not always supportive. The points we make are not always counted. *How do you win the game of life?*

The goal of life is not to win. It is to play the game with love. The rules of the game are: have a strong desire to win, believe that you are worthy of winning, have faith that you will win, and, as long as you are alive, never believe that the game is over. Go for the love and have fun while you are doing it! There really are no points to count. The fact that you are here means you have already won the most important race. Play the game believing you cannot lose. Play the game for the love of it.

The game of life is rigged in your favor. There are angels playing on your side. Learn how to cooperate with them. The team you were born into really doesn't matter, because there is only one coach for all teams in life. His name is God, and he has been cited for his consistent winning record.

Until today, you may have been working so hard to reach the goal line that you lost sight of the meaning of the game. Just for today, do not keep score. Remind yourself of the rules; love what you are doing. Listen to your coach because with him you are assured victory.

*Today I am devoted to renewing my commitment
to win the game of life!*

MARCH 28

I open my heart and mind to be aware . . . I must believe
that whatever it is, I can handle it.

You have earned the right to be exactly where you are.
Whatever the situation, circumstances, predicament or
challenges that face you at this very moment, you have
earned the *divine right* to be where you are. You have earned
the right to go through what you are going through based on the way
you got through, got over, went around or handled a similar situation.
You learned something then that you can surely use now. Think about
it! You have already demonstrated your ability to get up. You have clearly
exhibited your desire to get over. You have made it perfectly clear that you
can handle the rough times and hard stuff as you navigated through the
tight places. Now you have the opportunity to demonstrate how your
skills have improved.

With all that you have been through, have been challenged by, have
confronted and have overcome, you have earned the right to live with
this, make it through this, overcome this and benefit from the divine opportunity that now stands before you. Think about it! You have always
been there for you. You have always demonstrated you have what it
takes. You know how to make it through the ups and downs, the in's and
out's, the good times and the hard times. You have done it before. You
will do it again! Why you? Because you are a good student. Why now?
Because you have earned the right to do what it takes. Now get to it!

Until today, you may not have realized just how good you are. Just
for today, see everything that lies before you as a divine opportunity to
remember.

*Today I am devoted to reminding myself of the good
I have done and the goodness that I am!*

MARCH 29

I open my heart and mind to be aware . . .
when I do not open up, I set myself up to blow up.

Keeping things inside does not make them any better. In fact, holding on to secret fears, secret feelings and secret fears makes them seem a lot worse than they probably are. When you keep things on the inside, the weight of it all can tear you up, hold you down, push you into situations that do not serve your best interests. Holding on to things can cause all sorts of disease, chemical and emotional imbalance, complete confusion and plain old despair.

When you have a lot going on inside, you must find some way to let it out. You can talk about it. You might cry about it. If you are alone, you can shout about it. You can run it out, walk it off or go to the gym and work it out. You can call a help line, a hotline or a prayer line, but you must let someone know what is going on inside of you. It is tempting to eat about it, drink about it or blow it up in smoke. A better strategy is to write about it.

Each of us comes to that point when we must trust someone enough to open ourselves up for review and examination. It's not always easy! It is a challenge to admit or acknowledge your own faults. It is even more difficult to accept that we have made some costly mistakes, poor decisions and bad choices. For some reason it seems that we don't want people to know that we are human. But we are. We cannot hide what we feel forever. It is essential to our sense of well-being that we find a way to open up and let someone know what is going on inside.

Until today, you may have been holding on to secret thoughts and feelings. You may have been afraid to open yourself to self-examination or outside scrutiny. Just for today, be willing to release those things stored in your heart and mind that are causing you discomfort.

Today I am devoted to opening myself and my heart in order to find relief!

MARCH 30

I open my heart and mind to be aware . . . as long as I am
holding on to what I have, what I desire cannot get in.

If someone has offended you, insulted you, disappointed
you or upset your apple cart, let it go! If someone has
pushed your buttons, pulled your chain, or gotten on your
last good nerve, let it go! If you are remembering all the ways
you have been hurt or forgotten, betrayed or misunderstood, let it go! If
you are thinking about all that you have lost, had stolen or given away,
let it go! Ask yourself, *what good does it do for me to hold on to this?*

If you are feeling lost or left, mistrusted or misguided, misunderstood or as if you have missed out, just let it go! If someone has lied to
you or about you, if they act as if they have forgotten you or what they
promised they would do, let it go! If you have been falsely accused or unjustly abused, let it go! If someone has set you up or let you down, let it
go! Ask yourself, *what harm am I causing by holding on to this?*

Make a choice to let go of the things or people that cause you grief or
pain. You must *choose* to be pain free and free of grief. You must *choose* to
be more loving than the people involved in your experiences. You must
choose to be open to receiving something better. You must *choose* to be
self-sustained, self-contained, self-directed and self-affirming. When
you choose to let go, you are making room for a new vision for yourself
and of yourself that is more powerful than anything anyone can do or
say to you or about you. You are choosing to be upheld by and upright in
all the things you know are true about you.

Until today, you may have been holding on to what has caused you
pain. Just for today, make a new choice! Choose to move beyond the
things and people who have not honored the truth of who you are. Once
you make the choice, the Universe will give you something better.

*Today I am devoted to making new choices that will work
in my best interests!*

I open my heart and mind to be aware . . .
how my ABCs will lift my spirit.

Almighty Creator of the Universe;

Beloved Father, Mother, God;

Create in me a clean heart this day.

Deliver me from the limitations of the ego.

Exalt Your presence in my mind.

Forgive all that I have held against you, myself and others.

Grant me peace this day.

Hold me steadfastly within the boundaries of your truth.

Inspire my heart to know you, my ears to hear you and
my eyes to recognize you.

Justify me in the presence of all enemies.

Knead my heart with words of kindness.

Let no harm befall me or my loved ones.

May all I do this day glorify you.

Nourish me with your wisdom.

Open my eyes to know your truth.

Purge my heart of all things that are offensive to your law.

Quiet my soul in the midst of confusion.

Renew my connection to you.

Save me from my secret fears.

Teach me to trust you at all times.

Use all that you have given me to serve you.

Victory for your cause is my desire.

Walk with me so that my strength will never be diminished.

Xamine my heart continually.

Your love and grace are my good fortune.

Zealously I commit myself to your will for my life.

Until today, you may not have been aware of the power of knowing the alphabet. Just for today, practice making each letter in the alphabet come alive in your life.

Today I am devoted to relearning the entire alphabet of life!

APRIL

ACKNOWLEDGMENT

When you can look a thing dead in the eye,

acknowledge that it exists,

call it exactly what it is,

and decide what role it will play in your life,

then, my Beloved,

you have taken the first step toward
your freedom.

APRIL 1

I am willing to acknowledge . . . there are things
in my life that I have left undone!

One of my favorite stories in the Bible is about the man at the pool of Bethesda. The man had been an invalid for thirty-eight years. Once a year, the energy of the Holy Spirit would enter the pool. At that time, anyone who entered the pool would be healed. When Jesus saw that the man had not gone into the pool, he asked why. The man responded, *"I have no one to help me."* Jesus didn't buy it! He asked the man "Do you want to be healed?"

Some of us have long-standing situations in our lives that we have failed to address. We make excuses for why we haven't done certain things and why we did other things. We make excuses for the unfinished business, incomplete tasks, ongoing drama and the absence of well-being in our lives. We move from one situation to the next, leaving a mess behind us, wondering why we are not further along the path.

The truth of the matter is, when we are afraid, we act in fear. When we are angry, we react to the things that anger us. When we are lazy, we simply don't try. When we are self-sabotaging, self-defeating, or self-defiant, we blame other people for our lack of progress. We conveniently forget our habitual reactive behaviors that leave things unsaid, tasks incomplete, dreams unfulfilled, goals unmet and people hanging on. We use reason and excuses to explain why we still can't walk. Although we hate to admit it, the only reason we haven't been blessed by the ever-present energy of the Holy Spirit is that, for one reason or another, we have not stepped into the pool!

Until today, you may have made excuses for the unkempt and incomplete areas in your life. Just for today, be devoted to acknowledging the things you have left undone, unsaid, and incomplete. Acknowledgment is the first step toward healing!

*Today I am devoted to honestly acknowledging the things
I have not done in my life!*

APRIL 2

I am willing to acknowledge . . . I must pay more
attention to the messages I receive from my life.

Are you listening to your life? Are you listening to the subtle
messages contained in every condition, situation, and relationship in your life right now? In which area of your life are
you having difficulty? Do you understand what your difficulties are saying to you and about you? If you are talking back to the
difficulties in your life, are you being offensive or defensive?

Is your life telling you that it will always be this way? Or do you hear
that it is time to let go and move on? In what areas of your life have you
discovered energy leaks? A scarcity of resources? Repetitive motions that
result in little or no advancement? Perhaps your life is showing you that
you are struggling with all the wrong things, for all the wrong reasons. Is
your life peaceful? Fulfilling? Rewarding? Or is it strained? Draining?

Your life is always talking to you. Sometimes we listen to our lives
and pay very close attention to what they are saying, but more often we
are afraid to hear what our lives are saying to us and, more important,
about us. Then there are those times when we do not know how to hear
what we hear. We do not know how to do what we know we must to
change the dialogue in our lives.

When the conditions of your life are not peaceful and abundant;
when the relationships in your life are not harmonious and fulfilling;
when you do not feel good about yourself, what you are doing, and
where you are headed, it becomes quite obvious to everyone that you are
not a good listener!

Until today, you may not have taken the time to listen to your life.
You may be avoiding what your life is saying about the adjustments and
improvements you need to make. Just for today, make it a point to sit
down and listen to your life. Listen to every experience, situation, condition in your life and be willing to respond as a good listener would.

*Today I am devoted to listening to what my life is saying. I
am committed to making the adjustments that are needed!*

APRIL 3

*I am willing to acknowledge . . . the information that
I need is readily available to me.*

The Holy Spirit is the activity of God. It is the powerful
presence, the divine knowing, the merciful management of
God's love and grace. The Holy Spirit is the order and fulfillment of God's divine will for you and through you. The
presence of the Holy Spirit is revealed as thoughts, ideas, insights and
understandings that you never would have had on your own. The Holy
Spirit is present in situations, people and circumstances that you have
difficulty facing or accepting. In the presence of the Holy Spirit you
know, you believe and you understand exactly what is going on. Most
important, when you are in the presence of the Holy Spirit, you know
why it is going on. Some people are not aware of this presence. Some
people do not believe in this presence. Some people are aware and believe, but choose to be *disobedient* to the presence. The question you
must ask yourself is, *Are you ready and willing to accept information as it is
presented to you by the Holy Spirit of God?* If you have any questions beyond this one, you are not ready.

Until today, you may have been wondering how you would know
what you need to know. Or you may have been shocked at the times you
knew exactly what you needed to know. Just for today, be aware that the
Holy Spirit within and around you knows everything you need to know
and will let you know when you need to know.

*Today, I am devoted to receiving and accepting
information from the Holy Spirit!*

APRIL 4

I am willing to acknowledge . . . everyone is completely
capable and equipped to take care of themselves
and handle their own problems!

Today you can be the good news! Refuse to think negative
thoughts, speak negative words or engage in any negative
behavior. No rolling of eyes, sucking of teeth, wringing of
the hands or giving of the finger for you today! Oh, no! You
are going to be the good news! You are going to have something good to
say to yourself, about yourself and to every living person you meet. No
worry today! No doubt today! No gossip, criticism or judgment today!
Not for you! Oh, no! You are the good news today!

You are going to be the compliment someone needs to hear. You are
going to be the encouragement someone has been waiting for. You are
going to be the smile someone needs to see. You are going to be the big
tip someone needs to receive. You are going to be a prayer today. You are
going to be a blessing today. You are going to make something out of
nothing and do something good with it.

You are *not* going to focus on what is not right with your life. You are
not going to complain. There will be no crisis, no drama, no victim stories for you today. There will be no sadness, no gloom and no doom. On
this day you are going to be the good news! You are going to show up
with something good to say, something good to give, something good to
do for somebody. Today you realize that *when you are the good news,* you
can only receive the perfect reflection of who and what you are.

Until today, you may have been waiting to receive some good news.
You may have been listening to or spreading gloomy, dismal or bad
news. Just for today, be devoted to being the good news in your own life.

Today I am the good news!

APRIL 5

I am willing to acknowledge . . . a good word supports
and encourages good work!

Keep up the good work! Keep on putting one foot in front of the other, taking one step at a time, moving at a pace that may seem slow but is steady and sure. Keep on doing what you are doing to improve your life, to enhance your status, to improve your standing. Keep up with your vision, your goals, and your dreams. They are very important to you. You know that, don't you? Don't deny yourself the joy of your dreams. Don't doubt yourself or your ability to do what you are doing to reach your goals. Don't beat up on yourself for what may seem like a mistake or a waste of time. Keep on believing it was necessary for you to walk that path and to learn those lessons.

Keep on telling yourself that you can, you will, you are getting better, being better, making better choices than you once did. Keep on deciding for yourself who you are, what you desire to express and experience. Keep up the good work! Remember that you are doing just fine. Remind yourself right now that no matter what it looks like, you are doing the best you can. And getting better.

Until today, you may have doubted your progress, regretted your choices, put yourself down or ignored your progress, as minimal as it seemed. Just for today be devoted to encouraging yourself, supporting yourself and celebrating every little thing about yourself.

Today I am my own encouragement!
I am my own support! I am celebrating myself!

APRIL 6

I am willing to acknowledge . . . in some battles,
victory is won with the element of surprise.

Many people ask, *"How can I get the negative thoughts out of
my mind?"* Or, *"How can I get these negative feelings out of my
heart?"* Few of us realize that everything we do in life is experienced by our entire being—that means mind, body, and
spirit. What you know, you know on all three levels. What you desire,
you must desire on all three levels. When you are trying to accomplish a
task, all three levels of your being must be in harmony. If or when they
are not, one or more aspects of your inner being will be working against
you. When this happens, it is difficult to accomplish the task.

It is not enough to think about the good things you want; you must
also feel good about what you want. It is not enough to try to forget unpleasant experiences; you must also work to change how you *feel* about
them. In order to eliminate negative thoughts and feelings, you must
shift what you think. When you shift what you think, you change how
you feel and what you believe. This shift is called *learning.* When there is
harmony among all levels of your inner being, then you have learned the
lesson of the experience. Once you have learned a lesson, your behavior
will change.

If you are working to eliminate negative thoughts and feelings, think
before you act! Stop yourself from walking down the path of reaction.
Examine your beliefs about yourself and your experiences. Be willing to
release those things that are in conflict with your goal to release negative
thoughts and feelings. Only when you participate on all three levels of
your being can you break habitual responses that repeatedly produce un-
wanted experiences.

Until today, you may have tried to clear your mind and heal your
heart in two separate steps. Just for today, treat your mind and heart as
partners.

*Today I am devoted to having a surprising new response to
the same old thoughts and feelings!*

*I am willing to acknowledge . . . it is safe for me
to acknowledge and honor my feelings!*

It is standard operating procedure among human beings to act as if everything is all right, all of the time. No matter how sick, sad, upset, frightened, or confused we may be, if someone asks, *"How are you?"* the standard response is, *"Fine!"* Nothing destroys self-worth, self-acceptance and self-love faster than denying what you feel. We humans need to realize whatever we feel is just fine and that we are just fine, no matter what we feel.

Without feelings, you would not know where you are in your life. Nor would you know what areas you need to work on. When something doesn't feel right, you are motivated to change. Feelings keep you alive. They invigorate and educate. Feelings are like hound dogs. They sniff out what you are hunting down. This means that your feelings are inspirational and motivational. When you deny what you feel, you are not grounded. You let your guard down, sometimes to your own detriment.

It is true that your feelings can deceive you. You can feel good in a bad situation. You can feel bad in a good situation. This is what happens when you stifle your feelings. You cannot tell one from the other. Feelings are sensors. When you learn to keep the channels clear with the full expression of your feelings, your emotional essence develops and matures. It is also true that you do not want to be a slave to your feelings. Feelings that go up and down like a roller coaster are often the result of a physical or chemical imbalance in the body. The key to the development of a healthy emotional essence is to acknowledge what you feel.

Until today, you may not have been honoring your feelings. You may have been afraid, unclear or unsure as to what to do about what you feel. Just for today, be devoted to honoring your feelings. Allow yourself to feel them. Admit to yourself what you feel. If you really want to give yourself an opportunity to grow and heal, admit exactly what you are feeling to one other living person.

*Today I am devoted to honoring what I feel
until I feel better!*

APRIL 8

I am willing to acknowledge . . .
what I know, when I know it!

If you really want to get yourself in trouble, act like you don't know, when you know that you know! This usually happens when you base your clarity on the response you get from others. When you have to convince yourself that what you see, what you feel, what you think is not true, not right, not real, *you know,* but you are acting like you don't know. When you are seeking validation from external sources, you are acting like you don't know, and you could get into a lot of trouble!

You will know you are acting like you don't know when you try to act and that action is in conflict with what you know. At that time, your mouth will become dry. Your stomach will tighten up. Your heart will begin to race, and your mind will scream, "STOP! STOP NOW!" Your mind is simply responding to your self-denial, which is always a sign that *you know* but are trying to act like you don't know. This is also a sign that the Spirit of life is on your case, and it is not going to give up!

It is an insult to life, to your inherent power, to the blessings that God has given you to act like you don't know, when you know that you do know. *You know* what people are doing. *You know* why they are doing it. *You know* because you see how they are behaving. *You know* what you need to do. *You know* what you must stop doing. If you insist on acting like you don't know when you do know, you are going to find yourself in a lot of trouble! You know what I mean?

Until today, you may have judged your own clarity based on how others respond to what you know. Just for today, be devoted to knowing that you know. Be willing to act like you know! Talk like you know! And the moment you find yourself being lulled into the *stuff* of what someone may tell you that they know, remind yourself that you do know what you know.

Today I am willing to acknowledge, admit and accept that I know what I know!

APRIL 9

*I am willing to acknowledge . . . there are things
in my life that do not smell quite right.*

What does your life smell like? At first it may seem like an unusual question. On second thought, the question will probably reveal to you some things you may have overlooked. If you were to take a whiff of your life, which response mechanism would be activated? A gag reflex? The laugh button? A sigh of relief? Or unspeakable joy? If you were passing by your life, what would you smell? A bed of roses? Or a gym locker full of sweaty socks? Perhaps some of Grandma's home cooking? Or is it more like popcorn that has been left in the microwave too long? If you were to throw open the front door of your life, what would hit you in the face? The scent of Carpet Fresh or the stench of a moldy basement? The aroma of a cake that's just about done? Or the smell of trash that needs to go out? Most of us are very familiar with the way our lives look. Few of us have ever taken the time to make sure that our lives *smell* as clean as they look.

Quite often, what our ears, eyes, and hands miss, our nose can detect. The sense of smell is also quite useful because it evokes memories. With a whiff of something, you can be thrown back into a memory of something that happened, how it happened and whether or not you liked what happened. From there, you are motivated to encourage or discourage the same thing from happening again in your life. Most important, the sense of smell evokes feelings. If something in your life doesn't smell right, you will not feel right. If you don't like what you feel, you know it is time to clean up!

Until today, you may only have been concerned with the way your life looks. You may have ignored certain things you heard or saw, but you cannot ignore a smell. Just for today, be devoted to sniffing around your life. Be on the lookout for rotting things you need to discard and fragrant things you can put on display.

*Today I am devoted to sniffing around all aspects
of my life!*

APRIL 10

I am willing to acknowledge . . .
I am at the point of no return.

When you reach the point of no return in a particular situation, it means you have given all you can give, taken all you can take, learned all you can learn, taught all you can teach, been all you can be. You realize there is no hope of things getting any better, and you have done all you know how to turn things around. When you finally reach this point, please remember, this is not a bad thing. It is simply time to move on.

You will know you have come to the point of no return when your joy is gone, your peace is at risk, you are groping for some meaning, you are looking for a reason. You are no longer mad. You can't even get angry.

When you come face to face with the point of no return, remember the good times, appreciate the joyful times, be grateful for any support, encouragement or contentment you experienced. Pack all of those things in a corner of your heart and take them with you as you move forward. Acknowledge and accept that you may not be able to go back to what you had but that you have something to take with you on your new journey.

Until today, you may have resisted the need to move beyond the point of no return. You may have been looking for reasons to stay in an experience that no longer suits your needs. Just for today, acknowledge your needs and prepare your Self to pack and move on.

*Today I am devoted to packing up the good things
and moving on!*

I am willing to acknowledge . . . there are some things
I could be addicted to experiencing.

There are some of us who are recovered "I'm not good
enough" addicts, and some of us who are still recovering. As
addicts we think not good enough, feel not good enough,
drink not good enough, eat not good enough, and shoot
ourselves up with a daily dose of not good enough. Sometimes we ex-
pend a great deal of time and energy chasing things and people that are
not good enough for us. Often, to get these not good enough people, we
will sleep with them, only to discover they are not worth the time and
energy we spent trying to get them.

When you are a not good-enough addict, you can't do the right
thing because you are not good enough. However, you will beat yourself
up because you are not good enough to do what you know you need to
do. If you are a not-good-enough addict, you will overcommit yourself.
You will try to do more than you can possibly do, and when you can't do
it, you become resentful of the people who expect you to do what you
know you cannot possibly do. When a not-good-enough addict is overcommitted they feel overwhelmed, which of course intensifies the feelings of inadequacy, unworthiness, hopelessness and helplessness from
which the whole addiction cycle springs.

The truth is, as long as you *believe* that you are not good enough, you
will never *feel* good enough. And as long as you are not good enough, you
cannot, will not, take responsibility for the truth of who you are.

Until today, you may have been addicted to thinking of yourself as
not good enough to accept total and complete responsibility for yourself
and your life. Just for today, no matter what you are faced with, confronted with, challenged by or asked to do, have the courage to accept
that you are good enough to handle it.

*Today I am devoted to seeing myself as good enough
to be exactly who I am!*

APRIL 12

I am willing to acknowledge . . . if I am not giving my all to myself, I am not giving my all, at all.

If you were to poll fifty average people on a street corner in almost any city, asking them what they wanted to do in their lives, chances are the predominant answer would be, "To help people." When you consider how rude, abusive, violent and unloving we humans have demonstrated that we can be, this answer might surprise you. The natural instinct among most human beings is to reach out in support of one another. It is a wonderful concept; however, there is one small problem many of us have yet to overcome. While we want to help other people, most of us cannot help ourselves!

There are people out there who want to help save the world who have yet to master a sinkful of dirty dishes. Others want to save the children and feed the poor, yet they cannot seem to conquer the dustbunnies beneath their beds and in the bottoms of their closets. Yes, some of us want to fix all that is wrong in the *world*, but we cannot seem to fix our broken hearts or our shattered minds. We don't recognize that we cannot give what we do not have. Until we clean up the small places in our own lives, we will experience extreme difficulty doing what the world so desperately needs done.

Anger is a *little* thing. Hate is a *little* thing. Order is a *little* thing. Each of these *little* things have a major impact on the big picture. Right thinking, right action and right response to the little things will help us conquer the big things, like injustice, inequality, poverty and dis-order. Until we are each able to conquer and master the little things in our own hearts, minds and lives, the big things will remain undone.

Until today, you may have been attempting to do some things in the world that you have not yet done in your own life. Just for today, take care of the little things in your heart, your mind and your life that have a major impact on your ability to help and give to the world.

Today I am devoted to addressing all the little things about me and in my life that I have not mastered!

APRIL 13

I am willing to acknowledge . . .
there are certain realities I must face about my life.

It is amazing, the stories we tell to avoid facing the realities in which we live. People drink, they say, for medical reasons. Abused women say they fell down stairs. Abused and battered children needed the discipline. Rather than face what is really going on, we will sit in the middle of a *mess* and call it a garden. We ride our boats down the river of denial and refuse to acknowledge the stench in the river. Even when the stench becomes unbearable, we say it is a good place to fish! We seem to have a really hard time calling things what they are, which is probably why we spend so much time in bad situations. The longer we resist facing whatever it is, the easier it is to forget that we are equipped to change it.

The Bible offers us a story about a man who sat at the gate of the city begging for coins. When two of Jesus' disciples passed him without dropping anything into his cup, he asked, "Why?" The beggar explained his situation. He pleaded with the disciples for help. They refused! The disciples refused to believe his story because they knew the truth.

Instead of seeing the man as a beggar, they saw his power, his strength, his inherent right to stop begging and claim his Divine inheritance. They knew he was in denial. The disciples knew that the man had called himself a beggar for so long he now believed it. The disciples refused to help their brother hold on to his limited ideas and beliefs about himself.

Wouldn't it be wonderful if you could stop buying into your stories and face the truth?

Until today, you may have been avoiding, denying, resisting the truth. You may have forgotten that you can do anything you choose to! You can have the kind of life you desire. Just for today, stop telling stories! Put the begging cup away! Look at yourself. Look at your life. Tell the truth about what you see.

*Today I am devoted to telling the truth about
the realities in my life!*

APRIL 14

I am willing to acknowledge . . . there are certain things
about me I'd rather others did not know.

Marriage is not for punks! You must be *really* strong, *really*
courageous, *really* grounded, and *really, really* ready to stand
naked as your most vulnerable self before another human
being. You must be strong enough to be open and *to be
opened,* to see the powerful parts of your self and the weakest ones. You
must be courageous enough to stand in your power yet be willing to
compromise. You must be grounded in a sense of who you are and be
willing to give the other person the opportunity to do the same. You had
better be ready to see and learn some things about yourself that you may
not have realized, may have forgotten, may have denied or would rather
not know. When you join in union with another person, whether or not
sex is involved, it is a Holy Union, a union with the Holy Spirit. Wherever the Holy Spirit is involved, the truth *will* be revealed!

The good thing about personal and intimate relationships is that
you have an opportunity to be *born again.* As you learn to acknowledge
the areas in which you are undeveloped or underdeveloped, the false you
falls away and the true, authentic you is born. The people with whom
you have relationships encourage and support you in this process by
constantly *making you aware* of how you are growing and where you
need to grow. It may feel like they are nagging you, criticizing you or
picking on you. The truth is that they are helping you heal. They are
helping you grow into your truth and your power, and don't forget, you
are doing the exact same thing for them.

Until today, you may have been afraid to reveal your weaknesses,
fears or shortcomings. Just for today, make a commitment to tell the
truth about what you feel to the people who love and care about you.
Allow them the privilege and opportunity to help you heal and grow.

*Today I am devoted to loving myself enough
to acknowledge the things about myself which need
a little work!*

APRIL 15

I am willing to acknowledge . . . in some areas of my life,
I have been less than honest.

Some people tell big lies. Some people tell little lies. Nice
people tell little *white* lies. Mean people tell vicious lies.
Some people lie for the fun of it. Some people lie to prove a
point. Some people tell so many lies that they no longer remember the truth. Some people lie to themselves. Some people lie to
other people. People think that some lies are fine to tell and others are
not. A lie is a lie! No matter who is telling it or why it is told.

At times we lie to protect ourselves. Or we may lie to cover something
up. Many people lie to keep from hurting someone's feelings. Others lie
knowing it will hurt someone's feelings. A lie is a sign of fear. It is also a
means of control. When you withhold or distort the truth, you have an
impact on how someone can or will behave. If you have ever told a lie,
you know how it can haunt you. You live in constant fear that someone
may find out. If and when that happens, chances are you will lie again.

How do you lie to yourself? Where are the lies in your life? What are
you afraid of? Who are you trying to control? Do you tell lies to make others think you are better off than you are? Do you lie to protect yourself because you think you have no choice? Or do you lie in the midst of a temper
tantrum just to prove a point? Lying does not have to be active. There are
passive lies too. A lie is a lie! There are no good ones, and it is never necessary to tell one. Every lie that is told puts a damper on the Spirit.

Until today, you may have thought that you could get away with
telling little lies, or you may not have acknowledged the little lies you tell
yourself. Just for today, make a commitment to yourself to tell the truth,
the whole truth and nothing but the truth to yourself, about yourself
and to others. Also take a look at some of the little lies you have told and
ask yourself what you were trying to accomplish. There may be some
valuable information buried beneath a lie!

Today I am devoted to taking an honest look at myself
and my excuses for not always being honest!

APRIL 16

I am willing to acknowledge . . . there may be some parts
of my story that I have left out or changed.

Are you telling the *whole story?* Are you telling what happened,
the way it happened? Or are you only telling the parts that
will make you look good? Are you telling what you said?
What you did? Are you blaming someone else, everyone else,
for your role in the story? Are you adding a few things here and there to
accomplish a hidden agenda? Or are you telling what you *wish* had happened? Are you adding characters? Omitting characters? Putting characters in roles that they did not play? Perhaps you are telling the story for its
dramatic effect? Or could you be telling the story to create drama? Are you
telling the story to hear yourself talk? Or are you telling *a* story because
you don't know what else to say? Are you telling the story the way you see
it? Believe it? Or are you telling the story to make someone else believe it?

Your life is like a story. It has a beginning, a middle and an end. One
part leads to another. One part affects the rest. Each character in your
story plays a significant role. Each event in your story determines your
role in the next part. Wherever you are in your story, you really don't
know what is coming next. You don't know what characters are leaving
or coming in. You don't know how the next event in your story will unfold. When you do not tell the whole story, when you alter the actual
events, when you omit certain characters, you do not learn the lessons
your story can teach you. How you tell your story can keep you
wounded and stuck, or it can help you grow in understanding.

Until today, you may not have been telling your story or certain stories the way they were actually written, they way they occurred. You may
have overlooked, changed or omitted certain characters and events in an
attempt to make your story better than it is or worse than it was. Just for
today, review all the stories you are telling yourself and others. Make sure
what you are telling is an accurate reflection of what actually occurred.

*Today I am devoted to checking into the details
of the stories I am telling myself!*

APRIL 17

*I am willing to acknowledge . . . it is not my place
to tell other people what to do.*

You cannot tell other people what to do! You can tell them what you have done and how you did it. You can encourage them in what they are doing by sharing with them your experiences in similar situations, under similar circumstances. However, you should hold all this information in reserve until they ask for it. When they ask, if they ask, remember they trust you and respect you. What you say can have a tremendous effect on what they do. Put your fears and judgments aside and speak with a loving heart.

Until you have walked someone else's path, stumbled over the stones, fallen into the ditches and pits, felt the sunshine on your face, found your way to new paths and on new roads, you cannot tell another person what to do! Until you have fallen, gotten up and navigated the path they are on, you really don't know what can happen. You cannot tell them about the challenges and victories that lie ahead of them. They are not yours to tell! They are not yours to know! For each of us, there are things we must see and things we must do. There are falls we must take and things we must learn in the process of rising up from a fall. If you try to tell someone about a path you have not walked, either they will not be able to hear you, or you could send them off in the wrong direction.

Until today, you may have thought you were being helpful when you told other people what to do. You may have tried to steer them in the right direction. Or you may have been trying to steer them away from harm. Just for today, don't tell anyone what to do! Share your experiences, your insights, your understanding, but acknowledge that all paths are not the same. When you are sharing information about your path, always be sure to leave enough room for the other person to make up their own mind.

Today I am devoted to minding my own business!

APRIL 18

*I am willing to acknowledge . . . it may be difficult
to pick through my experiences to find the things
that will nourish me.*

When you sit down at life's table, you don't know what the chef will serve you. It is quite possible that life will serve you filet mignon on a silver platter with all of the trimmings. Or life may serve you a hearty chicken soup, with lots of veggies, in a china bowl. The china bowl might be chipped, and it could be sitting on a plate it does not match. Life could serve you burned roast chicken with half-raw potatoes on fine china that sits on an exquisite linen tablecloth. You might be served all fattening foods or low-fat treats. The point is, no matter what you are served in life, or how it is served to you, it is up to you to find the nourishment.

Your experiences in life are food for your soul. They make up the meat and potatoes of your character. Some experiences are quite tasty and good. Others could lead you to believe you are starving! If you insist you should have been served steak when you've been served chicken, you could miss the fact that it was served on fine china.

Don't get caught up in *what* life has served you. There is a chef in the kitchen of your heart who knows exactly the kind of diet you need to grow strong and remain healthy. Don't get stuck on *how* you were served. Ask the chef how to eat it, how to digest it, and how best to make use of what you were served. Don't try to *figure out* why you got what you got. Be grateful that you got something. If you got it, you can use it, just ask the chef how.

Until today, you may have been more concerned with why you have had certain experiences than you were with how they have nurtured and nourished you. Just for today, remind yourself, *"He* has prepared the table before me." *He* must know what I need.

*Today I am devoted to discovering the nourishment
in all of my life's experiences!*

APRIL 19

I am willing to acknowledge . . . all little boys need
guidance and direction from the Father.

When a little boy doesn't have a father to show him the way,
he can never be quite sure about the *manhood things* he
needs to know. He's never quite sure about how strong is
strong enough; how soft is too soft; or how much doing or
giving is enough from a *man's point of view*. He's never quite sure how to
push forward or when to pull back. When a little boy doesn't have a father to guide him, he's not sure when to speak up or when to shut up. A
little boy who does not or did not have a father is never quite sure what
other men will think about what he has to say.

Some little boys grow up never feeling quite sure about the things
their fathers did not or could not teach them. Sometimes they figure
things out on their own, by trial and error. Still, they are not quite sure
about themselves, within themselves. They grieve silently in their hearts,
which does not make them feel good about the man they are or are becoming. Many little boys grow up to be men who do not realize that
they have a heavenly Father who loves and supports them unconditionally. This is the Father who knows them inside out and will always be in
them and with them. Many little boys do not recognize that the wise,
courageous, loving fatherly advice they need, they already have at the
core of their being. They don't understand that the Father put it there for
them to use when they thought they could not reach him, see him, or be
with him. Like a good Father, the heavenly Father has given little boys
everything they need to grow into men.

Until today, you may have been one of the earthly sons grieving the
absence of an earthly father. You may have quietly, secretly yearned for the
loving embrace of a father. Just for today, spend some time sharing your
thoughts and needs with the heavenly Father who lives in your heart.

*Today I am devoted to acknowledging and spending
some time with my Father!*

APRIL 20

I am willing to acknowledge . . . a little girl needs
a father to help her grow into a woman.

Little girls need a big, strong daddy to hold them, protect
them and to let them know that *they matter* to him. They
need a daddy who will talk to them, listen to them, who will
speak up for them and teach them how to speak up for themselves. Little girls need a daddy that they can depend on and put their
trust in. They need a daddy who will discipline them, instruct them and
trust them to make decisions on their own. They need a daddy to tell
them they are pretty, to demonstrate that they are valuable, to teach
them that they are worthy and to acknowledge that they deserve respect.
Little girls need a daddy to teach them what to expect from men.

Unfortunately, some daddies do not know how to give little girls what
they need. They may want to, even try to, but somehow they never seem
to get just what it is that little girls needs from them. As a result, some little girls grow up searching for the daddy they believe they never had.
Some little girls grow up full of regret, sadness, fear and sometimes anger,
believing they will never get the things they need and wanted from daddy.

All little girls have a heavenly Father who understands them, loves
them, values them and knows their every need. The heavenly Father has
always protected, spoken to, listened to and spoken on behalf of his
earthly daughters. The heavenly Father has always and will always be
there to comfort, protect and provide for his little girls because he
knows, sometimes better than they do, just how precious they are to
Him and the world.

Until today, you may have believed that you missed out on a good relationship with your earthly father. Just for today, be devoted to spending
some time and sharing your thoughts with your heavenly Father. If you
do, you'll feel a lot better about the father you had here on earth.

*Today I am devoted to spending some time and
sharing some thoughts with my daddy!*

APRIL 21

*I am willing to acknowledge . . . the fear of fear
leads to a struggle for control.*

When people are hurt or afraid of being hurt, they will try to gain control of a situation. They may even try to gain control of you! If a person doesn't trust her ability to control herself or to stay in control of herself, she will try to control everything and everyone around her. That includes you! When a person feels wrong or, is afraid to be wrong, he will do everything and anything he can do to ensure that everything goes the way he thinks it should go. He also realizes that the only way to have that kind of power is to be in control.

Control can be difficult to recognize. It can be harsh and abusive or, it can be gently convincing. It can be so sweet and encouraging that even when you see it for what it is, you are unsure about calling control by its rightful name. It is, therefore, imperative that you are able to identify the many disguises of control so that you will recognize them when you see them. More important, you must understand the tricks of the trade employed by control so that you can stop yourself when you use them.

Rest assured that control is in control when:

You are fighting to prove you are right; you will lie to prove you are right; you have a need to be right; you are yelling in order to be heard; you won't say anything believing you won't be heard; the only view that makes sense is yours; the only thing that matters is what matters to you; you are still giving reasons *why* after someone has said no; you think if someone gets what they want or need you will not get what you want or need; you jump on someone's "case" to keep them off your "case"; you believe someone can or will hurt you and you are trying to avoid it.

Until today, you may have been unaware how the fear of being hurt or being wrong has influenced how you behave. Just for today, check yourself for the symptoms of control listed above.

*Today I am devoted to becoming aware of the things I do
to obtain and maintain control!*

APRIL 22

*I am willing to acknowledge . . . there are times when
I need to be alone.*

Why is being alone so bad, so frightening, so intolerable that
you would rather stay in a situation that is causing you pain
or harm? When you think about being alone with yourself,
what unbearable thought convinces you that it is okay to be
unhappy, unfulfilled or dissatisfied with someone else? When you are
alone, what do you see in yourself that makes it feel better to be treated
wrongly by someone else? What you may not realize is that you can
never fully be *with* anyone until you can *be* with yourself.

There is a very sacred sweetness about being alone that you will miss
if you fear it so much. When you are alone with yourself, you become
sensitive to and familiar with your own voice, your own touch, your
own sense of being. You learn to appreciate quiet times with you; special
things that you do for yourself. When you are alone, you can pamper
yourself, be extravagant with yourself, you can even talk to yourself
without being overheard. Being alone is an opportunity to examine your
thoughts, explore your feelings and allow yourself to feel all the things
you thought you could not feel because you were with someone else.

It is okay to desire a warm body in bed at night. It is perfectly fine to
want someone to talk to or share with or stare at across the dinner table.
It is human nature to congregate and communicate, to seek companionship and camaraderie. However, it is often detrimental to indulge your
human nature to avoid the sacred nature of being alone.

Until today, you may have done everything in your power to avoid
being alone. Just for today, allow yourself to explore the possibilities
and opportunities that being alone offer you. If it feels frightening or
sad, take a moment and ask God to show you how you can make it feel
better.

*Today I am devoted to exploring the sacred opportunities
of being alone!*

APRIL 23

I am willing to acknowledge . . . a mistake is a lesson
in humility and a powerful healing opportunity.

Very often we waste time, energy and readily available joy, because of our failure to acknowledge an error. We know that pencils have erasers. We know that computers allow us to cut and paste. We know that tests can be taken again, and that wrong sizes can be exchanged. Yet for some strange reason one of our greatest challenges is admitting to ourselves and others that we have made a mistake.

Perhaps as children we were spanked for breaking things, or criticized for shortcomings. Maybe those who raised us wanted so badly for us to be good that they left us little margin for error. Perhaps we believe that it is not safe to acknowledge or admit an error. Maybe we have heard so much about human errors that have caused great tragedy, hardship or heartache that we are simply afraid to say, "I made a mistake." This simple statement is a powerful acknowledgment that there is *spiritual power in human weakness!*

A mistake is a great opportunity for learning and for healing. A mistake reminds us that no matter how old we are, how smart we believe ourselves to be, regardless of how much we have accomplished, we are still human. A mistake is a lesson in humility. A mistake is the way we learn our limitations. It is a reminder that there is always more for us to learn about ourselves and our capabilities. When we grow in humility to a place where we can acknowledge, accept and admit our mistakes, we grow in compassion for ourselves and others as we learn to surrender and heal our judgments.

Until today, acknowledging a mistake may have caused you fear, anguish, anxiety or shame. Just for today, embrace your humanness. If you have made a mistake today acknowledge it. If you have made one in the past that has had lingering effects, admit it.

*Today I am willing to acknowledge and admit
I am human enough to make mistakes!*

APRIL 24

I am willing to acknowledge . . . I am powerful!
I am brilliant! I am the lover of my life!

Of course you have power! It is an internal force contained within and moving throughout your entire being. You may not be able to see it, but it is there. Just like the toaster and the television, the only thing you need is to get plugged into your Source. There is a light within you that the world is waiting to see. This light, your light, shines so brightly that it has probably blinded you! Your vision has probably been blurred because of *your own disbelief* that someone like you could give so much to so many by simply being turned on about who you are and what you do. The light within you, which is powered by an invisible Source, will guide, protect and supply you with everything you need, at all times, under all circumstances.

One of the most self-loving things you can do is to let your power be seen. If you are not sure of what to do and how to do it, love the process of learning how to love and accept yourself more fully, more completely. Love the process of living. Love the ups and downs, the ins and outs. No one is expecting you to get it right the first time around, but if you set the intention to love yourself while you are learning to love, the Source of the light of love within you will give you all the power you need to keep trying until you master the art of loving.

The shift that you must make in order to use your power, to see your light and to secure the key that will open all the doors of life is to move your attention from the outside world to the inside of you. Know how to plug into your power. Learn what it is, how to keep it flowing and, most important, how to use it. Accept and acknowledge your own brilliance. Stop waiting for others to tell you how great you are! Believe it for yourself and about yourself.

Until today, you may have been experiencing darkness caused by a power outage. Just for today, turn on the light of your inner power of love!

*Today I am devoted to allowing the power of the love that
I am to shine brilliantly.*

APRIL 25

*I am willing to acknowledge . . . the truth must be told
in a way it can be heard.*

Some people are very good at using a razor blade with a smile. Their words are so smooth, so sweet and so soft spoken, it may take you a moment to realize that you have been cut! While you are standing there bleeding, no, hemorrhaging, they put the razor blade away long enough to ask you, *"What's the matter, honey?"* Often the person is speaking the truth, but truth is not the issue here! How the truth is told is the issue. A sweet, gentle, smiling razor blade is still *a razor blade!*

Most people are open to hearing the truth when it is said in a way they can hear it. People cannot hear you when you make them wrong. People cannot hear you when you attack their weaknesses. People cannot hear what you are saying if by saying it you are making yourself better than they are. Do not make the mistake of believing that the people you speak to do not know what you *really* mean. They do! If there is one thread of judgment, of criticism, or denigration in what you say, they are not going to hear you. In fact, they are going to shut you out!

If you want to ensure that people will hear you when you talk about difficult or uncomfortable situations, speak to them from your heart. Speak to them from a place of compassion and concern. See yourself as their teacher, their healer, the step to their next level of spiritual and emotional growth. See them as the part of yourself that does not like to be wrong, does not like to be criticized, does not like to be cut to shreds in the process of learning.

Until today, you may have told the truth in a stinging, biting or cutting way that meant people could not hear you. Just for today, practice telling yourself some truth about yourself that is difficult for you to hear. When you master the art of telling yourself the truth lovingly, use what you have learned when talking to other people.

*Today I am devoted to learning how to tell the truth in a
gentle, compassionate and loving manner!*

APRIL 26

I am willing to acknowledge . . . there doesn't need to be anything wrong in order for me to be all right.

It is a sad thing to consider but some people seek out pain. Some people create pain. Some people just don't feel alive unless something is *wrong*, unless they are hurt in some way. When something has been *wrong* with you for an extended period of time, it can become a habit. It is the thing that makes you feel alive. It is the thing you expect and live for.

Pain gives you something to talk about with others. It can even make you feel important. You can use physical or emotional pain to demonstrate to yourself and others that you can handle whatever life throws at you. It attracts attention. When something is wrong with you, people come to your aid. If they don't, that too gives you something to talk about. It is not that you like pain. It's that it can give you something to do, and every living soul needs something to do.

Life doesn't have to be hard! It is not necessary to live in pain or to live eliminating pain. Without pain, we can learn to settle in to the beauty of life. When there is no pain, we learn to live without fear. When we learn to release pain and the anticipation that it can and will return, we become more comfortable with ourselves, which makes others more comfortable with us. We get the genuine attention and companionship we desire and deserve. It is at this point we discover that we do not need pain to feel alive or to enjoy life.

Until today, you may not have realized the role pain plays in your life. Perhaps the time has come to explore the idea that you may seek out, create and expect pain in your life. Just for today, closely examine all of the painful experiences or situations you are currently facing. Ask yourself, *"How do I support this and expect it to be a part of my life?"* Write down your answers. Next, ask yourself, *"How can I approach this in a more loving and peaceful way?"*

Today I am devoted to discovering a pain-free way of life!

APRIL 27

I am willing to acknowledge . . . what I choose for myself
is very important to me.

*"My only purpose for being on the planet is to awaken to my
God Self! To celebrate life! And to do what brings me joy!"*
This statement, by Rev. Michael Beckwith of the AGAPE
Church of Religious Science, points out the three most difficult challenges we face in life. *Awakening to your God Self.* What is it?
Where is it? How do you find it? How do you know when you have
found it? Ask yourself, *"What is it that I really want for myself?"* Your answers will point you in the direction that God has designed for you. To
celebrate life! How can I celebrate the life I have? How can I turn my life
into something worth celebrating? How can I find the time to celebrate?
Ask yourself again, *"What is it that I really want for myself?"* Your answer
will move you toward doing things you will want to celebrate and away
from those things that prohibit your celebration. *To do what brings me
joy!* What brings you joy? How much time and energy do you spend on
that part of your life? How can you find more time or make more time
for more joy in your life? Ask yourself, *"What is it that I really want for
myself?"* Your answer will be all the motivation you need to move toward
a more peaceful, joy-filled life and away from the fear-based existence
that has kept you from asking the question. In return, you will have
something to celebrate. That will surely make your God Self happy.

Until today, you may have been living without a sense of purpose,
meaning or direction. Just for today, spend some time alone with a pen
and your journal. Ask yourself, *"What is it that I really want for myself?"*
Repeat the question over and over until you hit pay dirt.

*Today I am devoted to the discovery of my God Self
so that I can celebrate life and do all of the things
which bring me joy!*

APRIL 28

I am willing to acknowledge . . .
I Am!

Here is an affirmation filled with so much power it can turn your life around instantly, if you have the courage to use it. The affirmation of power being offered to you today is *I Am!* Don't say, "I'm hoping!" Or "I wish!" Or "I'm trying!" Do not say, "I want to!" Or "I would like to!" Open your mouth and say, "I Am!" That's right! I Am good! I Am good at all the good things I Am doing and dreaming! I Am good at doing good and being good which means I Am open to receiving good! ! I Am so good that good is looking for me to be good with! Good is on its way to me, and that is good for me! I Am now openly receiving good things in every aspect of my life! Now take a breath.

Let's try this one on for size. I Am grateful for my good! I Am grateful for good opportunities! I Am grateful for good experiences! I Am good at everything I do! I Am renewed to do more good! I Am invigorated by the good I do! I Am rejuvenated by the good things I do and the good experiences I have! I Am excited about being so good! I Am good at being powerful! I Am good at demonstrating the brilliant power of my goodness! Now take a breath.

If your feet are still on the ground, try this one. I Am surrounded by good! I Am engulfed by good! I Am completely good! I Am perfectly good! I Am totally good, inside and out! I Am richly rewarded for all the good I Am! I give off good and good returns to me! Who I Am is a good thing to be! Now take a breath!

Until today, you may have been focusing on all the things you believed you were not. Just for today, acknowledge that who you are is good by speaking these affirmations into a tape recorder. Play the tape over and over until good comes alive in your consciousness and spills forth into your life.

Today I am devoted to acknowledging
the good things that I am!

APRIL 29

I am willing to acknowledge . . . the ups and downs
of life need not get me down.

There are days you wake up feeling bigger than life. You are
on a natural high! Then the very next day, you can wake up
feeling helpless, hopeless and worthless. You may feel that if
you had the strength, you would bury yourself forever. Both
of these experiences are natural, normal and to be expected. They are
what we call the *ups and downs,* the *highs and lows* of life. There are, however, some very important things you must be able to do in order to
make it through these experiences without getting bruised.

When you are high, be aware of the commitments and decisions you
make. Discipline yourself to avoid taking on more than you can do because you feel like you can do it all. Restrain yourself, knowing that even
if you remain up for the next few days, your plate may be full, your days
may be scheduled. Take your time in doing whatever you are doing so
that you will not be forced to redo or overdo at a later time. Do not get
caught up in the high times, allowing a good feeling to motivate you to
take on things which could cause you to crash.

If on the other hand you wake up feeling low, lowly or low down,
allow yourself the luxury of the experience. Allow yourself to remember
that you are human and that life goes on. It renews itself each day, offering you the opportunity to do the same. Avoid the things you do to deny
where you are. Simply be! Perhaps you need the rest. Be present with
yourself and what you feel for at least forty-eight hours. After that, pick
yourself up, pump yourself up, spruce yourself up in anticipation of the
next wave of feeling good.

Until today, you may have questioned or dreaded the feelings of up
and down that go along with being alive. Just for today, take note of where
you are. Allow yourself to be there. Take precautions not to do or say anything that could convince you that this is a permanent state of being.

*Today I acknowledge and embrace the highs and lows
of my life!*

APRIL 30

I am willing to acknowledge . . . there is a part of God
in me that requires time, attention and care.

"God uses ordinary people." He uses them not because they
are special or because they have special abilities; he uses
them because they are *ordinary.* It is only His power that can
make the ordinary extraordinary! One of the ordinary things
you can do that will have a God-centered extraordinary impact is to take
care of yourself.

Self-care is an acknowledgment of God's divine presence in you.
Spending time caring for your mind enables God's light, love and wisdom to shine through your thoughts. When you make it a point to still
your mind and your body to care for your spirit, you open yourself to receive the power of God's wisdom. This wisdom leads to righteousness—
right thinking, right action and right response in all aspects of your life.
Caring for yourself demonstrates gratitude for God's presence in you.

There are people in the world who desperately need the presence of
God's light. You are a perfect source through which that light can shine
to them. People learn by example, and you are a living example. The
world needs living proof that God, his Holy Spirit and the light of his
love are available to all. The better you feel, the better you look. The better you look, the more inspiration you offer. The more inspiration you
offer, the more believable it becomes that there are benefits and rewards
for caring for the God in you.

Who in the world could not benefit from a little more wisdom? A
touch of love? Or a surge of power? All it takes is a little time. A little care.
A few moments of silence and stillness each day. Do it for yourself. Do it
for the world. If these reasons are not good enough, then do it for God.

Until today, you may not have realized that self-care is God care. Just
for today, care for your mind, your body and your spirit as acknowledgment of God and in service to the world

Today I am devoted to demonstrating my care
for the part of God that I am!

MAY

ACCEPTANCE

If you take the chains, bolts and locks

from the door

of your heart and let the monster in,

it will just sit there and be.

And at any given moment you can get up

and leave.

MAY 1

I am now receptive to the idea that . . . there are
some things that I can live without!

Anything you *need, must have or can't do without* has domin-
ion over you and your life. In other words, you are a slave of
sorts. We're not talking here about food, clothing and shel-
ter! We are talking about *anything* or *anyone,* from your
mother to your job, that you feel you must have, must help or cannot
walk away from for one reason or another. We are talking about the
gamut from food to sex, people to pets, shoes to butter on both sides of
your bread. If God didn't put it in you, but you believe you cannot live
without it, you are in a lot of trouble!

All too often, we turn our lives over to things and people, believing
that they are essential to our survival. *How does this happen?* How do we
become enslaved? *Why does this happen?* Why do we turn our lives and our
power over to things and people? Well, it's a trick! It is the trick of fear!

Fear will do anything, use anyone, to throw you off track, keep you
off base and move you in the wrong direction. Fear is very well aware that
as long as you believe there is something you cannot do without, you
have an excuse not to do the things you must! Fear also knows that as
long as you have an excuse for *not doing,* fear has something to do! Fear
will keep you running. Fear will keep you in hiding! Fear will keep you
hoping, wishing and trying! Fear will tie you down, beat you up and leave
you gasping for air! Fear is the master trickster! It will make you responsible to others! It will make you responsible for others! Fear is the very
thing that prevents you from letting go of everything and everyone else.

Until today, you may not have been aware of all of the things and
people you hold on to in response to fear. Just for today, accept that you
are afraid to let go! Make a list of all the things you believe you *need.*
Read the list and identify all the excuses you give yourself for holding on.
Then, mentally and emotionally, let go.

*Today I am devoted to eliminating all fear-based reasons,
excuses and habits!*

MAY 2

I am now receptive to the idea that . . . when I get there,
everyone will not be there.

If you really want to live your life to the fullest and realize
your greatest potential, you must be willing to run the risk
of making some people mad. Oh, they will get mad! Whenever you move beyond someone's opinion of you, they get
upset because *you thought more of yourself* than they thought of you.

If you want to know just how much you can do, how far you can
reach, how much you can stretch, you must be willing to leave some
people behind. You must be willing to do more, be more and have more
than those in your present company have. This does not mean you
should compare yourself to them. Nor does it mean you are *showing off*.
Oh, no! It means that you must be willing to step out on your own, try
life for yourself and claim your divine inheritance without guilt.

If you really want to know who you are and what you are capable of
achieving, you must be willing to live without the opinions of other people. That means you don't ask for opinions! And when they are offered,
you need not accept them. In order to find your identity, your authentic-
ity and a true sense of wholeness, you must develop your individuality
from the wealth of information that comes from within you. Of course
others around you can give you effective feedback. But you need not make
it your gospel. People may not like what you do, people may not like how
you do it, but these people are not living your life. You are! Until you are
willing to live beyond the opinions of other people, and without the company of other people, you will have no idea of what *your life* is all about.

Until today, you may have been holding on to other people's opinions about you and doing your best to keep people with you and on your
side. Just for today, take a risk! Tell somebody what you really want for
your life. Tell someone you do not agree with their opinion of you. Then
jump into the center of your own life and get comfortable being there!

*Today I am devoted to living my life without guilt and
based on my own opinions!*

MAY 3

I am now receptive to the idea that . . . I can make things more difficult than they need be.

It really isn't as hard as you are making it. It's really quite simple. Unfortunately, you have so much "stuff" attached to it, you are creating a burden where there need not be one. You are creating a problem where none exists. You are causing yourself a great deal of upset for no reason. There is really no reason to fight or argue about it; to explain or to demand an explanation. You are clear!

You did not like what happened. It did not honor you. It was a violation of your boundaries. It was not in keeping with the agreement you made or the agreement someone else made with you. What is happening or has happened is not of your choice, nor is it of your making. So it's really very simple! Stop looking and asking for an explanation. Stop demanding that people do what they have already demonstrated an unwillingness or inability to do. Accept what has happened and decide what you are going to do about it. Once you make the decision that honors you, move on!

Until today, you may have been prone to making the realities of your life a bit more difficult than they need to be. Just for today, accept what you know and feel to be right for you without trying to convince others that it must be right for them.

Today I am devoted to seeing things plainly and keeping it simple!

I am now receptive to the idea that . . . I must learn
to doubt my doubt and to negate my own negativity.

Doctors prescribe medication in an attempt to facilitate physical healing. In the Book of Proverbs, we find what many the-
ologians consider to be the ultimate *prescription* for living a
successful life. *"Trust in the Lord with all your heart and lean
not on your own understanding. In all your ways acknowledge him. And he
will direct your paths."* If only it were that simple! These words raise four
major challenges: *trust, heart, understanding and acknowledgment.*

We have a problem with trust! We can't trust people! We can't trust
that things will turn out the way we want them to turn out. So how can
you trust God? You don't! You let God trust you. You trust that God believes you when you say you will or will not do a thing. You trust that
God will support you in the things you say you want for your life. If you
learn to forgive yourself for all the ways you have let yourself down,
God's trust will grow in you and God will grow in your heart.

When you believe you know everything, you will never acquire understanding. If you think that the meaning of life is always evident in
what is on the surface, you will never understand yourself, God or life.
Unfortunately, far too many of us believe the truth only when we see it.
As a result, we cannot recognize the truth when it is revealed. These are
the people who want to be right! When you want to be right it is difficult
to trust your heart because you know how many times it has been wrong.

Do you acknowledge God? More important, how do you acknowledge God? Step 1: Accept that you do not know everything. Step 2: Open
your heart, even after it has been broken. Step 3: Trust that God wants for
you what you want for yourself. Then, you are acknowledging God.

Until today, you may have been resistant to taking divine medication. Just for today, accept that it will work, even if you don't know how
it works.

*Today I am devoted to following the divine prescription
for a successful life!*

MAY 5

I am now receptive to the idea that . . . no matter what
it looks like, I did the best I could.

What else could you have done? You keep turning the experience over in your mind. You are rethinking your actions
and responses, which leads to questioning and doubting
yourself. Instead of making yourself crazy, why not ask and
honestly answer this one simple question, *"What else could I have done?"*
Then take it one step further by asking, *"If you could have done it, why
didn't you do it?"*

Could you have been more considerate? Compassionate? Understanding? Probably. Could you have been more patient? More tolerant?
More cautious? Well, what do you think? Could you have said more or
less? Could you have listened a bit closer? Could you have planned better? Waited longer? Of course you could have, but you didn't.

When you feel sufficiently remorseful, overwhelmingly confused
and totally beaten down, you will be on the brink of a divine revelation!
You will be face to face with something you probably never considered.
Something too simple! Too easy! The truth is, *if you could have done it,
you would have!* The fact that you *didn't* means you *couldn't* for reasons
you may not be aware of right now.

Second-guessing yesterday will not help you today. Holding yourself
hostage to what was not will not propel you into what will be. As you accept the reality of what you did not do in the past, you open yourself to
the luxury of knowing it does not mean you will not do better in the
future.

Until today, you may have held yourself hostage with remorse over
what you could have done. In fact, you may be pushing yourself to a
point of *remorseful no return.* Just for today, realize you *did* all you could
have done. Take note of what you saw, heard, felt and experienced. Use
those notes as preparation to do better at some later date.

*Today I am devoted to accepting that I have done
the best I could do!*

MAY 6

I am now receptive to the idea that . . . I am capable
of doing everything better next time!

The prefix *re* means *to do again.* What a blessing! Just think,
you can re-*peat* a lesson, at no charge, until you get it right.
You can re-*group* after a setback, in order to gather your wits
and your strength. You can re-*structure* your life should it
happen to fall apart. You can re-*create* your image should *you* happen
to fall apart. You can re-*position* yourself in any situation once you re-
evaluate it. You can always re-*think* the evaluation once it is done. While
most of us are not fond of doing most things over, when you consider
the blessings of *re,* doing it again may not be so bad.

You can re-*deem* your character by re-*tracting* words spoken harshly.
You can re-*cover* from your losses through the power of re-*organization.*
At some point, we have all faced the pain of being re-*jected,* which is
actually just a divine opportunity to re-*flect* on who we really are. There
is never any reason to live with re-*morse* or re-*gret* when you consider that
every experience is a re-*hearsal* for the next. You can always re-*move*
yourself from a situation when you feel you can't re-*late.* It is a sign of
your re-*fusal* to accept less for yourself than the best. When you re-*lease*
habits, people and situations that do not honor who you are, you will
re-*generate* your power. You cannot re-*capture* your hairline once it
re-*cedes,* but you can always re-*lax* the re-*quirement* to look pleasing!
Re-*fine* your thinking! Re-*form* your life! Re-*search* what you need to do,
and do it without re-*sistance!*

Until today, you may have been re-*luctant* to do things more than
once. Just for today, re-*do* what you need to do and re-*collect* yourself!

*Today I am devoted to re-claiming my power, re-charging
myself and re-cuperating from the past!*

MAY 7

I am now receptive to the idea that . . .
God is on my side!

Be a witness to God growing *in* you. Be a witness to the love, the grace, the kindness of God growing in you and blooming in every aspect of your life. Be a witness to the breath and the beauty of God moving in your being. Be a witness to God moving in your life, shaping, shifting, molding every moment of this day. In order to be a witness, you must trust God enough to stop moving, stop doing and just *sit a spell,* in order to call forth the presence of God in you. Then watch it do its divine work as you.

Be a witness to God growing *as* you. Be a witness to how you have changed, how you have grown, how you have blossomed into your goodness and greatness. Be a witness to how you touch others. How you teach others. How you serve and love others. Be a witness to the power you have to transform, to purify and rectify any signs of destruction in yourself and in the world immediately around you. Just be a witness by standing back, taking a look around and by remembering the truth of who you are.

Be a witness to God growing *through* you. Be a witness to what you thought you had to have that you no longer need. Be a witness to what you thought you could not do that got done with grace and ease. Be a witness to your ability to see all that is behind you as part of the path to where you are heading. Be a witness to the gifts you have, perhaps the one thing you can do that has sustained you and at some time been a blessing to someone else. Be a witness to the multidimension abilities of God moving through you that allow you to be in the past, the future and the present to make choices about which way you intend to go. In order to be a witness to the power of God, as you stop judging, start forgiving.

Until today, you may have been a blind witness to the glory of God in you, as you and through you. Just for today, take a moment, or several moments, to become aware of how good God looks on you.

Today I am devoted to being a witness and to seeing myself as God sees me!

MAY 8

I am now receptive to the idea that . . .
in God, there is no time or space beyond now.

There is an old saying "Tomorrow is not promised." But neither is the next moment. If that is the case, why not step
into *now!* Right here, right now there is a miracle waiting to
happen. Step into the present moment in which the pain,
shame, anger, guilt of the past are not present. Where the fear, doubt or
anxiety of the future cannot touch you, unless you bring it into the now
with you. Step into this moment in time in all of its fullness, and declare,
"This is good!"

Step into this moment, because it is the only one you have right
now. It is not wasted or thrown away. This divine opportunity could be
stolen unless you tell yourself it is here right now; available to you this
moment, to make of it anything you choose. Why not choose this moment, right now, to be available to yourself by declaring, I AM GOOD!

Are you present in this moment, right here, right now? Or are you
remembering what you didn't do yesterday, thinking about what you
have to do tomorrow, regretting what you did last week. If you are in any
of these places, you are not, right now in the fullness of this moment. The richness of the present is here. The fullness of *now* is present.
If you are not here now, it means you could be missing the love, joy,
peace and brand-new ideas that are here right now. Why not take a moment to gather yourself, to pull yourself together, to collect all of your
thoughts and feelings in this time and place. Take a nice deep breath. Put
the book down and spend just a few moments with yourself in the richness and fullness of now.

Until today, you may have spent all of your time moving away from
one thing to something else. Just for today, be in the presence of the now
of the moment: As a matter of fact, do it right now.

*Today I am devoted to being present and available
to every moment, moment by moment.*

MAY 9

I am now receptive to the idea that . . . everything I am
seeking is on its way to me.

When you least expect it, the very thing you want, the thing you have been praying for with all of your heart is going to come to you from nowhere. *Nowhere* is a spiritual location that leads to now here! The thing you have wanted for so long is going to drop right into your life without your having done or having to do anything. In fact, it will probably show up on the very day you did not pray, the day you did not work yourself into a frenzy trying to make something happen. In fact, it will probably slip into your life so quietly, with such grace and ease, you may not believe it at first. In fact, you might be a little frightened! It is frightening to think that life could be so easy, so graceful, so almost uneventful as to have the thing you have been praying for show up without you rough riding it!

You may not believe that just wanting it was enough because, in order to accept that notion, you would have to believe that you don't have to struggle or work hard in life. You will not believe that after all of your effort and trying, this thing shows up—just like that! When you weren't looking, watching, working or waiting for it to happen. For just a moment, you might even be a little *annoyed.* You might feel like you have wasted your time and energy and money! Oh! You don't even want to think about the money you spent! Or, you might think to yourself, No way! No way this can happen like this for me when I didn't have or don't have the money to make it happen. This can't be happening! But it is. And when it does, your reaction will answer a very important question, *How much confidence do you place in your prayers?*

Until today, you may not have accepted that one prayer is all it takes. Just for today, try praying for something with all of your heart and soul, then don't do anything else.

*Today I am devoted to placing my full confidence
in my prayers!*

MAY 10

I am now receptive to the idea that . . .
I am the only one who can determine how people
see me and remember me.

If your life were to end today, how would your obituary read? Now don't get frightened! Thinking about your obituary will not kill you. It is actually a way to *start living*, to start being fully conscious of the moments you are alive. Every moment of your life writes a line for your obituary. Every action and inaction provides memories of you to those you will leave behind. They are the memories that the people you love and leave behind will want to include in the telling of your life story.

You are the author of your own obituary! Are you writing a history of misery, or a tale of tenacity? Were you up or *uppity?* Were you inclusive and supportive? Or were you exclusively out for yourself? Did you lift others up, or did you allow them to knock you down? Did you stay down just long enough to recover? Or did you stay down, complaining and whining? What will your obituary say about the way you treated people and how you made them feel about themselves? What will your obituary say about the way you treated yourself? What will be said about your attitude? How you handled yourself in a crisis? It's true that people can lie. They can say things to make you look good to all those who didn't know you. But *they* will know and *you* know the truth. Perhaps now is the time to consider how you are living and what you want to be said about you when you are not.

Until today, you may not have realized that your life provides the content of your obituary. Just for today, examine your life. Think about all the things you want to leave behind. Remember, the good thing about doing this today is that you still have time to rewrite your life's content if necessary.

*Today I am devoted to writing a powerful history
of myself and my life!*

MAY 11

I am now receptive to the idea that . . . it is time
for me to stop whispering and to start living out loud.

Stop hiding! Stop holding yourself back and playing yourself
down! Stop worrying about how you look and what people
are saying. Stop listening to what people are saying and trying to find out if they are whispering about you. Stop waiting
for someone to tell you that you are okay or to make you feel special. Life
is special! It is a special gift. This is your life! Now take your gift and live it
out in the open! Decide today that you are going to *live out loud!*

Living out loud means having the courage to be exactly who you are
without apology. It means admitting your mistakes without beating
yourself up. It means not taking who you are and what you have for
granted. Release all shame! Release all guilt! You cannot live out loud if
you are hiding behind what *was.* Living out loud means focusing on
what is, right now, and that is *you!*

To live out loud means showing up as your authentic Self, without
your makeup or your toupee. It means acknowledging your shortcomings and celebrating your strengths. Living out loud means broadcasting
your needs, your likes and your dislikes as they relate to your fears and
frustrations. It means that you let people know exactly who you are and
expect them to be as thrilled as you are about who you are.

In order to live out loud you must have faith in yourself and in the
process of life. You must have principles you live by and standards by
which you can govern and gauge yourself. Most important, in order to
live out loud you must love yourself enough to tell yourself and everyone
else the absolute truth about you. When you can do that, you can live
out loud and be very proud about what the world will hear about you.

Until today, you may have been living your life in a whisper. Just for
today, take one step toward pumping up your volume. Stand up in yourself! Stand up and be yourself!

*Today I am devoted to broadcasting the truth
about myself!*

MAY 12

I am now receptive to the idea that . . . if I don't ask for what I need, the need will keep getting bigger!

HELP!

HELP!

HELP!

HELP!

HELP!

HELP!

HELP!

HELP!

Until today, you may have thought you had to do it all alone. Just for today, ask for what you need.

Today I am devoted to asking for and receiving what I need!

MAY 13

I am now receptive to the idea that . . . sometimes people do things that have nothing to do with what I have done!

What if someone you loved and respected suddenly stopped speaking to you? With no reason or explanation, they simply tuned out and turned you off. How would you feel? What would you do? Most of us would probably search for a reason. We would search our most recent words, trying to find the reason why someone, particularly this someone, would turn their back. When the search turned up nothing, we would make the next most obvious leap. We would ask ourselves, *"What did I do wrong?"* It is at the precise moment that we ask ourselves that question that we are going to get ourselves into trouble.

People have a right to do what they want to do, when they want to do it, in any manner they choose to do it. You don't have to like it, and sometimes it is very hurtful. It does not mean, however, that you did anything wrong. People see the same things in different ways. Certain people may process information in a different way than you do. They may feel different than you do about certain things. And even when you think you know a person, they may surprise you!

Each time you make yourself wrong for the way someone treats you, you diminish your sense of self. At times, you can be so willing to be wrong about what has happened that you make yourself wrong for simply being who you are. At some point in life, you may simply be faced with the painful reality that, for whatever reason, someone has chosen to move you out of their life. Accept that as their choice. While you may feel hurt and bewildered, it does not mean you have done anything wrong.

Until today, you may have considered yourself wrong about something that has nothing to do with you. Just for today, accept the fact that not every painful experience means you have done something wrong.

Today I am devoted to moving myself out of the position that I must be wrong because of the way others may treat me!

MAY 14

I am now receptive to the idea that . . . when I am afraid
to hear the truth, I make up the truth
the way I think it should be.

There are some people who can only hear what they want to
hear. It is, however, extremely hard on the people who are
trying to communicate with them. People who hear what
they want to hear usually miss the point, misinterpret the
meaning and are not above making up things that make them feel more
comfortable with what is said and who is saying it. When challenged
about their interpretation of what was said, people who hear what they
want to hear will get mad or upset about the things they heard that were
never spoken.

People who hear what they want to hear can feel accused, degraded
or criticized regardless of what is said. They are extremely defensive,
which makes it difficult to talk to them, even about important things.
People who hear what they want to hear know how things should be
said, but even when they are, they can't seem to hear them.

People who hear what they want to hear are mind readers and body-
language experts! They can read meanings into the speaker's tone of
voice. They often derive some meaning from the speaker's hand gestures.
They believe there is some relevance to how fast or slow the speaker's eyes
move, and they intuit meanings from the direction in which the speaker's
head is tilted. They challenge the integrity and intelligence of certain
speakers because there are only certain people they can hear. This alone
gives them a reason to blame what they do or don't do on someone else.
It's not their fault! But it is. They did not hear what was being said.

Until today, you may have been a person who hears what you want
to hear rather than what is being said. Just for today, practice not adding
meanings or diminishing the value of what is said to you based on who
is saying it.

*Today I am devoted to hearing the truth in what is said
and not giving the truth my own meaning!*

MAY 15

I am now receptive to the idea that . . . I may be blocking
myself from receiving more than I am holding on to.

As long as you are holding on to what you have, your path of
possibilities is blocked. The holding can be mental, emotional or physical. In any case, it is a sign of fear. If you are
afraid to lose what you have, it means your consciousness is
grounded in *lack*. Somewhere in the back of your mind, there is a belief
that there is not enough to go around. There may also be a belief that
when *it* comes around, you will not be on the receiving end.

Holding on is not the same as taking care of what you value or protecting that which is yours. Holding on is what most people do when
they are afraid they don't deserve more. Holding on is what we do when
we settle for less than we want. Holding on is what we do instead of asking for what we want and then taking responsibility for creating it.
When you really believe that you are worthy of the best, that you deserve
the best and that there is enough of the best for you to have plenty, there
will be no need for you to grab or clutch or squeeze what you have. You
won't worry about what you have. You will not watch over what you
have. You will no longer live in fear that by losing what you have, your
life will somehow be diminished. When you can stop holding on, you
begin to realize that your blessings cannot be taken away, nor will they
go away until the Universe is ready to *up the ante*.

Until today, you may have been holding on to things and people in
fear that they could not or would not be replaced in your life. Just for
today, allow yourself to imagine what your life would be like if your
hands and heart were to receive something better than what you are
holding on to right now.

*Today I am devoted to opening my hands, my heart and
my life to receive bigger blessings!*

MAY 16

I am now receptive to the idea that . . . whenever I see
a hole, I am to move around it.

Somebody left you, and now there is a gaping hole in the
middle of your soul. The question is how are you going to
fill that hole? Are you going to fill it with the painful memories of how you got hurt or got left? Or are you going to fill
it with memories of the many moments of joy and laughter you had together? Are you going to fill the hole with anger, resentment, fear or
shame directed toward the one who left? Or are you going to fill the hole
with appreciation that you do have an opportunity to choose how you
are going to fill the hole? Are you going to fill the hole with the countless
reasons why it should not have happened to you? Or are you going to fill
it with the courage it will take to accept that it did happen to you, in this
way?

Are you going to fill the hole with at least one ounce of confidence
that you can handle this, whatever it takes? Or are you going to fill the
hole with the self-defeating belief that you can't or will not make it
through or over this hole? Are you going to empty all of your self-value,
self-worth and self-esteem into the hole until it becomes a pit of self-
pity, self-doubt and self-inflicted nonsense that keeps *you* in a hole of despair? Are you going to throw yourself into a hole and dare life to try and
move you?

You can cover the hole with love and prayer and acceptance of your
ability to step over or walk around the hole. You can also step back, take
a little break and wait to see the *Self* that emerges from the hole. The
choice is yours!

Until today, you may have believed that you had to stay in the
painful hole of hurt caused by the loss of a loved one. Just for today,
make a conscious effort and choice to cover the hole and move on.

*Today I am devoted to covering the holes and filling in
all the gaps in my life!*

MAY 17

I am now receptive to the idea that . . .
if people really know who I am, they will probably
like me anyhow.

Until you are willing to be vulnerable, you will not be able to trust yourself. You will not know how far you can go or how much you can do. You will not know what makes you tick or what will make you crack. Until you are willing to let down your guard and lay down your defenses, you will not know how far you can push yourself or how you will handle what happens when you get there. Unless you are willing to be vulnerable, to let people know that you don't know how, but that you are headed *there* anyway, you will not be equipped to deal with the reactions of those you will meet when you get there. Unless you are willing to be vulnerable, to make a mistake, to be taken advantage of, to look stupid, to fall down and stumble when you are trying to get up, you will not know how durable or dependable you are. And as long as you don't know how strong you are, you will not benefit from the power or realize the beauty of your authentic Self. It is only through your vulnerable authentic Self that the world comes face to face with the true lasting power and undeniable beauty that you are.

Until today, you may have been afraid to be your authentic Self, to admit what you did not know or could not do. Just for today, allow yourself to be vulnerable with just one person, yourself.

Today I am devoted to seeing and accepting myself
exactly as I am!

MAY 18

I am receptive to the idea that . . . I always have a choice
about how I respond to experiences in my life.

If you have ever thought of yourself as a victim, you will have difficulty
trusting yourself, God or anyone else. As long as you are a
victim you will have someone to blame, someone to hold
accountable for what went on and what is going on in your
life. Sure, something unpleasant happened! That was then,
this is now. There is no need for you to remain a victim. As long as you
are a victim you can take no share of the responsibility for who you are,
what you do or how you feel. You see, victims do not respond in choice,
they react in fear. As long as you are in fear, you cannot trust.

As long as you are a victim, you cannot see the lesson. In fact, you
may not want to see the lesson. You want an explanation! You want the
whys answered, but no matter what anyone says, you will not believe it
because you don't trust anyone. As a victim you cannot admit that you
have grown and are growing in response to your experience. Rather than
choosing to see and celebrate your own growth, you choose hurt, anger,
fear, indignation and self-righteousness. In fact, the taste of anger is
probably rising in your throat right now because you *don't trust* that anyone knows how horrible it was for you. Nor do you trust that anyone
other than you understands how that horror is still very active in your
life. They do. They also realize that the reason you cannot let go of being
a victim is because to do so means deciding for yourself what else you
can be. And victims do not trust that they can do that.

Until today, you may have been singing a *victim song* so loud that
you did not realize that there is a *redemption song.* Just for today, trust
yourself enough to sing your own praises about how far you have come,
how much you have done, how much more you are willing to do, in
spite of all you have experienced.

*Today, I am devoted to trusting myself to break the chains
and shackles that have made me a victim!*

MAY 19

I am now receptive to the idea that . . . God's inner
vision of me can be the outer vision I create for myself.

There is nothing you need to do to make yourself more acceptable to God. You don't have to work harder, nor do you
need to change the kind of work that you do. You don't have
to give more money to more charitable organizations. The
reality is, God doesn't want you to give anyone anything if you only do it
to impress God! God does not love you or find you acceptable because of
anything that you *do*. God loves you and accepts you because you are a
part of God.

You can now give up any neurotic beliefs and activities associated
with perfection. That's right! You can stop trying to be perfect! You can
stop trying to do everything perfectly. You can save the time, energy and
money you are spending trying to make the world or other people perfect. You can stop trying to figure out how to make yourself greater,
grander, more acceptable to God today because you consider yourself to
be damaged by the mistakes you made yesterday. Nothing you can *do*
will make you look better, sound better, smell better or in any way be
better, more acceptable than the person God made you to be.

God has an *inner vision*. God is looking at you from the inside out.
When you are accepting of yourself as a divine creation of God, undeni-
ably connected to God, filled with the love of God, you become acceptable to yourself. That is really all that God is concerned with.

Until today, you may have believed that there was something you
needed to do to make yourself more acceptable to God. Just for today, examine and explore the aspects of yourself you believe are unacceptable.
Identify the behaviors and actions you are engaged in, and make a list of
those things you choose to eliminate. Just remember that God is happy
when you are happy. So do it for yourself.

*Today I am devoted to eliminating those things about
myself and my life that I have determined are
unacceptable!*

MAY 20

I am now receptive to the idea that . . . a spiritual master
is a master of self.

For the price of this book, you are about to receive a master's
degree in spirituality. What you are about to learn will carry
you through any situation life brings your way. Once you
have mastered this day's lesson, you will have everything you
need to realize everything that you are. Your divinity! Your nobility! Your
presence in life as a gift to humanity will be so evident, people will want
to know you! They will want to be just like you. The lesson may seem
very simple, but to truly master it may take a lifetime. Take all the time
you need. A master knows that rushing leads to nowhere. Ready for the
lesson, your key to freedom, joy and peace? Here it is:

Know Your *Self!* See Your *Self!* Accept Your *Self!* Be Your *Self!*

No matter what you may be faced with in life, know your *Self!*

No matter what someone may do to you or against you, see your *Self!*

No matter how many times you try and fail, or fail to try, accept
your *Self!*

No matter whose company you are in or what they have the ability
to give to you or take away from you, be your *Self!*

And if for some reason you are tempted to believe that you cannot develop mastery of these lessons, you might want to try this one: Trust
your *Self!* Trust that you really can do it. Trust that your *Self* will provide
you with all the tutoring you need. Trust that your life is a classroom that
will continue to provide you with the opportunities you need to master
all of the lessons. Trust that you cannot fail this course!

Until today, you may have believed you had to take a class or a
course to discover the tools of spiritual mastery. Just for today, work with
the tools you have. Know your *Self* as a divine being! See your *Self* as
connected to God! Accept your *Self,* even if you don't do well on today's
lesson! Be your *Self,* a loving and compassionate being!

*Today I am devoted to studying and mastering the steps
toward spiritual mastery!*

MAY 21

I am now receptive to the idea that . . . what I did not do
cannot stop me from doing something else.

We already know who and what we are not. We talk about it
every chance we get. We highlight it when people give us
compliments. We point it out to ourselves to make sure we
don't forget. We already know about all of the times we have
been weak and indecisive, the times we have lacked clarity. We fret end-
lessly over our errors in judgment. We talk down to ourselves every
chance we get, just in case we might begin to believe we are the somebody we have told ourselves we are not.

We already know what we're not doing and why. We already know
where we haven't been and why we cannot go there. We already know
what we don't know and why we haven't learned it. We already
know how we messed up and what happened because of it. We already
know who we hurt and how we did it. We already know the chapter and
verse of what is *wrong* with us. We know it so well that we have probably
lost sight of all the things that are *right*.

For some strange reason, it is not always easy to give yourself credit
when and where it is due, to give yourself the benefit of the doubt or to
take your neck out of the noose so that you can move forward. In his
book *Love Without Conditions*, Paul Ferrini wrote: *"If you do not take responsibility for bringing love to your own wounds, you will not move out of
the vicious cycle of [self]-attack, [self]-defense, [self-imposed] guilt and [self-
imposed] blame."* In other words, do your very best to see the right beneath your wrong.

Until today, you may have been focused on all of the things you are
not and the things you have not done. Just for today, offer yourself the
love and acceptance you need to move yourself beyond who you have
not been and what you did not do.

*Today I am devoted to bringing love to the places in me
where I do not feel good about myself!*

MAY 22

I am now receptive to the idea that . . . parents can see
the hidden parts of themselves in their children.

There are no such things as *problem children*. There are, however, *problem parents*. The problem with parents is, when
they recognize the suppressed parts of themselves being
acted out by their children, they go nuts! When parents see
their children daring to do things they were convinced could not be
done, they may feel insecure. When parents recognize that their children
are willing to take risks they were not willing to take, or to overcome ob-
stacles they believed were insurmountable, parents may feel inadequate.
When parents understand that their children have the power to do what
they make up their minds to do, parents feel that their authority is being
challenged. When parents believe their authority is being challenged,
they will do anything and everything to keep a child in line. They will
even run the risk of destroying the child's spirit.

When a parent is confronted by a child's opinions, they can make the
child feel insecure. When a parent is confronted by a child's insights, they
can make a child feel inadequate. When a parent is confronted with a
child's ability to see the truth, know the truth and speak the truth, a parent can make a child doubt their inner authority. When a parent is confronted with a child's sexuality, they can become totally confused,
disoriented and afraid! Parents know that they are powerful. At times, they
don't trust themselves because they remember what their own parents said
and did to them. They are so very afraid that they might do the same.

Until today, you may have been raising your children with the same
fear and disregard with which you were raised. Or you may be doing
your best to make sure your children are not raised like you. Just for
today, take a good look at your children. Listen to them. See them for
who they really are. Realize that your children offer a divine opportunity
for you *to give* and *to get* some of the things you may have missed.

*Today I am devoted to allowing myself to see my children
as they are, for who they are!*

I am now receptive to the idea that . . . there comes a
time when a parent must stop parenting.

Some parents never give up. They never give up directing,
controlling and interfering in their *grown* children's lives.
They never give up talking to, talking about, criticizing or
chastising their children, long after they are *grown.* Just in
case you were wondering, anyone who is of voting age or drinking age, is
sexually active and who demonstrates the responsibility and means to
pay their own rent, is *grown!*

Sometimes parents are in their *grown* children's lives in inappropriate
ways. They pay their *grown* children's bills. They buy their *grown* children's food. There are even some parents who allow their *grown* children
and *their lovers* to live in their homes. Some parents are so concerned and
afraid that the kid won't make it, they never give the kid the opportunity
to try. We are not talking about the parent who helps out when a child
has hard times. We are talking about those parents who will not allow
their children to face the hard time. We are talking about those parents
who *don't believe* that their grown children are capable of handling difficulty, so they constantly interfere. Running interference for your children can interfere with their ability to figure things out on their own.

It is a parent's *right* to worry. It is a *parental obligation* to be concerned. It is also a parent's *duty* to know when to let go and step back from
the front page of their child's life. A parent *knows* when a child is ready to
go out into the world. A parent *knows* when a child is in trouble and
needs some help or assistance. A parent also knows that some of the fears
they have about the child failing or falling *has nothing to do with the child!*

Until today, you may have been involved in your grown children's
lives in ways that were not appropriate. Just for today, take a breath! Let
go! Offer your grown children the opportunity to meet life on their own
terms. While they are doing that, learn how to knit!

Today I am devoted to offering my grown children
the opportunity to grow up!

MAY 24

I am now receptive to the idea that . . . what I see in
others represents the fears I have about myself.

See everyone in your family for the truth of who they are; spiritual beings on a spiritual journey that does not always follow
a straight or narrow path. See your family members as souls
on a journey, struggling through their lessons, just like you.
See them as vulnerable and innocent children, as afraid of their challenges
as you are of yours. It would be helpful to see that they are working
through their "stuff" in the same way you are working through your stuff.
They don't always do the *right thing,* in the *right way,* for the *right reasons.*
But neither do you. And there are times when they need a second chance.
Even if it is the *fifty-ninth* time they have needed a second chance. Haven't
you been in the same position on *sixty-two* separate occasions?

See your family members, even those you hate to see coming in your
direction, through the memory of your own fears and pains. Remember
being afraid to look at yourself? Remember feeling guilty or ashamed of
what you saw when you did look? Remember how you tried to cover up
the parts of yourself that you determined were bad? Remember how you
hated to hear the things people would tell you when they saw the pieces
of you that you tried to hide? Remember how you acted and reacted?
Well, let those memories be the looking glass through which you see those
whom you consider to be the undeveloped or underdeveloped members
of your own family. Look at them through compassionate eyes and see
their pain, their wounds, their futile attempts to hide their silent truth.

Until today, you may have viewed certain members of your family
through judgmental, harsh or hostile eyes. If so, you were seeing them
with your own fears. Just for today, see your blood, community and
world family with the compassion, support and love you know it will
take to inspire them to want to do better.

Today I am devoted to seeing all of my family members
through eyes filled with compassion and love!

MAY 25

I am now receptive to the idea that . . . the need to be
liked is a reflection of what needs to be healed.

Sit down. This one is going to be rough. It may rub you the
wrong way or upset your ideas about some things you
thought were important. It may even ruin the activities you
had planned for today, which means you are going to have to
shift gears and find something else to focus your life on. You may think
you know this already. Perhaps you do, but I bet each time something
happens to remind you, you scratch your head trying to figure out why.
What is it? Here it is: *Everybody does not have to like you!* In fact, everybody *can't* like you! Everybody must not like you! That is not their job!
Liking you is not anyone's purpose in life except yours.

There are times when, for no apparent reason or for no good reason
at all, people decide that you are not *likable*. They may even profess to
hate you! They will say things to you or about you that will hurt your
feelings. Sometimes, they will go out of their way just to be mean and
nasty to you. No matter how hard you try to make them like you, they
won't! This does not make them bad people. Oh, no! It simply means
that they may have "stuff" going on with them that has nothing to do
with you. And that *will trigger your stuff!* That's right! The behavior of
the people who don't like you will bring up your abandonment issues.
Your issues about being rejected. Your issues about *not being good
enough,* or *not doing things right enough.* The minute you discover that
somebody *you think* is important to you doesn't like you, all your *people-
pleasing stuff* will be triggered, and you will be forced to deal with it.
What a blessing! This is precisely the stuff you need to heal.

Until today, you may have been concerned because you know that
there are people who, for one reason or another, just don't like you. Just
for today, concern yourself with figuring out why you think they should.

*Today I am devoted to examining my need to be liked
and accepted by other people!*

MAY 26

I am now receptive to the idea that . . . the purpose of
living is to honor life, honor God and honor myself.

Life is not about *doing it right*. Life is the calling forth of your
soul by God, in order for you to live by principles that
honor God and see yourself as a part of God for the purpose
of doing good. God is good, you know? It is that same God-
goodness that life expects from you and will give to you when you live a
life of integrity.

Integrity. The good in you coming out of you as a statement of who
you know yourself to be. Integrity. The commitment to acting on what
your heart feels and knowing your heart feels good about who you are
and what you do in every situation. Integrity. The willingness to be diligent in giving your best, first to yourself and then to everyone else,
knowing that every moment of contact with another being is a gift from
God. Integrity. Yearning to know the truth. Seeking the truth. Learning
the truth. Spreading the truth. Acting in truth for the sake of honoring
truth for the good of everyone, including yourself. Integrity. Accepting
all that is and choosing to live by all that honors you and honors God,
without condemning the other parts. Integrity, not right or wrong.

Your integrity is the power that *records, rewards* and *restores* your position in the universe of life. Integrity records every thought you think.
Every word you speak. Every action you take. It is integrity that records
your motives at the root of each of these. When the thoughts, words and
actions you set forth in the universe do not honor the truth about you or
the truth about the universe, integrity rewards you accordingly.

Until today, you may have been so concerned with doing your life
right that you have moved out of integrity. Just for today, define your integrity. What are you doing? Why are you doing it? How are you doing
it? What are the rewards you are receiving? What are the rewards you are
expecting? How are you honoring God and the universe?

*Today I am devoted to defining and living in integrity
as the way to honor myself and honor God!*

MAY 27

I am now receptive to the idea that . . . a spiritual path is
a heart-centered path that cannot be found in a book.

Intellectual spirituality will not save you. People often turn to
the spiritual path in an attempt to find the deeper meaning
of life. People usually look to *things spiritual* in order to gain
a better understanding of *things physical*. The search may
begin with a book or a seminar or a profound personal experience that
leads to the reading of a book or attending some sort of gathering where
things of a spiritual nature are discussed and explored. Usually what is
read or what is heard strikes a chord somewhere deep in the inner self,
and the person knows they are on to something. This *on-to-something*
feeling usually results in the reading of more books, the attending of
more seminars and a broadening of the search to discover more materi-
als that will deepen the feeling of being on the spiritual path. It's nice,
and it may be fulfilling for a while, but ultimately it can become an intellectual, rather than a spiritual experience.

This is not to say that you should not read things of a spiritual nature. Nor does it mean that you should not attend events with the intention of broadening your spiritual understanding. This is to say clearly
and openly that reading books, writing notes on index cards, profess-
ing to know what you have read and written, *will not save you!* Knowing
what to do and doing it are not the same. Reading leads to knowing.
Doing leads to experience, and only *your own experience* will ultimately
save you.

Until today, you may have believed that all you needed was an
in-depth knowledge of spiritual principles and ideals. Just for today,
practice grounding your spiritual philosophy in your heart. Don't forget!
Ask the Holy Spirit to assist you in discovering whether or not you are
on the path that is most beneficial to you!

*Today I am devoted to getting grounded on a spiritual
path that is heartfelt and heart centered!*

MAY 28

I am now receptive to the idea that . . . nobody can really
love me until I really love me.

What I'm going to ask you to do may sound silly at first, but
it could save your life. If you take your life seriously enough
to do this one thing, you will see such a difference in yourself
that you may not recognize yourself. Here it is: Each day for
the next forty days, write a love letter and send it to yourself. Before you
shake your head and refuse to do it, just think about it. When was the last
time you had hot, passionate, steamy love coming at you on a daily basis?
When was the last time you received an expression of pure, totally accepting, noncritical unconditional love, love without any strings attached? An even better question is, "How much love can you stand?

Can you believe that there are people who have never had someone
tell them that they will be protected, supported and loved until the end
of time? These same people may have received some pretty nice cards,
but receiving a card is not the same as knowing that someone actually
took the time to write a heartfelt love letter on beautiful, scented paper,
perhaps with dried rose petals added to the envelope. Opening a card at
the kitchen table does not evoke the same feelings as curling up in a chair
with a hand-written love letter that expresses how special, how wonderful, how absolutely perfect you are. I'm telling you, if you were to receive
forty love letters, it wouldn't matter who had written them! You would
be so wrapped up in the true nature of love that you would be able to
recognize a love impostor as soon as you saw one!

Until today, you may have been willing to accept any little expression of sentiment as the true expression of love. Just for today, and for
the next forty days, be the object of your own love. Send yourself a love
letter and then take the time to read it to yourself. Once you get it down
to a science, you may feel loving enough to share some of the same loving thoughts with someone else.

*Today I am devoted to expressing my heartfelt love
to myself!*

MAY 29

I am now receptive to the idea that . . . it is possible
that I have been following the wrong directions.

Here is an interesting concept that could help you the next time you are faced with a challenge that you believe you cannot handle: Your personality is the *passenger,* not the *driver!* Your spirit is the driving force of your life. Most people believe it is the personality that matters. As a result, there are things they believe they cannot do or things they will not do because such things don't fit their personality. *Poor creatures!* As long as they insist on listening to the passenger, they will probably end up getting lost!

When it is time to make a life-altering decision, we allow the demands of the personality to govern the decisions and choices we make for ourselves. The personality, much like a backseat driver, is always giving unsolicited directions. Always questioning. Always warning. Always looking over the shoulder of the actual driver. If you're not focused, the chatter of the personality could cause you to *get turned around!* It could steer you in the wrong direction!

Your spirit is the only true navigational force in your life. Unfortunately, it doesn't talk as loud as your personality! Your spirit offers directions only when asked. Your spirit is not worried about getting lost, because it knows what to do, when to do it and what the final outcome will be. Your spirit knows the best time to travel. The best time to stop and rest. The best roads to take, and the weather conditions that lie ahead. Your spirit, unlike *your personality,* is not so concerned with your comfort. It is concerned that you have a safe journey on the path of growth.

Until today, the demands and controls of your personality may have led you down the wrong path. Just for today, closely examine yourself and your behavior to determine how the personality has driven you. Then invite your spirit to assist you in moving your life in the direction that God would have it go.

Today I am devoted to following the directions of the
indwelling spirit—the driving power of my life!

MAY 30

I am now receptive to the idea that . . . some things never
grow old. They just get better and go deeper.

The Ten Commandments for the New Millennium
    1. Thou shalt make it your business to get in touch
with God first each day.
    2. Thou shalt remember to pray for your mother and
your father as soon as you finish praying for yourself.
    3. Thou shalt honor thyself enough not to take things that do not
belong to you, and this includes other people's people.
    4. Thou shalt refrain from telling someone something about
somebody until you have told that somebody to their face.
    5. Thou shalt refrain from saying anything to anybody that you
would be ashamed or afraid to say to God, to God's face.
    6. Thou shalt do no less than two good things for yourself each
day.
    7. Thou shalt do one good thing for another each day.
    8. Thou shalt confine all whining, complaining and criticizing to
every other Wednesday, between the hours of 2:00 A.M. and 3:30 A.M.,
when the moon is full. When the moon is not full, oh, well, thou shalt
wait until it is.
    9. Thou shalt live fully, or thou shalt not. This choice is yours.
    10. Thou shalt believe the best about everything and everyone until
you have concrete evidence from God to the contrary.
    Until today, you may have believed the old ways and the old laws did
not apply to your life today. Just for today, apply each of these commandments to every aspect of your life.

*Today I am devoted to applying the old-millennium laws
to the new-millennium conditions in my life!*

MAY 31

*I am now receptive to the idea that . . . I am the body
that is the body of God.*

The Apostle Paul asked his followers a very important question when he wrote, "Don't you know that you are the temple of God; and that the Spirit of God dwells within you?" Many of us today are still wrestling with the notion that we are divine. We can't seem to grasp the concept that God is actually in us. His presence is our true Self.

What does it mean to be the temple in which God dwells? It means that we are sacred. It means that we are imbued with God's purpose and power. While many profess to know this, when faced with the distractions of everyday life, we forget. We get so busy trying to do physically the things we can only do spiritually that our true power often lies dormant in the temple. In essence, we don't utilize the God-ness within us. We waste our sacredness, our divinity and time that could be spent listening to, honoring and remembering God.

God's mind is your mind, God's power is your power. Knowing and accepting this as the truth of your being means learning to let *God work through you!* If you believe that God created the world with a word, surely you know that God can handle the mundane stuff, like your finances, your relationships, your kids and a hellish supervisor! As you learn to acknowledge God's presence as your true identity; to accept God's presence as the source of your power; to honor God's presence as the foundation of your own sacredness, your temple, your life will become a place where you will want to worship.

Until today, you may not have accepted that the presence of God in you creates the truth about you. Just for today, perhaps right now, allow yourself to be filled with the presence of all that is good and powerful and peaceful and joyful. Take a breath. Allow yourself to become the living embodiment of God.

*Today I am devoted to experiencing and expressing
the powerful and peaceful presence of God in me!*

JUNE

FORGIVENESS

Forgiveness is not something you do.

It is a state of being that when offered

brings forth the truth of who you are.

JUNE 1

I am now willing to forgive myself . . . because I am not always aware of what I am doing to cause myself harm.

There is a prayer being offered on your behalf at all times. This prayer is offered by the angels—your guardians, who live in the unseen realms of the universe. It is a universal prayer offered on behalf of everyone, even those who do not believe in the power of prayer. It is a prayer that operates most effectively when you don't know how to pray for yourself. The angelic prayer is this: *"Father forgive them. For they know not what they do."*

Each time you deny yourself the joy of loving or being loved, some angel pleads on your behalf, "Father forgive them. For they know not what they do." In those moments when fear, anger or the struggle for control motivates you to behave in a mean, nasty, inconsiderate or spiteful way, the Divine Mother opens her heart to pray on your behalf, "Father forgive them. For they know not what they do." In response to this prayer, God is willing to give you another chance any time you need one.

When you allow self-defeating beliefs to hold you in a place of pain and suffering, one of the archangels prays for you, "Father forgive them. For they know not what they do." When you lack the courage to move beyond habitual responses that do not support the divine unfolding of your true identity, the master teachers lift you up by praying, "Father forgive them. For they know not what they do." When you believe that what *you think* and what *you do* is more powerful, than what *God knows* and what *God can do*, some being somewhere pleads on your behalf, "Father forgive them. For they know not what they do." Perhaps it is time for you to pray this prayer for yourself.

Until today, you may have believed you had all the answers, that what you did not know or could not do was impossible. Just for today, write 109 times, *"Father forgive me. For I know not what I do."*

Today I am devoted to forgiving myself for believing that I know it all and can do it all alone!

JUNE 2

*I am now willing to forgive myself . . . for remaining
loyal to inaccurate information about myself.*

As children, everything we learn about ourselves comes from those around us. The most important thing we learn is the nature of our *value* and the depth of our *worth*.

In far too many situations, children are given inaccurate information about themselves and the world. This information becomes the looking glass in which we see ourselves. Long after we discover that the information we have received is inaccurate, even when we have concrete *evidence to disprove or contradict what we have been taught, we* remain loyal to that information and the *people* who gave it to us. Many people struggle their entire lives trying *not to contradict* what they were told about themselves as children. This results in "self-sabotage."

There comes a point in our lives when we must examine what we are doing and ask ourselves, "Why? *What would a person who does this need to believe in order to justify doing it?*" Until you are willing to contradict the impressions etched into your consciousness, you will find yourself struggling with what you *know in your soul* about yourself, and what you have been told.

Until today, you may have been struggling to reconcile what you know and feel about yourself with what you were told about yourself by parents and childhood caregivers. Just for today, examine the unconscious loyalties you may have to the inaccurate information you may have been provided. In your journal, write the first thought you have in response to the following questions: (1) What do I believe about myself? (2) How do I demonstrate this belief? (3) What do I remember being told about myself? (4) How does my behavior support what I have been told? Your responses will provide you with important keys to creating a more positive and productive self-image.

*Today I am devoted to breaking all loyalties to inaccurate
information about myself!*

JUNE 3

I now am willing to forgive myself . . . for believing
my worth is established by what others have told me
or believe about me.

Review your responses to the four questions offered in yesterday's "Just for today" message. Allow yourself to remember the things you were told that were wrong with you.
Remember the names you were called that limited your concept of yourself. Allow yourself to remember how you were scolded and
what response you got when you asked for what you wanted. Examine
how your behavior today supports or contradicts those responses.

If you have difficulty with the above steps, examine how you conduct yourself in realizing your goals and dreams. Are you just dreaming?
Always hoping? Forever trying? Or are you actually doing what needs to
be done? What do the tapes running in your mind say to support your
responses to difficulties or opportunities? Once you have a clear memory of the information you were given as a child that supports your self-
sabotaging behavior, you can begin the forgiveness process.

Forgive yourself for believing things about yourself that are not true.
Forgive yourself for believing that you were anything other than a child
of God. Then, after forgiving yourself for believing the things you were
told, forgive the people who told you. Forgive them not for what they
said or did. Forgive them because they did not know any better. Forgiveness is the only way to eradicate the inaccurate information given to you
as a child that you remain loyal to long after you know that it is causing
you harm.

Until today, you may have experienced difficulty in moving beyond
the information you received as a child. Just for today, forgive yourself
for believing inaccurate information and remaining loyal to the patterns
that have supported the information.

*Today I am devoted to forgiving myself for believing things
about myself that were not true!*

JUNE 4

I am now willing to forgive myself . . . for forgetting that
I am not in charge—Spirit is!

Very often, when things do not turn out the way we hoped
they would, we start labeling things right or wrong, good or
bad. Whenever *our way* is not *the way* things seem to be
going, we get caught up in fear, and jump to forgone conclusions of doom. There is a way to avoid these dangerous reactions. It is to
remember at all times, nothing can be hidden in the Universe of Spirit!

We all live in the Universe of Spirit, where time and forgiveness always reveal the truth. There is never a need to prove that you made the
right choices and are unjustly receiving the wrong results. When results
appear to run amuck, shut up! Back up! Pray for yourself. Forgive yourself for forgetting that Spirit is always in charge. Forgive yourself for
thinking that someone or something can stop your spiritual destiny
from unfolding at the perfect time in the perfect way.

The Spirit of good will always work on your behalf if you are willing
to let it do its thing! If someone has stepped into your path in a foolish
attempt to disrupt Spirit's plan for you, know that the divine plan cannot remain hidden for long! Spirit will reveal to you what you need to
know to get back on track. When that happens, don't gloat! Remember,
those who challenge the power of the Spirit of life "know not what they
do!" Forgive them and be grateful that the loving Spirit that is the power
source of the universe is always on the side of good. Spirit will always reveal what needs to be revealed, teach what needs to be taught and do
what needs to be done.

Until today, you may have been caught up in situations that appear
to be going badly. Just for today, practice forgiving yourself for believing
that bad things can happen where the goodness of Spirit reigns supreme.

Today I am devoted to remembering that at all times,
in all situations Spirit is in charge!

JUNE 5

I am now willing to forgive myself . . . for the judgments
I have held about myself and against myself.

Here is a prayer for you today.

Blessed and Divine Holy Spirit, today I forgive myself.
I forgive myself for judging my true Self less than a perfect
creation of God. I forgive myself for judging my Self not
enough and not good enough. I forgive myself for not asking for what I
need and want. I forgive myself for believing I do not deserve to be
happy. I forgive myself for all of the things I have done and not done in
support of this belief. I forgive myself for judging my Self unworthy. I
forgive myself for all the things I have done that supported this belief.

I forgive myself for all the judgments I have held against my Self. I
forgive myself for all of my behaviors that supported me in holding judgments against my Self. I forgive myself for the judgments I have held
against my body. I forgive myself for believing I have any inabilities. I forgive myself for the judgments I have held about my Self and against my
Self that have not allowed my God-given abilities to shine through me.

I forgive myself for judging my Self weak. I forgive myself for judging
my Self to be anything other than perfect and complete. I forgive myself
for being angry with my Self. I forgive myself for the things that I have
done and not done to justify remaining angry with my Self. I forgive myself for not trusting my Self. I forgive myself for all the things I have done
to support the belief that my Self was untrustworthy. I forgive myself
completely and unconditionally for all judgments I have held about and
against my Self, for I now realize how these judgments have diminished
the perfect unfolding and development of the divine Self I am.

Until today, you may have thought it was important to learn how to
forgive others. Just for today, be devoted to forgiving yourself for all of
the infractions you have committed against your true Self.

*Today I am devoted to accepting forgiveness
from myself to my Self!*

JUNE 6

I am now willing to forgive myself . . . for believing
I am not worthy of love.

Here is a prayer for you.

Blessed and Divine Spirit of Love, I ask for and accept your forgiveness for anything that I have done in violation of the law of love. I ask for and accept *Self*-forgiveness for anything I have done in violation of the law of love. I forgive myself for all of the ways I have chosen fear instead of love. I forgive myself for all of the ways I have chosen anger instead of love. I forgive myself for all of the ways I have chosen guilt over love. I forgive myself for holding on to thoughts and feelings that have blinded me to the presence of love. I forgive myself for doubting, denying, dodging and undermining the power of love in my life.

I forgive myself for denying myself the joy of a loving relationship. I forgive myself anything I have done and not done to support the belief that I was unworthy of a loving relationship. I forgive myself for anything I have done to remain in relationships that were unloving. I forgive myself for denying myself the joys of prosperity and abundance. I forgive myself for anything I have done and not done to support the belief that I am unworthy of prosperity and abundance. I forgive myself for all of the ways I have denied, doubted, wasted and abused prosperity and abundance when it has presented itself in my life. I forgive myself unconditionally for anything I have done, in any way I have done it, to deny the prosperous and abundant presence of God's love in my life.

Until today, you may have been preoccupied with the ways and times others have denied you love, or thwarted your efforts to attain prosperity and abundance. Just for today, forgive yourself for being the one and only one who has stood against you on your quest to realize the abundance of everything good and loving.

*Today I am devoted to forgiving myself for denying my
Self the prosperous and abundant blessings of love!*

JUNE 7

I am now willing to forgive myself . . . for believing there
is something wrong with being wrong about some things!

Are you so afraid of doing things wrong that you won't do
anything at all? How many times have you convinced yourself that something is right for you to do, only to allow
yourself to be blown off course by someone else who says,
"That's wrong!" Is it possible that you dwell in a past of things wrong to
such a degree that you now believe that anything you do will probably
go wrong? If you have answered yes to one or more of these inquires,
here is another question for you, *"What's wrong with being wrong?"*

When you take a step in a direction that could ultimately lead you
off course, *wrong* lets you know that you need to change directions. If
you choose something or someone that is less than worthy of who you
are, *wrong* lets you know that you need to make another choice. If you
decide to take on something that you really are not prepared to handle,
wrong lets you know what skills you need to build, what information
you need to acquire, what things you can do well and what things you
cannot. When you get right down to it, *wrong* is life's way of letting you
know what you need to know in order to get the *right results* for your efforts. Now what's wrong with that?

If you have a fear of being wrong, go back into your history. Allow
yourself to remember the first time you were told you were wrong. Allow
yourself to hear the words, feel the feelings and remember the experience. If you can place yourself in the midst of that experience, forgive
yourself for believing that there is something wrong with being wrong.

Until today, you may have allowed yourself to believe that if you did
the wrong thing you would not recover. Just for today, take a risk! Do
something you fear might be wrong. You may discover that you were
wrong!

*Today I am devoted to forgiving myself for believing
I could ever do anything wrong!*

JUNE 8

I am now willing to forgive myself . . . for believing there was something wrong about needing correction.

If you are a human being, there is something for which you need to be forgiven. There is something you have thought or said or done that you knew at the moment you were doing it was not the most loving or honorable thing to think, say or do. Oh, sure! You had a good reason for it. We can always come up with an excuse or rationale for our behavior. However, in the quiet moments when you are alone with yourself, you know you have done things that were not kind, nice or loving. These are things for which you need to be forgiven.

Often, we deny that we have done anything that requires forgiveness. Nothing scares a human being more than the acknowledgment of *wrongdoing*. We have been convinced that *to commit a wrong is bad*. Who wants to be bad? You get spanked for being bad. You can get hurt for being bad. Some of us even believe that if you are bad enough, you cannot be forgiven. The truth is, the things we call wrong or bad are actually our cries for correction. The way to correction is through the acknowledgment of the truth. The way the Spirit of love and life corrects the spirit of human beings is through forgiveness. When you are willing to acknowledge that you can do better, you become willing to admit to yourself those things for which you need to be forgiven. The good thing is, if you admit them to yourself, it may never become necessary for anyone else to find out!

Until today, you may have resisted acknowledging those things about you which you know require some correction. Just for today, acknowledge them to yourself. Forgive yourself for them. Then, ask forgiveness from anyone else who may have been involved.

Today I am devoted to acknowledging those things about myself that are in need of correction!

JUNE 9

I am now willing to forgive myself . . . for engaging in actions and behaviors I now believe are unforgivable.

Are there things you feel in your heart you cannot forgive yourself for doing? Things you have done in moments of weakness? Things you have done in response to fear? Perhaps there are things you have said or done in anger that have caused harm to yourself or others. Things you believe or have been led to believe are so horrible that you can never or should never be forgiven for them. Do you still hold yourself accountable for the lies you have told? Are you holding yourself hostage for the acts you committed because you simply did not know what else to do? If any or all of these are true for you, know that you are not alone.

It's the major things we consider unforgivable. Things we do that cause harm to others. Things we do when we are at a loss about what to do but are afraid to admit it. There are things we do without thinking that have a disastrous impact. There are things we do for revenge. There are things we do for money. There are things we do that dishonor and demean ourselves and others. These things, the things we consider unforgivable, are the very things we need to forgive ourselves for doing.

The things we hold against ourselves rest heavy on our hearts and eat away at our sense of worth. With an open and willing heart, you can be freed from the prison of self-damnation. If you sit still long enough and think about it hard enough, you will remember all of the things you have resisted forgiving yourself for doing.

Until today, you may have wrestled with thoughts and feelings of unworthiness. You may have convinced yourself that there were things for which you could never be forgiven. Just for today, open your heart to yourself, for yourself. Forgive yourself for everything you have thought, said or done that you may have told yourself could not be forgiven.

Today I am devoted to forgiving myself for my own resistance to forgiving myself!

JUNE 10

I am now willing to forgive myself . . .
for not being willing to risk proving that someone
may be wrong about me.

Many of us have a black hole in our hearts that sucks the fight, the life and the goodness from our lives. Sure, there are days when we can smile, laugh and almost convince ourselves that life is okay. Then, without warning, we are sucked down into the black hole of guilt. Some of us are guilty about believing that we have a right to be more than people have told us we can be. Every time we stand on the verge of proving them wrong, we throw ourselves into the black hole.

There may be a black hole in your heart that is full of fear, pain, grief, anger or shame. This is a deep hole! It seems so deep and wide that you may actually live in fear that it will swallow you. Many of us live in the constant fear that *we will be* more than we have been told we can be. Unfortunately, it is fear that sucks you deeper into the hole.

There is only one way to get out and stay out of the black holes. *Forgiveness.* Forgive yourself for all of the unkind, unloving, unsupportive things you have thought about yourself. Forgive yourself for the things you have done to yourself, that support the things you believe about yourself that are not true. Forgive yourself for being so hard on yourself. Forgive yourself for all the clever ways you have devised to deny that these holes exist in your heart.

Until today, you may not have been aware of the things you have done in response to the black hole in your heart. Or you may have done many things in an effort to deny, avoid, or ignore that the black hole exists. Just for today, step down into the hole and forgive yourself.

Today I am devoted to opening up the black hole
in my heart and forgiving myself for everything
I have allowed to be buried there!

JUNE 11

I am now willing to forgive myself . . . for all of the time
I have refused to follow Divine Orders.

Psssst! Come closer. This is a message for you. It is a message
intended to make you feel a lot better about yourself. It is a
message from the angels and the good spirits of life. The angels and good spirits of life are asking that you, STOP BEATING
UP ON YOURSELF FOR WHAT YOU ARE DOING OR NOT DOING! In other
words, they don't like it! They are also aware that it doesn't make you feel
too good either!

The angels and the good spirits of life have heard the things you have
said to yourself and about yourself. *They are simply appalled!* They know
that if you *could* have, you *would* have. They know that when you *can*,
you *will*. The angels and the good spirits of life would help you, if you
would allow them to. They also understand that when you feel bad
enough you will ask for help. It doesn't have to be that way, but the angels and the good spirits are aware that you have a few trust issues that require healing. *In the meantime,* they have issued a Divine Order that you
cease and desist all forms of *self-criticism, self-judgment, self-flagellation,
self-punishment* and *self-destructive* behavior. The angels and the good
spirits of life forgive you for partaking in such self-dishonoring behavior
in the past. Now they want you to forgive yourself and *stop it!*

Until today, you may have spent a good portion of your day beating
up on yourself for all the things you did not do to your satisfaction. Just
for today, forgive yourself for the way you have treated yourself.

*Today I am devoted to following the Divine Order to cease
and desist all forms of self-criticism and self-judgment!*

JUNE 12

I am now willing to forgive myself . . .
for being critical of my mother.

Forgive your mother! Forgive her *not* for the things she has done or not done, for the things she has said or has not said. Forgive her because it is the only way to open your heart to self-forgiveness. Forgive her *not* because you don't have a right to be upset about the way she has handled some things in her life and in your life. Forgive her *not* because she was *right* in making you feel *wrong*, or because she was *wrong* when she failed to acknowledge that you were right. Forgive your mother because until you do, there will be a void in your heart.

Forgive your mother for the many, many times she was not the mother you wanted her to be. Forgive her for the times she did not do things the way you needed them done. Forgive your mother for not protecting you or speaking out in your behalf. Forgive her for not guiding you in the right direction and for the times she totally lost her direction, dragging you along with her. Forgive your mother for demanding things from you that she could not provide for you or for herself. Forgive your mother whether or *not* she did anything wrong or bad to you. Forgive her *not* because you are excusing whatever she did or however it affected you. Forgive your mother because holding judgments against her has a devastating impact on *your soul.* The judgments you hold will eventually break your heart. Forgive your mother because *the truth is,* she did the best she could whether you would like to believe it or not.

Until today, you may have been harboring judgments or negative opinions about your mother and the way she did or did not mother you. Just for today, forgive yourself for judging your mother. Once you do, there will be nothing left to forgive her for.

Today I am devoted to offering myself total forgiveness for the judgments I have held about and against my mother!

JUNE 13

I am now willing to forgive myself . . . for the judgments
I have held about and against my father.

The universe does not edit your vocabulary. When you use a
word, it ascribes the universal concept to the word. For example, let us examine the word "father." In the spiritual
context, the word "father" means mind; provider; protector;
God, the one universal Divine Mind. Consequently, when you use the
word "father," the universe does not search out your meaning. You say
"father," the *universe hears* God, Mind, Provider, Protector.

Forgive your father! Forgive him *not* because you want to *get right* or
be right with God. Forgive him so that *you can be right with yourself!* Forgive your father whether or *not* he said all the *right things*. Forgive him
whether or *not* he gave you the *right* amount of time and energy. Forgive
him whether or *not* he was there to teach you what you needed to know
about life. Forgive your father because you are confusing the universe.
The judgments you hold against *your father* may be construed as judgments you are holding against *the Father.*

Forgive your father because holding judgments *about him* and
against him are construed as judgments about Divine Mind. These are
the judgments that cause the confusion, anger and shame you experience or harbor in *your own mind.* Forgive your father because until you
do, the love you are seeking, will continue to elude you. If you cannot
forgive him, how can you ever forgive yourself for the things you have
told yourself about you?

Until today, you may not have realized that what you think, feel and
judge about your own father is construed by the universal intelligence as
judgments about the one true Father. Just for today, open your heart to
the Father. Ask him to give you the courage and compassion to forgive
yourself for judging your father.

*Today I am devoted to opening my heart to forgive myself
for the judgments I have held about my father!*

JUNE 14

I am now willing to forgive myself . . . for allowing the
shadows of my past to eat away at me.

Native American folklore teaches that the crow is a bird with
visionary power whose curiosity sometimes gets the best of
her. According to lore, when the crow saw its shadow, it
began to stare with amazement. The crow pecked at the
shadow. It even left food for the shadow. One day, in response to the
crow's fascination, the shadow came to life and ate the crow.

The story of the crow teaches us about the danger of being fasci-
nated with things that are behind us. We are mesmerized by the shadows
of our past. We examine them often. We feed our shadows with mental
and emotional energy. We can never seem to move beyond the images,
memories, and fears caused by the shadows of the past. We give the
shadows of yesterday the power to swallow our today.

When she does not succumb to her fascination with the past, the
crow, unlike us, has the ability to see beyond the shadow. The crow is an
omen of change, with no sense of time. It does not matter to the crow
what has happened, she looks beyond the shadow *to create what will
happen.* She determines the path of her flight based on what she can see
now. When the crow's feathers are ruffled, she smooths them out. If her
wings begin to droop in flight, the crow rests. Unlike humans, the crow
has learned how to use her past to determine which way she will go.

Until today, you may not have used the sacred crow energy of vision.
Just for today, use the shadows of the past as a mirror. Look for the talents, skills or abilities that you can use to chart your flight forward. Use
what you see in the shadows of your life as your encouragement to move
beyond an old way of being into a new vision of yourself.

*Today I am devoted to viewing all the shadows of my past
through forgiving eyes!*

JUNE 15

I am now willing to forgive myself . . . for holding on
to grievances and grudges.

You are not guilty, and neither is anyone else. Guilt is in the
eye of the beholder. What you feel guilty about, you will
project onto others.

Release all grievances! What you feel is your own guilt. Is it
possible that you feel guilty because you didn't see it coming? Or perhaps
because you didn't see it soon enough? Maybe you are feeling some pangs
of guilt because, when you finally did see it, you didn't recognize it.

Stop blaming people! It is quite possible that you are placing blame on
others so that you won't be forced to blame yourself. Why would you
blame yourself? Perhaps because you moved too fast, you moved to slow
or you moved in the wrong direction. Rest assured that you are not
above blaming yourself because you failed to move at all.

Stop judging people! The things that you judge are *wrong* with them
could be the very things you find unacceptable in yourself! How many
times have you demonstrated that you can be undependable? In some cir-
cles, could you be called overly sensitive? Of course you are always honest
and forthright—even when you talk about your dress size or your salary.

Forgive yourself for believing you are guilty! Forgive others for the
things you believe they are guilty of! Forgive others for the things they
say that trigger feelings of guilt in you. Admit it when you have been
unloving. Acknowledge it when you have been unkind. When you begin
to focus on yourself, everyone else will start to look pretty good.

Until today, you may have been holding against others things which
are difficult for you to admit about yourself. Just for today see yourself in
everyone else, knowing that they are mirroring the inner you. If for some
reason you believe they are not, bless them and move on.

*Today I am devoted to not being a judge or critic of anyone,
and that includes myself!*

JUNE 16

I am now willing to forgive myself . . . for acting like nothing when the truth is I am everything.

You are being called accountable, not because you have done anything wrong, but because *you are divine!* You may have allowed yourself to believe that you are mediocre, meaningless, average or usual. You are not! Your divinity, your nobility, your divine Self is on the verge of bursting forward into the light of the world, and you will be held accountable for it and to it.

You are now in the process of a massive communal *soul surgery!* All the souls on the face of the planet are being opened in order to be healed, in order to have their divinity revealed and their divine power restored. There will be no more excuses, rationales and reasons for not shining in the light of truth and standing in the power of your divinity. The time is now! The process has begun!

The soul surgery process is a spiritual process. It is a process grounded in truth. It is a process of accountability and responsibility. The most challenging part of the process is that you will have to walk in the depths of all that you have done in order to heal it. You will have to tell yourself the truth. Once this is done, you will have to choose how you intend to demonstrate the magnificence of your divinity from this point forward.

It is useless, absolutely futile, to try to diminish yourself any longer. You know what to do. Now it is all up to you now, *you divine creature you!* It is up to you to make the new models for the way you intend to live. From this point on the focus is on you, for you and about you. Once you recognize yourself as the divine being you are, it will be easy to forgive yourself for all the time you wasted trying to be anything else.

Until today, you may have been waiting for something to change. Just for today, work on changing yourself and your ideas about yourself.

Today I am devoted to stepping into my divinity, my power and my true position in life!

I am now willing to forgive myself . . . for my inability to accept people exactly as they are.

Your opinion of another person affects how you treat them and what you expect of them. Believe it or not, how you see another person usually has very little to do with them!

Your views, *your* opinions, *your* perceptions and *your* judgments all stem from you! They are a function of who you believe you are or are not. How you see someone else is an outgrowth of what you want and what you believe they have that you need. What is inside you ultimately determines how you approach other people. In a very large part, your approach and your expectations determine how people respond to you.

In his book *The Seat of the Soul,* author Gary Zukav writes, "When you release the wants of your personality in order to accommodate and encourage others, you attune yourself to that person's soul." When, in your daily interactions with others, you can see someone else from a soul level, you can feel their need for love and support. When you look beyond what you think about someone, it is easy to see the truth.

We are all here in this life to help each other grow into our greatness. When you can see someone at the soul level, you become their teacher and their student. You are teaching them how to move beyond the fear and judgment of the personality, into the divine light that rests at their core. As students you are learning to move beyond your fears and judgments into the loving strength and power that is the truth of who you are.

Until today, you may not have realized that your thoughts about others were filled with a multitude of things that may not be true. Just for today, see everyone as your teacher. Realize they are teaching you things about yourself. See everyone as your student. Remember you are learning to see everyone through the eyes of love and truth.

Today I am devoted to seeing the truth about myself in everyone else!

JUNE 18

I am now willing to forgive myself . . . for taking on
more than is necessary or required for me to take on.

It is quite possible that you may be working so hard not to do
worse, that you are actually missing out on the opportunity
to do better. Or maybe, just maybe you are so caught up in
what someone else may be thinking about you that you are
not thinking for yourself. Whenever this is the case, you are going to stay
exactly where you are, doing exactly what you are doing—no worse! No
better! If this is your case, you may need to call on "grace."

Grace can catch you before you fall and pick you up if you do. Grace
is so powerful and sufficient that even when you don't know what to do,
grace is your insurance that whatever you do will be better than what
you did! Grace will close your eyes to what you don't need to see and
open your eyes to things that *only you* can see. Grace will close your ears
to what everyone is saying while she opens your heart to what *God* has to
say that *only you* need to hear. You see, grace knows that there are some
things just for you. Grace wants you to have those things. Grace, however, can only give you what you are willing to have. In other words, she
will only come when you call on her. And, by the way, Grace always
brings her sisters, Hope and Mercy.

Grace, Hope and Mercy will do for you what you cannot do, have
not been able to do, do not know how to do. Grace, Hope and Mercy
will go where you are afraid to go. They will show you what you are
afraid to see. The good thing about calling on Grace, Hope and Mercy is
that eventually you come to realize you don't have to do everything
alone.

Until today, you may not have realized the presence of Grace in your
life. Just for today, call on Grace to work through you. And please, try
not to tell her what to do. Women really don't like that.

Today I am devoted to acknowledging and accepting the
power of God's grace in every aspect of my life!

JUNE 19

I am now willing to forgive myself . . .
when I stumble.

When you are walking down the street and you stumble, do you criticize yourself? Do you keep reminding yourself of how horrible it was? How foolish you must have appeared to those watching? Do you stop walking or refuse to move any farther? Of course not! You probably gather yourself and your wits, give thanks that you didn't fall flat on your face and move on. Why then do you freeze, refusing to move when you stumble in your choices or decisions about your career or relationships?

When you stumble or lose your footing in your career, it is not the worst thing that could happen. Losing a loved one can sure feel like the worst experience you have ever had, but it is not. The same way your heart pounds when you just miss being hit by another car on the highway, meeting one of life's challenge may leave you shaken. It should not, however, leave you broken. You may have faced some difficult things in your life, and you will face more. These things may make you angry. They may cause you to question your skills or abilities. They may even knock you down for a minute or two. Under no circumstances should you allow anything that happens in your life to lead you to believe that life, with all of its challenges, is not worth living. That would be more than a stumble. That would be the same as *throwing the fight!*

Until today, you may have allowed yourself to believe that human mistakes, the challenges of human life and the things you have experienced in your humanness were greater than your spirit as a human being. Just for today, forget that! Stumble, fall, crawl or hitch a ride all the way to the finish line.

*Today I am devoted to relying on the Spirit of life
to catch me when I stumble or fall!*

JUNE 20

I am now willing to forgive myself . . . for being hard,
rigid, unable to bend or give.

Is it worth it? Is the anger, resentment and stress you feel in
your body paying off? In other words, is the way you feel
getting you what you want? Is holding your ground, defending your position, promoting your opinion making you
feel any better? How is what you are doing paying off? Is it paying you
enough to go through what you are going through to get it?

It is true that static, friction and challenge can lead to breakthroughs
of new insights and information. However, new insights can only happen when you are flexible. Being flexible does not mean you are weak.
Nor does it mean that you are caving in or giving up. When you are flexible, you are open. Open to doing what is best for yourself and everyone
involved. Flexibility is a reflection of your willingness to do what needs
to be done with no attachment to how it gets done. *Done is the key!*
DONE is an acronym for Divine Order Now Expressing. When you are
willing to honor divine order, you will learn how to be flexible.

Flexibility means surrendering, giving up your preconceived notions about people, circumstances and the ways things should be.
"Should" is a judgment! When you find that you are "shoulding," know
that you are in a struggle for power and control. You will not win! When
you are not flexible, chances are you will be broken or torn down. Flexibility means seeing the good in everything and being open to gaining an
understanding of how things work. When you find yourself fighting to
get what you want, to have your way, drop your hands to your sides, take
a deep breath and ask yourself, Is this worth fighting for?

Until today, you may have believed that it was necessary to stand
your ground and fight to get what you want. Just for today, bend *your
way,* asking the divine forces to show you *the way.*

*Today I am devoted to remaining flexible and in alignment
with the divine order of all things!*

JUNE 21

I am now willing to forgive myself . . . for holding on to the need to be right.

There are some people you are never going to be *right* with. No matter what you say, how you say it, what you do or how you do it, there are people who are going to find something *wrong* with everything. *This includes you.* There are some people who can take what you say and twist it into something you did not say in order to be right. By the time you realize you are fighting a losing battle, it is too late! They are *right* and you *feel wrong!* You see, the challenge with being confronted by an *I gotta be right* person is they have a way of bringing out the *I gotta be right* in you.

When you have the smallest glimmer of *I've gotta be right* in your eyes, people detect it. Even when you couch your need in care or concern, those you approach recognize in you what they know about themselves. In response, they become as determined as you. They have a need to be *right,* and they are not afraid to *sacrifice you* in pursuit of their own needs. If you have the same need, somebody is going to go down, *hard!*

The *need to be right* is nothing more than the need for external validation. The conflict created when one *need to be right* person locks horns with another *need to be right* person is really a blessing in disguise! The one who can back down first, without feeling they have lost anything, is the one who is well on their way to self-acceptance, self-forgiveness and self-love.

Until today, you may not have been aware that you may still need external validation to feel good about yourself. Just for today, *surrender!* Drop your hands to your side. Take a deep breath. Ask yourself, *"What is it that I believe is wrong with me or about me?"* Answer that question, and you will never again need to be right. You will know when you are. Nothing else will matter.

Today I am devoted to healing my need to be right!

JUNE 22

I am now willing to forgive myself . . . for believing that
people who do not agree with me are wrong.

Some people do things completely differently from the way
you would do them. It does not mean that they are right or
that you are wrong. It means that people are different.
There are things that people say which you would probably
say in a different way, at a different time. It does not mean that people
are wrong to speak up, to speak out or to speak their minds. Nor does it
mean that you are wrong for choosing not to do so. It means that people
are different. Different is not right or wrong. It is a reality. Differences
become problems only when we choose to measure ourselves by our difference in an effort to determine who is right and who is wrong.

It is not loving, healthy or necessary to make people wrong for what
they do, what they say or the way in which they do it or say it. Nor is it
self-affirming to feel wrong when you see things differently, do things in
a different way or express a difference of opinion. All people are different
from one another. Our different points of view shape our vantage point
and our vision. Where we *sit* is a function of where we have *sat*. What we
can see is a function of what we *have seen*. No one person's experience,
point of view or view point is more accurate, more acceptable, more
righteous than another. It is simply different. Our differences sometimes
make agreement difficult to achieve. They should never make us feel
wrong. Nor should they lead us to believe that what others believe is
wrong.

Until today, you may have questioned, opposed, resisted or even de-
tested differences. Just for today, open your heart. Be willing to embrace
different points of view, different habits, different responses, different
opinions and the differences that exist between yourself and others.

*Today I am devoted to embracing and celebrating
differences and to forgiving myself for believing
that they are wrong!*

J U N E 2 3

I am now willing to forgive myself . . . for believing
I could offer something to others before I have offered
it to myself.

If you have been working on forgiving someone for something and you still feel the anger, consider this: you probably want *revenge!* Forgiveness will not bring you the relief
you seek when you really want payback. Forgiveness only
works when it is offered with compassion.

When you experience the trauma of betrayal, abandonment or rejection, the normal response is anger. Your anger is directed first at the
offender. Your next logical target is God, who allowed the trauma to
happen. For this, you are in need of forgiveness. You need forgiveness for
holding onto thoughts and emotions that have caused you so much pain
and anguish. You need forgiveness for believing that you needed to stay
mad and seek revenge because God *has not!* You need forgiveness for believing that by forgiving the other person, you were somehow letting
them off the hook. The truth is, by not forgiving them, *you have kept
yourself hooked!*

When forgiveness has not worked for you, try compassion. Have
compassion for yourself for feeling wounded. Have compassion because
you have been unable to let go. Compassion is the ability to feel sorrow,
coupled with the deep desire to alleviate pain. When your desire to feel
better is greater than your anger, you will have opened the door to compassionate forgiveness.

Until today, you may have been seeking revenge. Just for today, ask
yourself, Is the need for revenge greater than my desire to feel better? If it
is, you are not ready to be healed. If it is not, call forth compassion and
forgive yourself for choosing anger over forgiveness.

*Today I am devoted to experiencing and expressing a spirit
of compassion in myself and for myself!*

JUNE 24

*I am now willing to forgive myself . . . for believing that
telling the truth can hurt me.*

You can have the best intentions in the world, but there are
those times when you can be led to believe that telling the
truth is not a good thing. You can tell the truth from a pos-
ture of loving care and concern and be accused of creating a
problem. In response, you may be convinced that telling the truth is the
worst thing you could do for yourself or anyone else. This would not be
a good thing.

There was once a man who told the truth. He told the truth to help
save people from the pain and darkness of ignorance. He told the truth
because he knew that the truth would set people free from physical,
mental and emotional bondage. He told the truth because he did not
know how not to tell the truth. People heard what he was saying, and
they hung him on a cross. Conclusion: when you tell the truth, people
will be upset with you. They will be afraid of you. In fact, if you tell too
much truth, too often, people will crucify you!

When you tell the truth, it upsets the apple cart! It brings light to
darkness. More important, the truth makes people think. For people
who believe they have it all figured out, thinking is not a good thing! In
fact, they know if they think too hard, they may bump into some truth
they have already rejected or are not yet willing to accept. None of this
should be of any concern to you. If you are attuned enough to embrace
light over darkness, then you are powerful enough to handle whatever
happens as a result. Always choose the truth because only the truth will
set you and keep you free. Telling the truth not only affords you internal
and external freedom, it keeps you in good company.

Until today, you may have avoided the risks associated with telling
the truth. Just for today, forgive yourself for believing that telling the absolute truth, *as you know it,* could bring you anything other than good.

*Today I am devoted to claiming my freedom!
I am willing to tell the truth!*

JUNE 25

*I am now willing to forgive myself . . . for not being
willing to acknowledge my own anger at myself.*

 When people treat you badly, harshly or inappropriately and you accept it, there is an important question you must ask yourself; *"Why am I still so angry with myself that I would subject myself to this kind of treatment?"*

Many people live with a shroud of hidden internal anger. They are angry at themselves for things they have or have not done in the past. Intellectually, they can convince themselves that they are no longer angry. Yet, deep down inside, they cannot, will not forgive themselves or forget what happened. At the same time, they are no longer willing to beat up on themselves. They find someone else to do the job. They allow themselves to be treated badly by others because they believe they deserve it. Often, unexpressed anger shows up as ill-treatment by others.

Unexpressed anger is like a red neon sign etched on the soul which reads: *Beat me! Kick Me! Treat me bad because I've been bad!* Silently, we broadcast this energy into the world, attracting those who are willing to comply with our unspoken, often unconscious wish. Because we are not aware of what we are broadcasting, we make excuses for ourselves and for those who are abusive. In all cases, accepting verbal, emotional or physical abuse is a cry for self-healing and self-forgiveness. This cannot happen until you are willing to recognize the abuse you accept as a symptom of anger you are directing toward yourself.

Until today, you may have been unable or unwilling to recognize that how you allow yourself to be treated is a reflection of how you believe you should be treated. Just for today, examine the people and situations in your life in which you feel abused. Ask yourself, *"Why am I still so angry with myself that I would subject myself to this kind of treatment?"*

*Today I am devoted to forgiving myself for all the things
I may have told myself are unforgivable!*

JUNE 26

I am now willing to forgive myself . . . for believing that
I have the power to create victims.

We have all done something that has caused someone pain or
discomfort. Often, we are aware of the consequences of our
actions. Then there are those times when we don't have a
clue about what we've done until someone brings it to our
attention. When they do, we feel bad. We believe that we must forever
be indebted to the people who have been the victims of our thoughtless-
ness, negligence or abuse.

You cannot see people as victims of something you have done. If you
do, they will allow you to continue to feel bad. You cannot see people as
victims of who you were or of who you are. If you do, you are declaring
yourself to be more powerful than you have a right to be in anyone's life.
Seeing someone as your victim says that you are somehow responsible
for what people believe and do. Thinking this way or feeling this way is
going to cause you a tremendous amount of grief *unnecessarily!*

Regardless of the impact your actions have on anyone, they are not
your victim! Think of it this way: we are all dancers in the ballroom of
life. Some of us are accomplished dancers. Some of us can't find the beat.
When you ask someone to dance, they, not you, choose whether or not
they will dance with you. If you step on their toes, ask for forgiveness.
Don't buy them a new pair of shoes! If the experience leaves them with the
impression that life is not worth dancing, ask for forgiveness. *Do not
spend the rest of your life trying to force them to dance again!* You have no
victims! Ask for forgiveness. Make amends if you can. Then, waltz away.

Until today, you may have believed that you would be forever indebted to others. Just for today, acknowledge those times you have been
thoughtless, negligent or abusive to others. Forgive yourself. Ask for forgiveness and then continue to dance.

*Today I am devoted to forgiving my errors and to
acknowledging that there are no victims in my life!*

JUNE 27

I am now willing to forgive myself . . . for not taking
time to deal with certain unpleasant memories.

You don't have to be angry because you were not recognized
or acknowledged as a child. No matter how hard you tried
or how well you did, no one noticed. It may have seemed as
if those who were a little better, a little bigger, a little smarter
got all the attention. That may be true, but you don't have to be mad
about that today. You don't have to be angry because the love you needed
or wanted or sometimes demanded wasn't there for you. You were probably made to feel as if what you thought, what you knew, what you felt
was not important. But there is no reason to still be mad about it today.

As children, few of us were allowed to express anger. When we experienced anger, we had to stuff it, camouflage it or deny it. In essence, we
held on to it. That anger grew with us into habits, attitudes, beliefs, perceptions and decisions. Anger makes us anxious and impatient. Angry
people are, *"See, I told you so!"* people. They can also be, *"I knew this
would happen!"* people. They are always looking for reasons to be angry
and ways to express the anger they have been holding.

If you feel left out, unnoticed, unappreciated or you feel the need to
prove yourself, chances are you have some unexpressed childhood anger.
If you love to compete and hate to lose, if you are a yeller, a hitter and
perhaps a drinker, it may be time for you to deal with your anger

Until today, you may not have realized you were angry or understood why you are angry. Just for today, set an intention to heal any unexpressed anger that may be present in your life. Go to a quiet place with
pen and paper. Take a few deep breaths. Ask your anger to speak to you.
Write down the thoughts. Write about the feelings. When you are finished, forgive yourself for holding on to the anger for so long. Then, ask
the Holy Spirit to transform the anger into a passion for life.

*Today I am devoted to healing unresolved and
unexpressed anger!*

JUNE 28

I am now willing to forgive myself . . . for refusing to acknowledge what my life is showing me about myself.

Your life is a reflection of you. Everything that is coming at you from out there is coming to show you where work is required on yourself. As you shake your head No and point at all the people you can blame for what is going on with you, you miss another divine opportunity to examine what is really going on within you. Until you are willing to accept total and complete responsibility for every aspect of your life, your life will keep sending you experiences designed to get your attention.

It can be difficult to acknowledge your role in the annoying little messes and great big disasters in your life. *No one likes to take the blame!* Quite often, we confuse accepting responsibility for bearing the blame. When you are the one to blame, it means you are somehow at fault—and must be punished. To avoid punishment, we look for someone else to put the blame on. In doing so, we miss an opportunity for self-correction.

Rather than looking for who is to blame, think about who is responsible. Accepting responsibility means examining the choices made. A choice is usually made in reaction or response to some sort of stimulation. The outcome reveals what kind of choice was made. When you are trying to escape blame and punishment, the outcome will lead you to speak about others. When you are willing to accept responsibility for your choices, the outcome leads you to self-evaluation and self-correction.

Until today, you may have believed that if you were to blame, you would be punished. Just for today, take blame out of the *life evaluation equation.* Honestly examine the situations in your life about which you are not pleased. Forgive yourself for not accepting your full share of responsibility. Put yourself in the center of your life and accept full responsibility for all things that may be spinning out of control.

Today I am devoted to acknowledging my responsibility for every aspect of my life!

JUNE 29

I am now willing to forgive myself . . . for making life harder than it is meant to be.

How difficult have you made your life? Have you made it hard to get ahead? Have you created enemies and challengers who are bigger than you? Have you set yourself up for failure? What stance have you taken in life? To what lengths are you willing to go in order to prove the *rightness* of the stance you have taken? Have you taken on more than you could do just to prove that you were right about the fact that you could not do it? *Just how hard have you made life?* How far are you willing to go to prove that you are right about how hard life is?

Life is not hard. Life is a process. Life distributes itself equally among all living people. While all things in life are equal, all *things* in life are not equally distributed to all people. We are talking here about *conditions.* Not the essence of life itself. Some people have a little more of this, while others have a lot less of it. Some people are given opportunities that others must work to get and others may never get. These are conditions. They are situations and experiences. They are not the essence of life itself. Unfortunately, there is a tendency to confuse the *conditions of life* with the process of life. When that happens life itself becomes hard to live.

Life is a process of taking what you have and turning it into something worthwhile. Your willingness to do this determines the conditions of your life. The process of living encourages you to leap and to fly, to run and to soar, to meander and to piddle, to embrace and to release. What you tell yourself about your ability to do one or all of these things at any given time determines how hard life will be for you.

Until today, you may have held on to the position that life is hard. Just for today, make a distinction between the *process of life* and *the conditions in your life.* You just may determine that what you are telling yourself about the process is becoming evident in the conditions.

Today I am devoted to examining all the things I am telling myself about the process of life!

J U N E   3 0

I am now willing to forgive myself . . . for holding myself
hostage to things God has forgiven me for.

Dear God:

*Thank you for reminding me that I am not guilty! Thank
you for reminding me that I am worthy of love, I am enti-
tled to happiness and that you want me to have both.*

*Thank you for reminding me that while I have made mistakes, I
have learned from them things I needed to know about myself.*

*Thank you for showing me that when I judge myself, others will
judge me and when I condemn myself, others will support my efforts.*

*Thank you for showing me that when I complain about what is
missing, I miss the opportunity to be grateful for what I have.*

*Thank you for forgiving me for all the times I have spoken words
of blame and fault-finding. Thank you for allowing me to feel the
sting of my own words in the words others have directed toward me.*

*Thank you for being so patient with my impatience. Thank you
for being so giving when I was withholding. Thank you for being so
gentle and compassionate with me when I have been so hard on myself.*

Thank you for your mercy, God!

Thank you for your love, God!

*Thank you for showing me and reminding me that you are the
one who knows me, accepts me and loves me just as I am.*

*Thank you for reminding me that I am not guilty! I am growing!
I am learning! I am remembering the truth of you, God, which is
etched into my soul. I am a child of God! I am freed from all guilt.*

Until today, you may have considered yourself guilty for many
things for which God has already offered you forgiveness. Just for today,
pray for the ability to experience God's forgiveness toward yourself.

*Today I am devoted to receiving, experiencing and
expressing God's forgiveness as self-forgiveness!*

JULY

UNDERSTANDING

In all relationships, regardless of their nature,

there comes the moment when you understand

that there are some things you will
never understand.

When you are standing in that moment,

just be all right with it.

JULY 1

I will gain more understanding when I realize . . .
each person has an experience of the experience
they are having.

In life, certain people will impersonate understanding. They will smile at you. They will assure you that everything is just fine. They will make you fell all warm and fuzzy inside. They may even say, "Yes! I understand!" Yet, when the moment comes for a demonstration of understanding, what you will get is misinterpretation, misrepresentation, miscommunication, and you will probably get blamed for the misunderstanding.

Certain people will impersonate compassion and concern. They will have you convinced that they have your best interests at heart. However, when the moment calls for a demonstration of compassion and concern, what you will experience is abandonment, betrayal, rejection, insensitivity, abuse and/or neglect.

Do not be alarmed! Do not be shocked! Be aware that we all have different experiences and different definitions of the same experience. What we hear, do and expect in life is always based on our own personal experiences. When we interact with others, we must understand and expect that we may not be on the same page or in the same book of experiences. Unless we take the time to gain clarity in the beginning, we may find ourselves in the company of experience imposters at the end.

Until today, you may have assumed that just because they say so, others know what you know, feel what you feel and will do what you do. Just for today, be devoted to putting forth the effort and energy required to gain clarity at the beginning of all relationships. Define your words. Identify your expectations. Clarify what you are saying and what you understand about what is being said and what is expected from you.

Today I am devoted to gaining clarity!

JULY 2

I will gain more understanding when I realize . . . I must
open my heart to others if I want to stop hurting.

Very often, we shut our hearts or shut others out to protect
ourselves from being hurt. While we are on guard, we are
defensive. Often, we become unapproachable and unavail-
able. We look for, and usually find, an ulterior motive in
everything and everyone. The motives and agendas we see, whether they
exist or not, are the reasons we must protect ourselves. At the same time,
we are isolated and lonely. We don't want to be hurt. We don't want to be
alone, but we don't know what to do about how we feel.

In general, people are not out to hurt you. They hurt you because
you expect to be hurt. They hurt you because they are trying to tear
down your barriers. They hurt you because *your barriers* look and feel
very similar to *their barriers*. When people see their issues being reflected
back to them, they often become afraid of what they see and feel. In response, they want to get to you before you get to them. In the process,
you get hurt. You must accept that people are not out to hurt you. They
hurt you because they don't realize that what they do or how they do it
causes you pain. They don't know what causes you pain because you
won't come from behind the barrier long enough to share with them the
pain of your experiences. You believe that if you show them your
wounds, they will think you are weak or dumb.

It is important to understand that when you shut your heart down,
or live life on the defensive, there is absolutely no way healing or light or
love can get in. When you shut down, you are going to keep on hurting.

Until today, you may have believed that people are out to get you.
Just for today, let someone into your heart. Open yourself to the healing
light of love. Expect the best. You may be surprised by what happens.

Today I am willing to drop my defenses and
open my heart!

JULY 3

I will gain more understanding when I realize . . .
I cannot forget my pain or bury what is unpleasant.

There are some things we believe we have forgotten and others we choose not to remember. The truth is, these are one and the same. When we are not ready to face a situation, or if we believe it is unimportant, we *put it out of our minds.* We call it *forgetting.* A better choice of words would be, *we choose not to remember it.* The choice may be conscious or unconscious, but it is a choice.

Forgetting is a defense mechanism we use to eliminate or avoid pain. It is an escape route we use when we fail to honor our commitments. At times, we choose to forget in an effort to protect or defend ourselves from those things and people that drain our energy. In some cases, we choose to forget to protect someone else. Whatever we choose to call it or whenever we do it, chances are the things we forget are also the things we want to avoid.

It is quite common to get caught up in doing something to the point of forgetting you have made a commitment to do something else. It is more common that you rarely forget the things that are important to you. When you are stressed or pressured, you are likely to forget. The question is, why are you pushing yourself? Is it possible that you are keeping yourself so busy to avoid thinking about the things you really want to forget? Yes, to forget is human, but it is not divine. The truth is, we are too Divine to forget. You also have the divine power to move through all the things you would rather not remember.

Until today, you may have been unaware of your ability to remember and deal with all things. Just for today, be devoted to remembering all there is to know about you. As you remember, make a commitment to honor everything about you.

Today I am devoted to opening the bank of my memory to make withdrawals and deposits that honor me!

JULY 4

I will gain more understanding when I realize . . .
that when I withhold the truth of who I am, I cannot
receive the truth of what I want.

The thing we want most is often the thing we resist. At work, we want recognition and reward. However, we hold back our ideas and energy because "it's just a job." In our family, we want support and acceptance. Yet we go along with people or avoid them because "we know" how they are. In our relationships, we want fulfillment, passion and intimacy, yet we withhold from our partners the very thing we want to experience: intimacy.

The most important elements of any relationship are trust and respect. When you trust someone enough to be honest with them, you grow to respect them and yourself. Where there is trust and respect, intimacy resides. When you are afraid to let others see you exactly as you are, you are bound to lack fulfilment and satisfaction.

Intimacy is about openness and feeling safe. It is about the willingness to be just who we are, without defenses, excuses or expectations. For some reason we have reduced intimacy to sexual conquests. Yet, without trust and respect, sex can leave us feeling empty and unfulfilled. These are the same feelings we can experience in the relationships where we resist intimacy. We don't often think of intimacy in relation to our professional, social and family relationships, and therein lies the challenge.

There is something magical and mystical about the intimate truth of your being. When you allow it to come forth without fear, it creates an intimacy of hearts, souls and minds that leads to fulfillment.

Until today, you may have reserved moments of intimacy for the bedroom. Just for today, be willing to be honest about who you are and what you feel in every situation. In other words, go for the gusto!

Today I am devoted to having in intimate relationship with myself and everyone else!

JULY 5

I will gain more understanding when I realize . . . exactly
where I am is exactly where I need to be.

How many days of the week do you spend wondering why you are not further along than you are? If thinking about it makes you angry or frustrated, you are definitely not on the right track. *Exactly where is it* that you believe you need to be? Why isn't where you are just fine? You can only be where you are, and it is up to you to make the best of it. You cannot get to where you are going until you have learned all there is to learn about where you are. There are always powerful, insightful, sometimes shocking things we need to know about ourselves. Those lesson are not *over there*. The things you need to know about you are right where you are.

While you may think you know it all, there is some reliable information about your beliefs, your doubts, your stamina and your behavior patterns right where you are sitting. Right under your nose there is something you have forgotten, neglected, resisted or denied. At your right side, or on your left side, there is a blessing that has not been acknowledged, a hurt that has not been forgiven, a skill that remains underdeveloped or a good you have yet to do. Everything and everyone that is available in the place you are in right now has something to teach you or something to give you. The reason you may have missed the lessons to be learned, or refused the gifts being offered right where you are, is you are preoccupied with *where you want to be*.

Until today, you have missed the lesson, ignored the blessings or denied the truth about where you are in life. Just for today, devote yourself to answering the following questions: What do I believe about where I am? What do I think about where I am? What do I feel about where I am? What do I tell myself about where I am? In your answers, you will find your ticket to the place you need to be.

Today I am devoted to learning all I need to learn
about where I am!

JULY 6

I will gain more understanding when I realize . . .
as long as I have an emotional attachment to a goal,
I am attached to the fear of not achieving the goal.

How do you relieve or release the pain associated with a relationship or experience that goes sour? Try saying, *"It just didn't work."* You can make yourself crazy trying to figure out why, or you can simply accept that it didn't. The choice is yours. How can you overcome the pain of disappointment? How about acknowledging that perhaps you were not as clear as you needed to be, or perhaps you were expecting more than you knew you could get. Once you can muster up enough courage to acknowledge your part in what happened, try saying, *"It just didn't work."*

How do you live through betrayal by a loved one or someone you trusted? You can choose to see yourself as a victim and the other party as the villain, but is it going to make you feel any better? Probably not. How do you move out of the past and beyond the fear that what happened before could happen again? Why not take one self-loving, self-honoring step at a time. Admit what has not worked without any emotional attachment to why. Admit what you felt without any emotional attachment to who contributed. Admit to yourself that no matter how much you want them, or how hard you work to get them, some things simply don't work out the way you want them too.

How can you create a better more fulfilling future when the past has been so dismal? Well, if you want to do better today than you did yesterday, you simply must believe you deserve it.

Until today, you may have believed you had to run away from the past. Just for today accept your past by using what you have learned to create a vivid picture of what you want and deserve.

Today I will love myself, listen to myself and expect the best from myself and for myself!

JULY 7

I will gain more understanding when I realize . . . divine action is always working on my behalf.

It's a *God job!* There are simply some things in life you are not going to be able to do anything about. There will be those occasions when you simply cannot change what happens or how it happens. There will be those times in your life when your hands are tied, your mind is blank, your mouth is shut and you feel totally helpless. These are *God jobs!* These are experiences of God working on you, in you, through you and for you. Although you want to get involved, although you feel the need to do something, when God is working, your job is to be still!

There is nothing more challenging than sitting through a God job. Yes, you will feel weak. Yes, you may feel stupid. Unfortunately, there is nothing you can do nor is there anything you need to do except wait. In the midst of a God job, there is nothing you need to say. There is no place you need to go. There is no amount of fixing, figuring out or trying that will make what you want to happen happen the way you want it to happen. When God is on the job, working on you, in you and for you, there is no one and nothing on the planet that can help you through what you are going through.

On a God job, the only course of action is total, undaunted, microscopic trust. You must become a child again. You must trust that you will be fed, that you will be changed, that you will be protected, that every need you have will be met. It may feel like you are being passive, but the truth is, if you can trust God in the midst of a challenge, God can do more in five minutes than you could ever do in five years.

Until today, you may have been trying to do for yourself what only God can do for you. Just for today, be devoted to trusting that God is on the job—doing what needs to be done, the way it needs to be done, working toward the best possible outcome for your best interest.

Today I am devoted to remembering that God has a plan!
That's all I need to know!

JULY 8

I will gain more understanding when I realize . . .
I must feed my spirit if I want to stay alive.

Picture yourself sitting at a banquet table, covered with all of
your favorite foods. Imagine the sight! The smell! Antici-
pate the pleasure of sinking your teeth into all of your favorite foods, which have been prepared to perfection. Now
imagine that as you finish one delight, a well-mannered server brings
you the next. This continues until you are filled to capacity and thrilled
to ecstasy. You push back from the table totally satisfied and grateful.

Are you aware that your spirit needs to be fed? Did you know that
your spirit would be delighted to partake in a feast of spiritual food?
How about a plate full of prayer? Or maybe a few hours of succulent self-
reflection. Perhaps a piping-hot selection of spiritual literature, served
by the side of a lake or under a tree, would satisfy your spiritual hunger.
Can you imagine feasting for a few hours on spiritually uplifting music?
What about some forgiveness à la mode, topped with compassion? You
cannot imagine how much your spirit would enjoy it.

Would you believe that there are many eager angels, guardians and
guides just waiting to serve you? They have already set the table and
begun to prepare everything you need to satisfy your spirit. Need some
help? Look under appetizers. Want some more understanding? Check
the daily specials. If warm wisdom or scrumptious security would fill
you up, try the Chef's Specials. It's all there on life's spiritual menu. All
you have to do is simply raise your head, your heart or your hand and
ask. Like the body, the spirit must be fed. Your spirit not only requires a
well-balanced diet, it must be fed on a regular schedule.

Until today, you may have believed that your spirit could survive on
bits of information. Just for today, be devoted to preparing a spiritual
banquet for yourself. Take a moment to identify all the things that
would *fill-full* your spirit, and then ask the angels to serve it up.

Today I am devoted to having a spiritual feast!

I will gain more understanding when I realize . . .
spiritual malnutrition is a condition that can be cured.

What if you were forced to sustain yourself on a low-calorie, minimal-intake diet for rest of your life? Or worse, what if you were told that you could never eat again? No more chocolate! No more homemade soup! How would you feel? How would you survive?

If you did not eat to sustain your physical body, you would eventually grow weak and weary. As you used up the reserve resources of nutrients and vitamins, your vital organs would stop functioning. Your body would begin to shrivel up and waste away. A person can only diet or fast for so long before the body demands to be fed. The same is true of the Spirit.

Some people are suffering from *spiritual malnutrition*. Some people have deprived themselves of spiritual nourishment for so long, they no longer have the strength to handle the weight of their lives. Their vision is shot! Their sense of *Self* has been diminished to the point that it is a chore for them to do the simplest task in their lives. Spiritually malnourished people are fretful and frightened, worried and worrisome. They are drained and draining. They have their eye on someone else's plate, someone else's life, and they will stretch their shriveled and shaking hand out for whatever crumbs can be spared.

There is only one cure for spiritual malnutrition. It is a steady diet of spiritual food. Prayer builds the spiritual structure. Faith puts meat on the spiritual bones. Gratitude builds spiritual muscles. If you are feeling worn out, run down or weary, check your spiritual diet! You may need to increase your intake of spiritual nutrients.

Until today, you may have been suffering from *spiritual malnutrition*. Just for today, increase your intake of spiritual food. Engage in a few spiritual experiences. Test your spiritual muscles. Make the necessary adjustments to your spiritual diet.

Today I am devoted to increasing my spiritual intake!

JULY 10

I will gain more understanding when I realize . . .
little creatures can teach me big lessons.

Few people appreciate mice. To most of us, they are dirty, annoying little creatures who destroy property and invade our personal space. A mouse will make its way through the smallest of openings to come into your home and help itself to the best you have to offer, leavings its droppings behind. Ever try to catch a mouse? They will dodge your broom as they scurry into a hole you never knew existed, leaving you out of breath and out of control! Then there is another side of the mouse you may have never considered.

Because mice are so small, they have the ability to get into places and to see things that other creatures can't. In other words, mice see opportunities that other creatures miss. At the same time, mice are a source of food for many other animals. For this reason, they must be very careful about how they move, where they move and when they move. They don't eat from every hand. They must first know you and feel comfortable around you. Mice know that they must be flexible in order to get into and out of tight places safely. The mouse teaches us to pay attention to details. Things like cheese in a trap! Mice know that there are details, which if ignored, could cost you your hide.

Caution in movement. Focus of direction. Scrutiny of association. Flexibility. The mouse teaches us that it is possible to move in and out of the experiences of our lives without being trapped. The key is to be aware of what you are doing at all times.

Until today, you may not have had a healthy appreciation of the skills of mice. Just for today, set aside any dislike of little creeping things. Instead, examine how their example could help you.

Today I am devoted to moving with caution, focusing on what I am doing; and to scrutinizing everything and everyone, including myself!

JULY 11

I will gain more understanding when I realize . . .
who I am is Divine.

If you see a chameleon in the grass, it will appear to be green. If you see the same chameleon in the mud, it will appear to be brown. What a wonderful gift nature provides its creation: the ability to change its appearance in order to survive. For we human beings, the ability to *adapt* in order to *fit in* has one major drawback. If we do it too often we run the risk of forgetting who we truly are.

We have a business mask, a social mask, a home mask, a play mask and a Don't mess with me! I'm not playing! mask. Then there are the many masks of the many roles we play. There's the daughter/son mask; the mother mask; the father mask; the wife/husband mask. There is the Help me I'm lost mask.

Each of our masks carries duties and responsibilities, fears and frustrations, likes and dislikes, demands and desires. Sometimes the responsibilities of one mask conflict with those of another. Or, to hold one mask in place, there may be things we must do that are inappropriate for the other masks we wear. In fact, we can become so skilled at putting on the appropriate mask, at the appropriate time, in order to survive that we can eventually lose sight of our true essence.

Perhaps it is time to wear the mask of Divine identity. Find your true essence and allow it to show in all of the roles you play. If you wear it all of the time, there will be a lot less confusion about what to do and how to do it.

Until today, you may have allowed your environment to determine the mask you wear. Just for today, devote your self to discovering or rediscovering the truth about your Divine self, so that tomorrow you can show up in your true divine color.

Today I am devoted to remembering and demonstrating the truth about the Divine identity that I am!

JULY 12

I will gain more understanding when I realize . . . I must
maintain a power line into the power source.

We were late, my assistant and I, rushing around in the hotel
room, trying to put on makeup and get dressed before the
car arrived to pick us up. We had called for an iron. A half-
hour later, it had not arrived. By the time the iron was delivered, we decided that it, not our lying around watching television, was
the reason we would be late.

I laid my dress across the ironing board and went into the bathroom
to put on eyeliner. When I returned, the iron was still cold. Turning the
fabric selector to its highest position, I retreated to the bathroom to put
on some eye shadow. When I returned, the iron was still cold. It's broken! Now we are really going to be late! We called for another iron. I
went back into the bathroom to put on my blush. Another iron arrived.
Back into the bathroom one more time. When my *spit-on-the-finger* test
proved that the new iron was cold, I went ballistic! I stormed over to the
telephone, called housekeeping, blasted the unsuspecting person on the
other end. As I was standing there in my half-naked, self-righteous indignation, I noticed that the iron was not plugged in!

How many days have you left your house without being plugged in
to God? How many times have you been too busy to pray? How often
have you slept so late, you did not have time to ask for guidance, support
or protection? How many times this week or last week, have you met
with a challenge or a disappointment, only to get mad at God for not
warning you? If you want your life to run smoothly, it is in your best interest to get plugged in every morning and check your connection
throughout the day.

Until today, you may have tried to make it through life on your own
power. Just for today, make sure you are plugged in to the source of true
power. Pray a moment. Draw on the power of God at every moment.

*Today I am devoted to staying plugged in to the voice,
wisdom and love of God!*

JULY 13

I will gain more understanding when I realize . . .
I am an important part of the wholeness of life.

Author and teacher Eric Butterworth once said, "I am an *each-ness* in the *All-ness* that is God." His words convey the idea that we are all essential elements of all that God is. Sometimes we forget that every part of the whole is an important part. We fail to understand that every part of the whole contains the essence of the whole. When we forget this we lose sight of our power, our purpose and the essential role we play in life as a whole.

As children in school, we had to line up by size. At recess or dismissal time, a crooked line would delay the advancement of the whole class. If one person was out of line, the whole line had to wait. No *each-ness* could go out to play or go home until the *all-ness* was in alignment. It works the same way in life. What you do, how you do it and when you do it affects every person in front of you and every person coming behind you. That is how important you are.

It is so easy to get caught up in the day-to-day doing of the things required just to stay alive that you lose sight of the all-ness of life moving around you, depending on you and waiting for you. In reality, getting caught means forgetting your importance and your power to affect the world and to have an impact on life. If and when you get caught up, some part of life must wait or stop and is delayed in its ability to move forward.

Until today, you may not have understood how important you are to the forward movement of life. Just for today, think about all the people who are affected by what you do and what you do not do. Think about all the things you have not allowed yourself to do and what an impact you could have on the world if you allowed your *each-ness* to shine in the *all-ness* of life.

*Today I am devoted to recognizing the importance
of the power I have to impact all of life!*

JULY 14

I will gain more understanding when I realize . . . there is
an *i* in me that longs to become the *I* of Spirit.

There seems to be a war against the ego. People are cautious
about seeming to be ego-centered, ego-driven and ego-
based. As so many are moving toward a more spiritually
grounded life style, the ego is taking a pretty bad rap! Unfortunately, few people are talking about the power, the beauty or the purpose of the ego.

It is the ego that inspires you to brush your teeth and comb your
hair. It is the ego that makes you health conscious and body conscious.
Without your ego, you could not make steps toward self-improvement,
self-development or self-empowerment. The ego is the little *self* that desires to become the *Self* filled and fulfilled by the truth. It is the *i* of you
that will motivate and support you in becoming the *I* of Spirit. When
the *i* of you is tempered by the knowledge and love of I in you, the ego
becomes your source of grace and compassion.

When it is understood and disciplined, the ego is a safety net. It is
the ego that will warn you about walking alone down a dark street. It is
the ego that brings to your attention the fact that you are being spoken
to or treated inappropriately. The ego made Sojourner Truth stand up
and Rosa Parks sit down. The ego, when tempered by the guidance of a
well-nurtured spirit is an excellent source of guidance. It serves as a map
and a compass. It is only when the ego is *left to its own devices, when it is
not spiritualized* by the power of prayer, self-discipline and the influence
of the Spirit within that it becomes a problem.

Until today, you may not have understood the role the ego can play
in your spiritual development. Just for today, examine your ego. Determine if your ego is a little *i* searching to fulfill itself or whether it longs to
be a big *I*, destined to fulfill a grander purpose of Spirit.

*Today I am devoted to checking in with and
checking up on my ego!*

I will gain more understanding when I realize . . .
I am always in touch with all forms of life and
those who have lived.

People never really die. They leave their bodies. They end their physical existence in order to continue their spiritual journey in another form, on another plane. A person who has entered the realm of existence that we call *death* is never beyond your love. The thing we call death is not a cold or a dark or a frightening and cruel existence. It is an essential part of life that teaches us to believe in what we cannot see. Once you know a person, you will always know a person. Once you have loved a person, your love will keep them alive.

Life continues after death as long as you remember the warmth of another's smile, the gentleness of their touch, the meaning they brought to your life. In your remembrance of another, death cannot overtake life. Life simply changes its form. When you spend time honoring the dreams of one who has changed, when you continuing standing up for the things they believed in and doing the things you loved to do together, you are saying, "This life continues to touch my life."

Stay in touch with your loved ones. Send them your love. Use the memory of your time together as motivation to keep growing. Always remember to honor the special ways the one you knew and loved touched your life. Your remembrance offers them a victory over the thing called death.

Until today, you may have misunderstood death. You may have been grieving or mourning the loss of a loved one, believing they were forever gone from your life. Just for today, be devoted to being a living reflection of the dreams and love you shared with someone who has passed on.

Today I am devoted to living my life as a demonstration of how deeply I have been touched and loved by those who have changed the form of their lives!

JULY 16

*I will gain more understanding when I realize . . . I must
not allow the spirit of grief to take over my life.*

When you lose someone you knew or loved to the experience
we call death, grieving is what you do. You grieve because
you believe that the chance to do all that you *did not do,* or
to say all that you *did not say* it is gone forever. You grieve because you will miss the person. Quite often you believe that you will
never again feel the way they made you feel. If you are not careful, the
spirit of grief can take over your life, causing you to miss the joy, peace
and love that lies within you and ahead of you.

It is normal to grieve the loss of a loved one. In fact, you will grieve the
loss of any situation or experience that ceases to be the way you knew it or
want it to be. It is important not to grieve so long and so hard that you
begin to doubt your ability and desire to continue living. This is what happens when grieving becomes confused with *missing out.* When you are
missing out, you cannot connect with, create or enjoy all that you have or
have had. When you are grieving because you *miss,* you cannot recognize
what you have already received and what is coming your way.

Everything ends exactly when it needs to end. To grieve what you
think you have missed or will miss, is to doubt Divine Wisdom. Grieve
until you feel comforted enough to live in gratitude and without fear.
Grieve until you can accept what has happened without resistance.
Grieve until you can let go of what was, without forgetting all that is.
When you grieve in this way, you will realize you will not miss anything
that is meant for you.

Until today, you may have been grieving for what you did not do or
what you believed you would no longer experience. Just for today, embrace grief as a process of preparation. Know that you are preparing
yourself to be opened and to receive something more.

*Today I am devoted to shaking myself free
from the spirit of grief!*

JULY 17

*I will gain more understanding when I realize . . .
until I handle my unfinished childhood business,
I will behave like a child.*

When you face danger or frustration, do you regress in age?
When as children we did not get our way, when we were not
heard, we pouted, stomped and probably slammed a door.
When was the last time you turned on your heel or slammed
your hands on a table? In an instant, you, an able bodied, competent
adult, can become a fourteen year old, a nine year old or a five year old,
gripped by the hands of terror. You are regressing back to the time when
you first had a similar experience. When you are mentally or emotionally a terrorized child, you must handle yourself with compassion.

When children are afraid, they yearn for a mother, father, grand-
mother or some other *big person* to protect them. The same thing happens when an adult regresses. If we feel that comfort is not available, we
will do as an adult what we did as a child. We will cry. We will cower. We
will run for cover. Adults who regress beat up on themselves. They feel
ashamed or embarrassed. They make excuses for their behavior, and ultimately they miss the point. What you did not handle or complete as a
child, you will handle and complete as an adult.

We are all little people who grew into big bodies. The challenge we
face as adults is to resist the tendency to beat up on ourselves when we
act out. Rather, take a moment to soothe and comfort the *little you* inside of the *big you*. Do for yourself today what was not done for you yesterday. In this way, you will complete your unfinished business.

Until today, you may not have understood the temper tantrums,
panic attacks or fear that you may sometimes experience. Just for today,
be devoted to remembering and healing the little one inside you.

*Today I am embracing, protecting and honoring the
child that I still am!*

JULY 18

I will gain more understanding when I realize . . . there
are some things I need to heal before I can forget them.

There are some things in the back of your mind about which
you are still hurt, angry and even confused. These are not
things that you think about every day. In fact, for many of
us, these things are so far in the back of our minds, we no
longer remember them. Rest assured, however, that they remember us.
At times, these things become the source of the fear, anger, guilt, shame
or pain that can control what we do and how we do it.

You will know you are being controlled by a memory if you insist on
doing a certain thing in a certain way, because you are convinced your
reason for doing it is right. You can be pretty sure you are being controlled by a memory when you interpret the things you see or hear in
ways that cause you anger, fear or resentment. When a memory of something you have forgotten is controlling your life, you will say things that
are not true, you will do things that are not productive, you will hear
things that are not said, you will see things that are not there. You will respond in ways that are inappropriate and out of character. In these cases,
your soul is calling out for healing.

What was going on *then* will continue to happen *now* as long as you
forget to remember it. A repressed memory will push itself into your
consciousness to be healed. It will stand up until it receives the attention
and recognition it deserves. Everything you have experienced deserves to
be honored and embraced. Yes, some things also need to healed. Until
you are willing to remember the things you have learned to forget, you
cannot participate in or benefit from the joys of healing your life.

Until today, you may have been struggling with yourself to gain control of your life. Just for today, try acknowledging and healing the forgotten memories that do not increase your sense of self-worth and value.

*Today I am devoted to remembering the memories
that are controlling my life!*

JULY 19

I will gain more understanding when I realize . . . I have
been a captive audience for the reruns of my life.

Most of us have a story about why we haven't gotten around
to doing what we say we want to do. We can tell the story
with exacting precision, at any moment, for anyone who
will listen to the tragic details of our failures, disappoint-
ments, betrayals, which have led to our *seeming* inability to be the person
that we know we can be, want to be, need to be but can't be because of
how we feel about ourselves in response to the events of the story we
have been telling ourselves, including the ending statement about what
we like and don't like, have and don't have, using both as explanations
for why we are not where we say we want to be.

If you have a story you having been telling or like to tell about the
whys of why you are not, here is a suggestion: *live in simple sentences!*
Without a closing mark or gesture that signifies the end, a story can drag
on forever. You must put a period at the end of an experience. You must
bring closure to it and experience when it is over. The longer a story
drags on, the more complicated it becomes, the more people you become entangled with, the further away you move from your destination.

Live your life in simple sentences of what is now. Identify where you
are going now! If you continue to talk about what no longer is, you allow
it to continue. Focus on what you desire. Clarify what you need to do to
make it happen. Look forward rather than backward. Describe your past
in simple sentences. Look for the clear and simple lessons. Be open and
receptive to the pure and simple blessings.

Until today, you may have been living a run-on sentence, loaded
with excess baggage, high drama and explicit smut. Just for today, live
your life, create your dreams and set your goals with simple sentences.

*Today I am devoted to simply living, simply expecting the
best and simply putting an end to the things that are over!*

JULY 20

I will gain more understanding when I realize . . .
discipline is the one magical power I must develop
and use.

There is *magical thinking* and then there is *magical doing*. Magical doing is the result of personal discipline. You can think up a host of really great ideas, but if you do not have the discipline required to pull them off, you will not get very far. Some people are so good at magical thinking, they begin to believe that the things they want to do can be done, magically!

Discipline magically leads to results in your life. Discipline helps you plan. Discipline helps you to stay on the path to what you are planning. Only when you are disciplined will you follow through on what you are thinking. Only when you are disciplined will you coach yourself through all of your actions. Only when you are disciplined can you capture the magic of your spirit and put it into action in your life. Discipline cannot be forced upon you. It must be developed.

You must develop the discipline to think right. This will give you the discipline to act right. When you are disciplined in your thinking and acting, you always feel good. When you feel good, you want to share how you feel. You want to do good things. When you do, you set an example for others. They are inspired by you.

Until today, you may have been thinking great thoughts while demonstrating very little discipline to do anything about them. Just for today, practice discipline. Take one step toward doing something you have been thinking about. Speak to yourself calmly, firmly. Do things that are in alignment with your thinking. Feel good about any little progress you make. Support the progress you made today by disciplining yourself to do a little more tomorrow.

Today I am developing the discipline I need to make
something magical happen in my life!

JULY 21

I will gain more understanding when I realize . . .
a teacher is not one with many students but one
who creates many teachers.

There is a saying, *"When the student is ready, the teacher will appear."* For many on the spiritual path, this statement implies that a teacher will *show up in the flesh,* ready to teach us the things we need to know. In fact, some of us feel so ready, we mistake *other students,* who *believe* they are teachers, for the teacher we long to have. When this happens, we can follow the wrong people down the wrong path, learning very little. Unfortunately, by the time we discover our error, we are a little bruised and very weary.

A teacher, a true teacher is not one who gives you anything. A true teacher is one who *makes you aware* of what you already have and encourages you to use it. A teacher is not one who tells you anything. A true teacher listens to you, learns from you and uses what you have to inspire other students. A true teacher recognizes your brilliance and supports you in learning how to nurture it. Seeing your dilemmas, a true teacher walks through them with you. A true teacher will look you dead in the eye, call you out of hiding and celebrate with you in the joy of standing in your truth. A true teacher will not *do it for you.* Instead, they will sit with you as you figure out how to do it for yourself. A true teacher will not keep score for you. They will support you in moving beyond the need to know the score. If you are really lucky, you will happen upon the greatest teacher of all: the *student* who brings you to the realization the you are your own greatest teacher.

Until today, you may have been searching for a spiritual teacher in the flesh. Just for today, pinch yourself! Honor yourself for all the lessons you have taught yourself.

*Today I am devoted to being the best spiritual teacher
I can be!*

JULY 22

I will gain more understanding when I realize . . . there is
no light more brilliant than the light I am.

Let's keep it simple. When you put yourself on the path to
knowing yourself, embracing yourself and honoring exactly
who you are, without excuses or defenses, you will experience the illumination of self-enlightenment. Oh! That
sounds too hard! Perhaps it is too simple. Perhaps the reason you have
made it so hard is because you really do believe that if it is not hard to
get, it is not worth having.

Every being is born into enlightenment. We know everything we
need to know and are equipped to do everything we need to do. The
only awareness we need to have is, *I can do this!* These four simple words
are the key to knowing all and to doing everything. But for some reason,
they don't seem to be enough. We want it to be more complicated. So,
instead of saying *I can,* we say *I can't. I can't take it! I can't do it!* Each time
we say *I can't,* we dim our inner light.

The *light* of your en*light*enment is already within you. It is this same
light that will help you to realize the power of your being. The *light* of
your en*light*enment is powered by your thoughts and your words. Each
time you are able to acknowledge, accept and embrace the truth about
yourself, your light becomes a little brighter. The *light* of your en*light*enment never goes out. In fact, the light that you think you see in others is
a reflection of the light within yourself. When you realize your own
power and stop borrowing light from others, you will have reached the
perfect state of self-realized illumination.

Until today, you may have been following someone or something
toward the light of self-realization. Just for today, stand in your own
light! Turn on the power of your light by remembering who you are!

*Today I am devoted to turning on the light of self-
awareness, self-acceptance and self-illumination!*

JULY 23

I will gain more understanding when I realize . . .
to be on pause is a good thing.

Everything has to stop at some time in order to keep going. When driving, you must pause at stop lights and stop signs. On a train, there may be stops before you reach your destination. An airplane stops at the head of the runway before it ascends into the sky. Knowing this, why do we believe that we can move from experience to experience without stopping, refueling or resting?

Most of us will not leave one job until we have another. As soon as one romance is over, we begin our prowl to find another. We go from work to home to work some more. Even a quiet relaxing evening could mean reading, talking, playing with the dog. Some of us feel guilty about doing things that do not earn an income or meet some responsibility of our lives. We believe that doing nothing is not a good thing, when in fact it is the best thing we could do for ourselves.

To stop, to rest, or to *pause* means *to do no thing*. It means no thinking! No moving! No decisions! When you press the pause button on the audio or video machine, everything stops. No picture. No sound. No movement. The images and sounds of life must come to a halt if you want to have a clear picture about what to do next. What a blessing it is to push the pause button. To have the ability to stop and gather strength or to wait until things have passed before turning a corner and moving forward. A pause in life's journey does not mean that *nothing is happening*. In reality, it is a divine opportunity to be present and catch up with all that is going on.

Until today, you may have been afraid to stop moving or doing in life. Just for today, push the pause button. Be still. Shut down. Stop your movement just long enough to check up on yourself. Unless you pause, you may not know if you are fast-forwarding or going in reverse.

*Today I am devoted to putting my movement and
my life on pause!*

JULY 24

I will gain more understanding when I realize . . . . when I expect to experience pain, I experience things painfully.

Change doesn't have to be hard, and healing doesn't have to hurt. Often, because we expect a situation to be challenging, stressful or painful, we brace ourselves for the worse. The truth is, we are equipped to go through anything. *How* we get through it is the result of what we tell ourselves about going through it.

When a change is about to happen, or when some healing is about to occur in your life, you remember others, the many others who have been where you are going. You remember their pain, their tears and the hard times they had. You remember being there for them and being afraid for them. Now, here you stand, on the verge of a break-up, a breakdown or some other form of a healing or growth experience, and *all you can remember is the pain?* Stop the imagination train! It doesn't have to be that way! The question is, are you willing to allow it to be any other way?

Whether you are acknowledging something you have denied, accepting something you have resisted, confronting something you have avoided or healing something that once hurt you, *it doesn't have to be hard!* The only thing that will make the experience more painful and more difficult than it needs to be are the things you tell yourself about going through the experience. Surely by now you know that every thing happens for a reason! Knowing that, you must be aware that there is something better awaiting you on the other side of this! If you would stop telling yourself scary stories and stop imagining that monsters lie ahead, the fear, guilt and shame would go away.

Until today, you may have resisted the inevitable by bracing yourself against the pain. Just for today, stop imagining the worst! Give yourself permission to weather the storm of an emotional experience without telling yourself how bad or hard or painful it is going to be.

Today I am devoted to moving through all experiences without the expectation of pain!

JULY 25

I will gain more understanding when I realize . . .
how I interpret what comes at me is a reflection
of what is in me.

When something someone says or does upsets you, *your upset*
is not about the other person. Feelings are triggered *within
you* when an external source bumps into something that is already there. A *self-inquiry* will help you figure out what you are
hiding that is being triggered by what you are experiencing.

When you least expect it, truth will fly out of someone's mouth.
That truth will burn a hole in your defenses, and chances are it is going
to upset you. More than likely you will direct your upset toward the person who released the truth you were denying, ignoring or trying to excuse away. If, on the other hand, you turn inward, then you are opening
the door to a wholesome self-inquiry that will ultimately lead you to
something that needs to be healed.

A self-inquiry indicates your desire to take charge of rampant emotions so that you are not *manipulated like a puppet* by the things that go
on around you. A self-inquiry begins the moment you experience the
upset and ask the question, *What am I feeling?* Once you get the nature
of the feeling, you must ask yourself, *Why am I feeling this?* The answer is
likely to be, *Because so-and-so did such-and-such! WRONG!* Do not lay
your feelings in someone else's lap. Take charge! Call forth your issues so
that they can be healed. Doing anything less will leave you out of touch
with you and at the mercy of everything and everyone.

Until today, you may have been tricked into believing that people
can upset you. Just for today, be aware of what it is in you that triggers
toxic emotions. If your trigger is pulled, run to the nearest quiet place
and begin your healing process with a self-inquiry.

*Today I am devoted to healing myself of the need to react
to the actions of others!*

JULY 26

I will gain more understanding when I realize . . .
I have an ongoing relationship with things I cannot see
but can feel.

Today's message is a continuation of yesterday's message regarding self-inquiry. Self-inquiry is the process of discovering what it is within you that is hurt by what goes on around you. A self-inquiry is a healing process. Self-inquiry puts you in touch with vital information about yourself which you have ignored, denied or may not be aware of.

The third question in our self-inquiry is, *What is the memory that is the source of this feeling?* In other words, *When was the first time I felt this way?* If you take a deep breath and call forth the truth of your being, this will be the Bingo response! This is the question that will remind you of who it was that first made you feel this way. What the experience was that first triggered this feeling. What you expected or were denied that first gave rise to this feeling. How this situation reminds you of that situation. Armed with this information, your healing is imminent.

When you remember the first time you felt this way, *you must pray! Dear God: I now forgive myself for all beliefs, judgments, decisions, choices and agreements that have caused me to be attached to pain, hurt, shame, anger, guilt, disappointment and any other toxic emotions. I ask that you transform what I am feeling, experiencing and believing into an expression of love so that I may be healed. Thank you, God.*

Until today, you may not have understood how the first experience of a toxic emotion has influenced your responses to current experiences. Just for today, take the time to go back and heal your mind, heart and soul of the things which are no longer relevant.

*Today I am devoted to being freed from past beliefs,
judgments, decisions, choices and agreements
that trigger toxic emotions!*

I will gain more understanding when I realize . . .
I cannot force others to see that what I feel is real.

When you are hurting, it may seem that other people do not notice or that they do not care. They never seem able to recognize the depth of your misery or discomfort. You want them to see and feel what you are going through so that they can stop it. Unfortunately, your efforts to get them to acknowledge what you are feeling lead to more frustration. You conclude that they don't care and this sends you deeper into the very thing you are trying so desperately to escape.

You cannot force someone else to see your pain. Your pain is your pain. It is the result of what *you are telling yourself* about yourself, about others, about situations or circumstances. It is not necessary for anyone to see, know or understand that you are hurting. You know! Your experience is the only motivation required to let you know that something must change. That something is you.

When you are in pain, you must take responsibility for the elimination of your own pain. If you believe that someone's behavior is hurting you, move away! Move far enough away and for long enough to realize your pain is not caused by them; it comes from what you *tell yourself about them*. Often, pain is the result of the failure to acknowledge something that is staring you right in the face. What may be staring at you is the fact that in demanding attention from someone else, you are giving away pieces of yourself that are too valuable to lose.

Until today, you may not have realized that trying to force someone else to acknowledge your pain causes you more pain. You may have been blaming them when the truth is you are abusing yourself. Just for today, know that your pain is real and that your experience is the only legitimate reason you need to make some needed changes.

Today I am devoted to the elimination of all self-abusive,
self-negating thoughts and behaviors!

JULY 28

I will gain more understanding when I realize . . .
loving in unloving ways is not love at all.

You can usually tell when someone is afraid of love. They simply will not let you into their heart. A person who is afraid of love will behave in the most inappropriate ways in an effort to turn you off. A person who is afraid of love will find all sorts of things wrong with who they are and will point these things out to you. They will also find all sorts of things wrong with you, which they will also point out. People who are afraid of love cannot not give it, nor can they receive it. They will have so many barriers and defenses that you will end up asking yourself, *Why am I trying to get through this stuff*????

A person who is afraid of love may believe that they will not measure up to what you expect of them. Often, this is because they have not lived up to what they expect of themself. A person who is afraid of love will pull you in and out like a yo-yo! Today they want you. Tomorrow they won't. The closer you get, the faster they run. The more you give the more they want. You will never be able to prove yourself to a person who is afraid of love because *they do not want to believe you!*

When you find yourself trying your darnest to love a person who demonstrates that they are *not willing* to be loved, *stop yourself!* Stop trying to force them to accept what they obviously do not want or cannot handle. Stop making excuses for them. Stop accepting their excuses. It is very *unloving* to push someone beyond the point they are willing to go.

Until today, you may not have understood that trying to love someone who does not want to be loved is an invasion. Or that an invasion is not a loving act. Just for today, ask yourself if you are trying to force love on someone. If the love you are offering another is not being welcomed or invited in, back up!

Today I am devoted to recognizing the difference between loving someone and invading their heart space!

JULY 29

I will gain more understanding when I realize . . .
trying to hide what I feel does not work.

An unexpressed feeling is like a rubber band being stretched
to its limit. The longer you hold on to the feeling, the more
the tension grows. Eventually something has to give, or the
rubber band is going to snap. When that happens, someone
is going to get hurt!

More often than not, the reason you do not express your true feelings is because you believe what you feel is wrong. You may remember
the last time you felt this way about something or someone. When you
shared what you felt, it was rejected or challenged. That memory is now
hovering right below the surface of what you feel, and you are not about
to run the risk of making someone else angry!

Perhaps you are trying to protect other people from your feelings.
You may believe that *they cannot handle your feelings* You don't want to
hurt or upset them. Unfortunately, *your plan is not working!* They are already upset! They are constantly upset with you because somewhere *in
their being they know* that there is something you need to say. Keep this
in mind when you are withholding your feelings: you are always having
an unconscious relationship with people. This means that they already
know the very thing you think they don't know. In fact, they, like you,
know that there is a collective healing attached to the expression of feelings. The question is, *are you willing to be healed?*

Until today, you may have not understood that harboring thoughts
and feelings creates tension in a relationship. You may not have realized
that what you feel is important and that expressing it is an important
step toward healing yourself and someone else. Just for today, ask the
Holy Spirit's assistance and guidance in finding the appropriate words
and the right opportunity to share your feelings with others.

*Today I am devoted to sharing my feelings in an
appropriately healing and loving way!*

JULY 30

I will gain more understanding when I realize . . . there is
a place called home where I am always welcome.

Inside of you there is a place called *home*. It is not a house,
nor is it anything like the home in which you grew up. The
home inside of you is the place where God resides. It is a
safe place. A place filled with love. In this home there is
everything that you could need or want. There is support, comfort,
peace and unconditional acceptance. In this home, no one will judge
you. No one will deny you. You will never be rejected or abandoned. In
this home, your divine home, God is waiting to rock you to sleep. When
you awake from the dreams and nightmares of the world, God will still
be there, waiting for you.

At any time, in any moment, you can go *home*. You don't need to
pack or plan. You can get *home* if you don't have a dime to your name!
You can move out of frightening, threatening or challenging situations.
You can move away from difficult and unloving people and go *home*.
When you get there, you can receive the answers, insights, understandings and revelations you need to make your worldly life a more pleasant
place to be. You can build up the strength, stamina and courage you
need to deal with your world and the people in it. When the world and
your life become a bit too much for you to handle, simply go *home*.

It is always easy to get *home*. Here's what you have to do: take a deep
breath; close your eyes; see yourself as a young, vulnerable and lost child;
feel your pain, fear or discomfort. The moment you are in that place,
open your mouth and say aloud, *Father, Mother God: I am coming home!*
The doors of God's loving comfort will fly open. Miraculously, you will
be exactly where you need to be, *home* in the heart of God.

Until today, you may not have realized that there is a place in your
heart called *home*. Just for today, practice going home to get what you
need at any moment.

Today I am devoted to finding my way back home!

JULY 31

I will gain more understanding when I realize . . . there is
a divine purpose for my living and my being.

Your Creation Is a Good Thing

• In the beginning, you were created to be good, and you
  are still good.
• There is nothing about you that is inherently bad.

There Is a Purpose to Your Living

• Your Creator etched a purpose into your being.
• You have been born to fulfill that purpose in a way that only you can.
• You bring to life talents and gifts unlike those of any other person.

Every Experience Supports Your Purpose

• Every experience will facilitate your understanding of your purpose
  and will call you to use the talents and gifts you possess.
• Every person you have met has played an important role in facilitating
  your understanding of your purpose.
• You have been influenced by your environment to such a degree that
  you have lost touch with the truth of your self and your purpose.

You Must Choose to Live Your Purpose

• The guidance you need to recover your true purpose is available to
  you because you are worthy of having it.
• You can make the choice to fulfill your purpose at any time.
• Balancing your heart and mind is the key to bringing forth the talents
  and gifts you possess that will enable you to fulfill your purpose.

What You Choose for Yourself,
Your Creator Will Support

• If you want to know the purpose of your life and how your experiences fit into that purpose, ask your creator. God is available, accessi-
  ble and waiting for you.

Trust the Process

- Once you ask, listen for the response, and believe what you hear.

Until today, your life may not have made much sense. Just for today, be open to hearing and embracing God's purpose for your life and all of your experiences.

Today I am devoted to getting myself in alignment with my purpose!

AUGUST

FAITH

What you make in your own mind

is what you put your faith into just

to prove to yourself that what you believe

is correct.

AUGUST 1

I am faith-filled and fear-free because . . . I have more
than enough of what it takes to make it through
the rough times and tight places.

Life is never going to give up on you because there is something important for you to do. One of the primary purposes
and processes of life is the development of character. Your
character—your nature, the distinctive qualities of your
essence, what makes you you—is developed through experience. If you
do not understand that character development is an important process
of life, you may be tempted to give up when things get tough. You may
even begin to believe that life is against you. More important, you may
miss the fact that the very part of your character that requires development is being developed by your response to the things that you are
walking through. What you do when your back is against the wall speaks
volumes about the nature of your character.

Every human weakness is strengthened by experience. Every
strength that serves you well in those tight spots is remembered. When
things get a little rough, it is always good to remember that you cannot
stay where you are forever. Life is continually renewing and redesigning
the intricate pieces of your character. When life detects that there is an
opportunity for you to advance the nature of your character, it will send
the perfect situation and people your way. Your job is to respond to
everything in a manner that develops and strengthens your character.

Until today, you may have thought that what happens to you and
around you determines the nature of who you are. Just for today, devote
your time and energy to using every experience as a character-building
exercise. Allow faith, joy, gentleness, kindness, patience and peace to be
the character-building tools that determine your approach to situations
and your response to experiences.

Today I am devoted to demonstrating a better, stronger,
wiser expression of my true nature and character!

AUGUST 2

I am faith-filled and fear-free because . . .
God is always on duty!

What is the number you use to call God? Is it 411? Or 911?
Many of us are 911 callers. We don't call in for information.
We only call in when we need an ambulance, someone to
put out a fire, or a police car to take something or someone
away. We are in the habit of only calling God at 911 for emergency treatment. We call when we are broken down, torn down or on the way
down! We call frantically when we hit something we can't handle, when
we break something we can't fix or when some part of our lives isn't
working the way we set it up to work. And if, for some reason, we feel we
are not being heard, or that the line is busy, we keep checking. We keep
looking to make sure that what we need, what we have requested is on
the way. Yes, most of us use 911 because we forget to use 411.

When you use 411 to call God, you get preventive treatment, long-
term care and regular maintenance. You get local and long distance information. You talk to God about what is going on now and what is
coming. When you call God at 411, it is an indication that you recognize yourself as a product with a lifetime guarantee. You call to ensure
that there is an open line of communication between you and your
manufacturer. When you call 411 there is no need to wait. No need to
fear. No need too great. Why? Because you have paid your *life-care pre-
miums* on time. You know where the trouble spots are and what precautions you need to take. The good news is, God is always on duty! When
you call God at 411 you are less likely to need to call him at 911!

Until today, you may have placed God on your 911 emergency list.
Just for today, try contacting God for information only.

*Today I am devoted to asking God for the information
I need to give my life a clean bill of health!*

AUGUST 3

I am faith-filled and fear-free because . . .
the law is on my side.

There is an impersonal law of personal good that works on behalf of anyone who is willing to acknowledge it. Your mind is its mind. Your heart is its heart. The law is impersonal because it does not care if you are black, white, red or yellow. It doesn't care if you are old or young, male or female, married or single. The law doesn't even mind if you are still living at home with your parents! The law works for you, whoever you are, if you are willing to surrender your way of doing things to a divine way of being and doing. If you are willing to take your humanness out of the way, the impersonal law of personal good will work for you, on you and through you.

The impersonal law of personal good is all the good things that you seek, and it gives you all the good that you are. It is the law of *all* that will give you *its all* because *it is all* and *it has all*. The law is the source of your personal wealth, health and well-being. It is the impersonal source of all personal resources. Now, here is the way to get out of the way so that the law can operate on your behalf: Know that you are good. Know that you deserve to experience good things. Trust that good is on your side, and good shall be done unto you.

Until today, you may not have realized that you have the ability to experience anything and everything good that you desire. Just for today, live on the right side of the law. Expect good! Believe in good! Trust that something good in you will bring something good through you!

Today I am devoted to bringing my mind and life into alignment with the impersonal law of personal good!

AUGUST 4

I am faith-filled and fear-free because . . .
this day belongs to God!

Rev. Michael Beckwith of the Agape Church of Religious Science once said, "When you pray, *Give us this day, our daily bread* . . . the day no longer belongs to you. Your day belongs to God!" Your day and every action in that day belongs to the good of God, through the love that God has for you.

Today, there is absolutely nothing for you to worry about. You don't have to concern yourself with what has to be or what may not get done. This is God's day! And on God's day, everything takes shape and form in and through divine order. You will be guided and led, supported and protected. When God is in charge of the day, you need not concern yourself with anything that anyone is doing or not doing. God knows! God sees! After all, God is God! What do your opinions mean when they are measured against who God is and what God can do?

When you know that God is in charge, the polite thing to do is to mind your own business! Don't go sticking your nose into things that God is doing on this day. This is God's day! Listen to your own heart, in case God has something special to say to you. When your day belongs to God, you have only one thing to do, that is, to know. You must know that you can depend on God. You must know that whatever comes your way is coming through God first and that by the time it gets to you, you will know exactly what to do or say. So relax! This is God's day! You gave this day of your life to God. Now don't take it back!

Until today, you may have been reluctant to turn your life over to God. You may have been trying to do what only God can do. Just for today, open your heart to the all-knowing power of God. If things don't go the way you think they should, there is always tomorrow!

*Today I am devoted to allowing the presence of God
to control every aspect of my life!*

AUGUST 5

I am faith-filled and fear-free because . . . I know
that every experience opens my heart to a greater
and grander experience.

When you are attached to the way things are, it is very difficult to put your faith in anything else. You do not trust
yourself to risk experiencing anything other than what you
already know. You do not trust life to bring you the results or
rewards you desire. You do not trust that you can and will handle whatever comes your way. Without trust, there can be no faith. Without
faith, you will hold on to what you know. In the process, you will not be
making any progress.

Attachment is another way of saying, "I don't have faith in anything
else! I know what this is! I can handle this!" You want to control your experiences and your responses. You see, rather than fight with you for
control, life will send you into the pit of stagnation. This can be *extremely painful!*

Attachment reflects a lack of faith in your ability to learn. Learning
takes place three ways. You learn by force. You learn by choice. You learn
by being forced to make a choice. When you are attached to what you
know or what you can control, chances are you will be forced to make a
choice. You can choose to stay attached and be stagnated in pain and
confusion. Or you can let go in faith that your next experience will be
exactly what you need, but did not know you needed.

Until today, you may have been holding on, attached to the way
things are. Just for today, open your heart to the possibility that there is
something great waiting for you. Let go of anything or anyone you are
attached to, in faith that you will be pleasantly surprised.

*Today I am devoted to stretching my faith beyond
what I know!*

AUGUST 6

I am faith-filled and fear-free because . . . I know what time it is!

I could be wrong. In fact, I am willing to be wrong, but if my recollection serves me, I seem to remember that you have been talking about doing *this* or *that* for quite some time now. Perhaps I am mistaken. Maybe I have you confused with someone else. There are so many people who talk and never move, who wish and never act, who tell stories and never take risks, who wait until they are so *weighted down* that they never get anything done. I admit that it is quite possible that I thought that you were one of them. *Forgive me!*

Just in case you are interested, if I were talking to one of *those people*, I would know exactly what to say. I would make the point that they seem to always have a reason *why not*, rather than a motivation for *why to*. I would let them know that being *beat down* and *beat up* by their failed attempts seems to make them more comfortable than *standing up* and *taking charge*. I would have absolutely no qualms about challenging those people to make their *when* now! To make their *if* happen! To make their *because* disappear by doing what they can do *right now!* I would admonish them not to let *when* steal their right now! I would encourage them not to allow *if* to hold them back! I would ask them why they continue to allow *suppose, what if,* or *only if,* to stop them. So please forgive me if I have mistaken you for someone else. It's just that I thought I had already heard what you are saying

Until today, you may have been paralyzed by *when, if, only if,* or *because.* Just for today, remember that *now is the time!* Make something happen in your life and for your life.

Today I am devoted to being in tune with the time I have right now!

I am faith-filled and fear-free because . . . I am diligent!
I am patient! I am built for the victory!

Bad is not going to leave you alone just because you are a *good* person. Bad makes its living trying to make you forget about what is good! Bad doesn't care that you go to work on time, give to charitable organizations and help old ladies across the street. *Oh no!* What you call bad times, bad experiences and, sometimes, bad people are going to find their way into your life. Working its way into the lives of good people is what makes bad *so bad!*

Bad is not going to pass you by because you read self-help books, have an I LOVE YOU bumper sticker on your car, own a string of prayer beads or know how to meditate. *Get real!* Bad is going to show up in any disguise available in an attempt to beat you up, knock you down, run you over and tear you apart. *Good!* Show *bad* that you are made of *good.*

You are made of divine power! Infinite wisdom! Pure love and powerfully piercing insight! Show bad that you have unshakeable faith and staying power! Demonstrate to bad that you are put together with the unfathomable intelligence of the *Chief Architect* of the universe, who issued a lifetime warranty on the durability of your goodness. Ward bad off by showing it that you have everything you need, whenever you need it, to do whatever needs to be done. Demonstrate to bad that you know what to do by doing it! Put on your faith boots! Cover yourself with a faith shawl! Pull out your faith tools, and be willing to stand in the faith of good. If you feel a little weary, take a prayer break. Allow yourself to take a meditative pause. Indulge yourself with a deep breath and tune up your faith.

Until today, you may have forgotten that you are good enough to withstand anything that you may call *bad.* Just for today, flex your faith muscles and shake your good fist in bad's face.

Today I am devoted to showing bad just how <u>good</u> I am!

AUGUST 8

I am faith-filled and fear-free because . . .
God is still God after all of these years!

God has not changed His/Her address. Good was not a part
of the urban flight or the rural revitalization program. God
still lives where God has always lived: in your heart. God is
still doing what God has always done: loving you. God is still
who God has always been: the source and supply of all that you need and
desire. God is still doing things in the only way that God has ever done
anything, in the only way God can do anything: eternally.

Some of us don't think God is still around because we haven't visited
God in such a long time. With all the changes and challenges, ups and
downs, additions and subtractions in our lives, our faith in God may
have faded. Some of us may even have concluded that God has gone
away and that there is absolutely no way to find God in the midst of all
the pain, confusion, discontent, disharmony and discord in our own
lives. Nothing could be further from the truth! God is still in the same
place: in the midst of your need. Being the same way: merciful and forgiving. For the same reason: love. Under the same circumstances: waiting for you to acknowledge and accept how much you depend on God.

Until today, you may have been reluctant to visit with God. In fact,
it may have been so long since you have visited, you may have thought
God moved away. Just for today, pay God a visit, in your own heart, and
allow God to catch up with the details of your life.

*Today I am devoted to having a good, long,
visit with God!*

AUGUST 9

I am faith-filled and fear-free because . . . I know what
to do without doing anything at all.

Here's a news flash that will make your day. You don't have to
do anything to get your good in life! You must, however, be
open to *receive* it. For some of us, *receiving* is much more
difficult than *doing*, because we think we know what is required to *earn* our good. Earning puts you in control! Your *doing* is motivated by the belief that *the more you are able to do*, the more you will *get*.
Need we mention the countless numbers out there who are *doing* all that
they can and still do not *get* what they need, deserve or desire? Remember those who *do* very little and *get* more than they could ever need. The
difference between those who do and those who receive is *willingness*.
You must be willing to receive.

Receiving means trusting that God is aware of what you need, desire
and deserve. Deserving, according to God's formula *is a function of
being!* Being open! Being clear! Being grateful! Being focused! Being
committed! Being faithful, and being willing to receive. *Being* is a state
of consciousness developed through unwavering faith and trust. You
trust that you will always have what you need, and that is the foundation
of your faith. When you are open to receive what God is able to do for
you, you stop doing. You learn how to *"Be still and know!"* You know
that your good is on the way, according to God's nature and willingness
to give. You also put your faith in the fact that God is always on time.

Until today, you may have embraced the doing/getting model of living. Just for today, allow people to compliment you. Allow someone to
do something for you without feeling obligated to do anything in return.
Give yourself permission to ask God for everything you desire, faithfully
believing that once you ask, you are in a *divinely timed receiving line*.

*Today I am devoted to opening myself to receive the grace
and goodness of God!*

AUGUST 10

I am faith-filled and fear-free because . . .
I am willing to test what I know.

Life's trials are progressive in nature. They get bigger to make us better. Just when you think you've got it all together, things you have never seen or heard of will present themselves in your life. They will push you, test you and challenge you to do more growing, more learning, more of what we have already done. Very often, when this happens, we are tempted to believe that we have done something wrong or that we missed something. Rarely do we understand that you cannot get too much of a good thing—growing, learning, living are good things! They are good, even when we are forced to retest our skills and abilities over and over again.

Endurance reveals and strengthens character. It also builds faith. As your faith grows, it takes more than it used to to shake you up. It takes more than it did before to make you doubt yourself. It takes more pressure this time than it did last time or the time before that to make you consider giving up. Life always wants to be sure that you are sure! *What about you?* Don't you want to be sure that you can take it? Make it? Work it through it until you can work it out? Of course you do! You want to know that *you* depend on *you* when *you* need *you*. You want to know that you have the requisite amount of faith required to sustain you at all times, at any time. For this reason, it may seem that as you get better, the trials become greater. The truth is, the best students always get the hardest tests because they can handle them!

Until today, you may have thought that a retest in life was the result of a failure. Just for today, be a good student of life. Trust yourself! Rely on what you know! Do what you did before better this time! Be willing to take the progressive steps required to ensure the divine unfolding of your fully empowered Higher Self.

*Today I am devoted to knowing that I keep getting better
and better as I pass through the testing situations
in my life!*

AUGUST 11

I am faith-filled and fear-free because . . .
I can see in the dark.

Have you ever been in a totally pitch-black room where it seems as if there are things everywhere? Even when you know where everything is or where it was the last time you saw it, if the place is pitch-black, everything feels different. In a pitch-black room you stretch out your arms because you expect to crash into a wall or a piece of furniture. Even in a familiar place, once the lights go out you expect something to jump out and attack you. In other words, in the darkness, you expect to get hurt.

There are times in life when you can expect to be in the darkness, when you will not be able to see what is directly in front of you or what is over in the corner. In these times, you must rely on your instincts and your memory. You must also realize that you are not in control—God is! When you find yourself in the darkness of an unfamiliar experience, do not fight God for control! Do not grope, grab or swat off imaginary demons. Rather than shielding yourself from the expectation of pain, *surrender!* Drop your hands to your side. Take a long deep breath. Concentrate on one thing that you know. Remember that God loves you and will protect you no matter where you are. Remember that what you can't see, God can! When you invoke the light of God to lead you and protect you, you will miraculously be able to see the way in or a new way out.

Until today, you may have been frightened by the darkness of your past, the unknown future or the difficulty of the present. Just for today, move faithfully through those *experiences in which you cannot see what is to come. Affirm to yourself,* "Let there be light! Let there be light in my heart. Light in my mind. Light in all of my experiences!"

Today I am devoted to standing firm in the knowledge that God will light the blind spots in my mind and in my life!

AUGUST 12

I am faith-filled and fear-free because . . . I cannot lose
when I play life by the rules!

In a sermon, Dr. Barbara King of Hillside Chapel in Atlanta, Georgia, said, "You are playing on the court of life. Hopefully you have come to win!" She was saying you cannot go through life wondering whose game you are playing, by what rules you are playing or whether or not you are equipped to win. When you arrive on any of life's playing fields, you must know you have come to win! At the same time, you must accept the fact that there will be fouls thrown your way, that you may occasionally strike out. Strikes and fouls do not mean that you will lose the game. They mean you must remain alert! Fouls and strikes indicate that there are others on the field with the same thing in mind: winning!

Do not be surprised if you get pushed, kicked or tackled. Do not be upset if you have to lose a point here or there. Remember, the rules of life do not change, but some people think they can avoid playing by the rules. Know that everyone on the playing field has the same skills and the same opportunities. How they use their skills and approach the opportunities are a reflection of their knowledge of the rules. They cannot strike you out unless you let them! They cannot beat you down unless you let them! And no one can win what you have come to win!

The rules of the game of life are quite simple. Always tell the truth. Never live in fear of anything or anyone. Be conscious of what you are thinking so that you can always think positively. Do everything that you do for the love of doing it. If you devote yourself, your time and your energy to following these rules, have no doubt—you cannot lose!

Until today, you may have believed you had to cheat, cut corners, compete with others in order to win at the game of life. Just for today, try following the rules.

*Today I am devoted to playing life by the rules
in order to win!*

AUGUST 13

I am faith-filled and fear-free because . . .
I know exactly who I am.

How many times should you try and fail before you give up on trying? If you give up, how can you ever expect to succeed? If you give something your best shot, and it doesn't turn out the way you expected, what does it mean? Does it mean you shouldn't want it? What if you still do? These are all good questions for which there is only one answer: *know who you are!* Only when you know who you are will you find the faith you need to get where you are going!

Knowing who you are eliminates the *guess work* in life. Knowing short-circuits hoping, wishing and trying. When you know who you are, you are open to every experience. You know there is always room for self-improvement and that where you are is an opportunity. When you know who you are, you remain open to new insights, new information. You also know that what you learn at any given moment will assist and guide you on the path to where you desire to be. When you know yourself, you know your strengths. You embrace your weaknesses. You know that everything and everyone is pointing you in the right direction: the direction of learning more, embracing more information about exactly who you are. When you know who you are, you are always grateful. You are grateful for all that you have seen. All that you have done. All that you have lost and all that you have received. When you know who you are, you know in this very perfect moment that all that you are is more than enough to answer any question you might have about where to go and what to do.

Until today, you may have been badgering yourself with questions for which there seemed to be no answers. Just for today, allow the questions you ask yourself to teach you more about yourself.

Today I am devoted to allowing my questions about my life to teach me more about myself!

AUGUST 14

I am faith-filled and fear-free because . . . I am aware that fear of failure leads to failure.

What do you do when you have done everything that you know how to do and you are still not moving in the desired direction? How do you stay convinced that you are doing exactly what you need to do, in the way you need to do it? The short answer is, you don't! You don't keep moving when the movement is not taking you anywhere! You have hit a wall, and when that happens, you must not claw at it! You must back up. Take a look around. Let go of your needs and desires, and surrender.

When you hit a wall there is no need to give up! Oh no! We are not talking about that at all! However, when you hit a wall, you must acknowledge that *there is something* you cannot see or do not know about that is standing in your way.

Fear creates walls. Faith will tear down the walls of fear. If you are struggling to get something done and it is not getting done, you could very well be in the way. It could be that your fear of *not* getting it done is keeping it from being done. Your *frustrations* about *how* to get it done will not allow it to be done. Your *anxiety* about *when* it will get done or *if* it can be done are probably blocking the path to getting it done. When you hit a wall, don't attack it! Back up in order to see what it is.

Hitting a wall could mean that the Holy Spirit of life wants to show you something, give you something, or do something for you that it cannot do because you are in the way. If this is the case, the only way you can know for sure is to let go, back up and surrender your fear of the wall.

Until today, you may have believed it was noble or necessary to keep advancing your plans even after you hit a wall. Just for today, do not advance against any wall, human or otherwise. Back up! Let go! Surrender! Listen for your new and improved marching orders!

Today I am devoted to getting clear about any and all walls in my life!

AUGUST 15

I am faith-filled and fear-free because . . . God always
delivers what God has promised to deliver.

Psalm 138 in the scriptures of the Holy Bible reminds us
that, *"God's promises are backed up by the honor of God's
name."* This means, "God's got your back!" This means that
God is *with* you and *for* you. It also means that you can depend on God. It can be very reassuring to know that there is Someone
everywhere who you can rely on. Still, hearing the words may not be
enough. You must *understand* what they mean. When you understand
exactly what it means that God, the creator of all, is standing with you,
for you and behind you, a new realm of possibilities and opportunities
opens up before you. When you understand that what God *has promised
to do,* God *will do,* it takes a load from your shoulders. God has promised
us many things, the most important of all being, "I will *never* leave you
nor foresake you." Boy! What a relief!

Until today, you may have forgotten, or perhaps you were not aware
of all of the promises your Creator has made to you. Just for today, take
a moment to remember and reflect on the good things that God has
promised to do for you and in your life.

*Today I am devoted to remembering the things
that God has promised me!*

AUGUST 16

I am faith-filled and fear-free because . . .
I am never alone.

Do you remember your first day at school?

On the first day of school, you step out of a familiar environment into the mystery of the unknown. Those who you have loved and relied on take you to the door of something big, something pretty scary, and they leave you. You tell yourself you are not going to cry. Yet, at the critical moment, the moment you are forced to stand on your own, the breakdown comes. You stand there fumbling with the buttons on your brand new blouse or shirt, trying to be brave, wanting to run and hide. You might even kick and scream in protest. You may even lose your dignity by begging and pleading for things not to change. No one seems to be listening to you. They are all trying to convince you that it will be okay. Inevitably, one of the big people leans down. In that moment, regardless of what is said, the voice of God speaks directly to your heart, saying, "Fear not, for I am with you."

Each new day and every new experience is just like the first day of school. It is a renewal of God's promise to never leave you. If you can stop crying long enough to hear the promise, someone will take your hand and lead you to the classroom of life. By the end of the day, you may feel a little embarrassed about the way you behaved as you realize there really wasn't anything to be afraid of because you are never alone. God promised to stay with you and God has.

Until today, you may have thought you had passed through the first day of school with flying colors. Just for today, realize that each time you step beyond your comfort zone, it is like entering school for the first time. Also remember that God has promised, if you take one step, God will take two on your behalf.

*Today I am devoted to remembering God's promise
to always be by my side!*

AUGUST 17

I am faith-filled and fear-free because . . . I know that
my greatest challenge will strengthen me.

A promise is a promise! Let's take a look at the promises we
have broken. Perhaps in doing so we will discover why we
do not expect God to keep Her/His promises to us.

How many times have you promised *not to* do something and found yourself doing it anyway? How many times have you
promised *to do* something that you have never gotten around to doing?
How many times have you made a promise you knew someone was depending on, yet for one reason or another, *you failed to do* what you
promised to do? How many times have you made a promise to impress
someone? Or to get them off your back? How many times have you
made a promise knowing that you did not have the strength, courage,
stamina or resources to keep the promise you were making? How often
do you think about *your broken promises* when you need to rely on one of
God's promises?

Thank goodness God is not like you! Thank goodness God cannot
forget what S/He promised, nor can God go back on God's word. Thank
goodness that when God's promises were made, there were no people
around to impress or shake off. Thank goodness that when God made
promises, there was one and only one motivation. It was to remind you
that when you make a promise, you can keep it because God has promised you, *"I will strengthen you. I will help you."* Thank goodness God is
there to help you fulfill every promise that you make. Thank goodness
God doesn't get angry or upset when you fail to keep your promises.

Until today, you may not have realized the power of a promise. Just
for today, be aware of all the promises you make and be aware that God's
help is available to insure that you keep your promises.

*Today I am devoted to relying on God's help in keeping
all of the promises I make!*

AUGUST 18

I am faith-filled and fear-free because . . .
I know what I have to do.

Along with God's promises come certain *commands*. We are not talking about the Ten Commandments. Nor are we talking about those edicts that pertain to a particular faith or religion. We are talking about the *loving commands* that God continues to whisper in our hearts, even when we don't want to hear them. We are addressing those things that we know deep in our souls that we must do purely for the sake of our own good. These commands drive us, inspire us and motivate us. They keep us going. These loving commands instruct us to do things that we know are best for us, and when we find reasons and excuses not to do them, they echo in our hearts as soon as we get in trouble. They command us to do things that make us proud to be who we are, things we can pat ourselves on the back for doing even when those around us do not seem to take notice or care. Only God recognizes and rewards us for doing things that we don't always like to do but are in direct response to the command God has placed in our hearts: *"Never grow tired of doing good!"* The deeds we do in response to this command are the only things upon which we can build our faith in God, in ourselves, and in the process of life.

Until today, you may not have understood why you continue to do the good things that you do, even when it seems no one notices or cares. Just for today, do good knowing it is in response to a command from God.

*Today I am devoted to doing good for myself
and those around me!*

I am faith-filled and fear-fear because . . . I have
something to do and someone to be.

There is a saying that *"Your family tree can put a noose around
your neck!"* This means that some of us are born into families and experiences that are well below the place to which
we are destined to rise. Even when we know and understand
this, we may feel guilty about achieving what could be considered by
un-achievers as *"too much."* We continually question ourselves, wondering why we should be so lucky, so blessed to be able to crawl out of the
black hole of pain or dysfunction we have come to know as the norm.
We question if we are being selfish. Some of us wonder if our abilities
and talents are a fluke of some kind. Poor creatures! We have no idea that
every accomplishment, every success is the result of God's command to
"Come ye out from among them!"

We do not get *divine brownie points* for remaining with people who
are not moving. In fact, staying where we are may quell any motivation
others may have to move forward. *"Come ye out from among them"* is
God's way of saying go out! Do it! Use what God has given you to make
yourself better or make a better life for yourself. *"Come ye out from
among them"* is God's way of assuring you that you can depend on God's
promises. If you are not sure what the promises are, *re-read* the messages
of the past five days. Then, pass what you have learned on to someone
you know who is not moving.

Until today, you may have questioned why you seem able to do what
no one else you know has been able to do. You may have felt guilty about
your success or underestimated your accomplishments. Just for today,
remember and realize that you are the living embodiment of God's
promises. What you do teaches others what they, too, can do.

*Today I am devoted to moving out beyond what is normal
and what is expected!*

I am faith-filled and fear-free because . . . I know that
I don't have to know.

Most people will do everything in their power to avoid admitting *I don't know!* When you do admit *I don't know,*
some people respond as if you are crazy! Adamantly they
want to know *what do you mean you don't know?* Contrary to
popular belief, when you *don't know* and can admit it, you are in line for
a great healing or a magnificent blessing!

Few *know-it alls* are blessed with new insights or information. When
you are willing to acknowledge that you don't know, you open yourself
to all sorts of information and assistance from life. Not knowing may
send you on a search. It may open your mind and your eyes to things you
have never even thought of before. The things you discover in your
search may bless you at some later date, or the search may heal some
long-held fear. What a blessing!

An admission of *not knowing* is a sign of great faith and trust. It
means trusting that even when you don't know, *you know that when you
need to know, you will know!* An admission of *not knowing* is an act of
great humility that leads to the healing of the ego. It is the ego that fosters an internal sense of inadequacy. When you feel or believe you are in
some way inadequate, it will always feel as if you have something to
prove. Admitting that you don't know is a very loving way to acknowledge that you are absolutely fine with who you are and that you are not
afraid to admit it. What else do you need to know?

Until today, you may have believed that it was your duty and responsibility to know everything. Just for today, be open and willing to
admit what you don't know. Open yourself to receive new information
from expected and unexpected sources.

Today I am devoted to acknowledging what I don't know,
finding new paths of discovery and incorporating new
information into my data bank!

AUGUST 21

I am faith-filled and fear-free because . . . I am not afraid
to look at my life.

If someone wants to insult you, they might look at you and
say, *"Get a life!"* This is not a bad thing to consider. It is only
when you know that you don't have a life that the thought
of trying to get one will *freak you out!*

When you are twenty-something, the quest to *get a life* is your focus,
and you probably have fun doing it. When you are thirty-something,
you can expect to revisit this goal at various times in response to a variety
of transformational experiences. When, however, you are older, hearing
the words *get a life* could shock you. You could panic. You could become
seriously depressed. You could get angry. If you are one of those people
who have missed the *lifeboat,* or have been afraid of the *waters of life,* the
real question may be *what does it mean to have a life?*

When you *have a life,* you can stand alone in what is true about you
and what you believe to be true. You do what feels right for you, even
when it means that those around you do not agree with what you are
doing. You mind your own business, leaving it up to others to do the
same. To really have a life, a good life, means sticking with something
long enough to see if it works for you, admitting when it doesn't, moving on without fear or anger and exacting the blessings from the lessons,
because you know that every lesson is a blessing.

Until today, you may never have considered whether the life you
have is the life you really want. Just for today, check out your life. Ask
yourself, "Am I doing the things that are important to me?" *"Am I learning and growing in response to the things I am doing?"* *"Am I willing to
make the changes required to create the life that I desire to experience?"* In
asking yourself these questions, remember that the lifeboat sails best on
the sea of faith. *Are you sailing or sinking?*

*Today I am devoted to getting the kind of life
I desire to live!*

AUGUST 22

I am faith-filled and fear-free because . . . I am on a
search-and-recovery mission, led by a divine rescue squad.

Emergency! Emergency! Emergency! It is time for a search-
and-recovery mission! It is time to recover your *Selfhood!* It
is time to search out fear, doubt and anything else that promotes and supports self-sabotage. It is time to rediscover
your mission and purpose in life. It is time to recover your confidence! It
is time to recover your joy! It is time to recover your faith!

Emergency! Emergency! Emergency! The Divine rescue squad is
here with a dose of forgiveness and faith that will help you destroy all internal enemies. When you find the enemies that diminish your Self-
value, you will recover your divinity. Is that the enemy anger? *Where?*
Over there under the fallout of a break-up! Is that the enemy hatred?
Where? Right there! It's joining forces with the memory of what was
done and how it was done! Smash those memories with forgiveness! Do
you see the enemy resentment? *Where?* Right there! It is next to the
enemy comparing yourself to everyone else. What is that hiding under
the need to please? The need to be liked? Call in the troops! You need a
transfusion of self-love and self-acceptance!

Emergency! Emergency! Emergency! Search for your pride. Recover
it from the feeling of failure. Search for your honor. Recover it from the
feeling of powerlessness and victimization. Search for your purpose. Recover it from disbelief. Your life is depending on *you!* It is time to recover
the faith that no matter what happens, you will not be defeated.

Until today, you may not have realized that within your own
thoughts, there are enemies who could be destroying your faith and diminishing your sense of *Self.* Just for today, perform a search-and-
recovery mission. Think about what you are thinking about, and apply
the appropriate treatment to the enemy.

*Today I am devoted to searching for mental and emotional
enemies and recovering my Self!*

AUGUST 23

I am faith-filled and fear-free because . . . my heart
always knows what I need to know.

There are some things you simply must ponder in your own
heart. There are things that you would ask of others which
can only be answered in your own heart. There are things
that others cannot see for you and say to you. If they could or
would, their answers would have no meaning for you. You would not be
able to recognize the divine gift being offered just to you. Some things
are simply *matters of the heart*. In response to some things you face in life,
only your heart knows what is right for you, what is good for you and
what is best for you. *Have faith!* Your heart has the answer that you cannot seem to get from anywhere else. When your heart has something it
wants you to know, it will shut down all other means of communication
just to make sure that you can hear and will hear what it needs to say.

Until today, you may have believed that there is someone else who
knows or somewhere else you need to go to get certain answers about
your life. Just for today, ask in your own heart about those things for
which there seem to be no answer.

*Today I am devoted to making an inquiry and receiving a
divine answer from my own heart!*

I am faith-filled and fear-free because . . . I have
a wonderful imagination that imagines
wonderful things for my life.

Can you imagine what would happen if for just one moment, with every fiber of your being, you allowed yourself
to believe that you can have life exactly as you choose to
have it? Can you imagine what would happen if you believed
with your hair, your eyebrows and lashes, with your fingers and toes,
that every good thing you ever wished would happen, could happen
right now? Let your central nervous system and all the lobes of your
brain be filled with the grandest vision of life you can imagine. Allow
your feet, legs, arms and hands to think about all of the good things you
would choose for yourself in this life. Allow the thought to move up
your spine into the base of your neck until it spreads out across your
shoulders. At that point, let the thought of having a life filled with joy
and peace drop down into the pit of your stomach. Then allow it to
stream into your heart. If you could imagine your life in this way, for just
a moment, your life would be an experience of unlimited possibilities.

Feel the thought of a peaceful life, a prosperous life, nourishing your
body. All of its organs and systems. Feel it getting hot. Feel it rise up in
you. Feel it as it rushes through your entire being, growing in intensity,
forcing you to throw your head back and shout, OH YEAH!!! Think it! Feel
it! Do it! Can you just imagine what would happen?

Until today, you may have limited, edited or restricted your thoughts
about the good things that could happen in your life. Just for today, allow
yourself to be totally involved with just one good thought. Give yourself
permission to get your entire being involved. Then watch to see what
happens.

*Today I am devoted to being totally involved with good
thoughts about one good thing!*

AUGUST 25

I am faith-filled and fear-free because . . . every concern
I have is a concern of God's.

God knows all about your troubles. God knows why you are
crying and how long you have been crying. God knows
what you are struggling with and where you are stuck. God
knows why you continue to struggle with things God has already taken away from you. God also knows why you keep going back
and picking them up. God knows what you tell yourself and why you
believe this is the best point of view. God knows where you are, where
you are going and why you believe that you should be further along the
path. God knows all the questions you have and why you still have no
answers. God knows your challenges, and God knows your potential.
God knows all of the *ins and outs* of why you feel in or out of touch with
God. God knows *you*. Whether you know God is not important. What
is important is for you to *know* that when it feels most like there is no
one, it simply isn't true. There is always *Someone* who is as concerned
about your concerns as you are. God also knows that what you believe
and put your faith in can make a world of difference in what you know
and don't know.

Until today, you may have believed that your concerns were yours
alone. Just for today, consider that there is *Someone* who cares about
your concerns. Whether you call this *Someone* God really doesn't matter.
What matters is that you know and believe that there is Someone who
will share your concerns if you will let Them.

*Today I am devoted to sharing my concerns with
Someone who cares!*

AUGUST 26

I am faith-filled and fear-free because . . .
having one grain of what is true will eradicate
a million grains of what is not true.

The following is an affirmation. An affirmation is a statement that embodies the truth. If there is something you
want to know about yourself or your life, faithfully and rev-
erently repeat this affirmation three times and ask yourself
the question. It is best to ask questions about yourself rather than asking
about another person because their truth may be none of your business.
Once the affirmation is repeated and the question asked, remain still
and listen for the answer. If the answer does not come right away, have
faith! Sometimes the truth is more than you can handle at the moment.
At the right time, in the right way, the truth will make itself known
to you.

I believe in the power of truth.

I believe in the presence of truth.

Truth cannot be buried or hidden.

The truth must be revealed.

I now experience the essence of truth as it moves through me.

The Spirit of truth now envelops me.

The Spirit of truth now infuses me.

I am filled with the light of truth.

I am filled with the power of truth.

I am filled with the presence of truth.

The truth is revealed to me now.

Until today, you may not have known how to get to the truth of a
pressing matter in your life. Just for today, ask the truth to reveal itself to
you. Remember that what you ask for, you will receive!

*Today I am devoted to knowing the truth about
myself and my life!*

AUGUST 27

I am faith-filled and fear-free because . . . I know
the power of the truth.

You know something. You may not know how you came to
know it, or why you know it, but you know it must be told.
Finally, with all selfish motivations laid to the side, you tell
someone something about themselves that you know they
need to know. Much to your surprise, they act like they didn't even hear
you or that what you said was a *dose of poison!* Should this happen, *do not
be alarmed!* Just because someone did not hear, failed to respond or chose
not to acknowledge or accept the truth you offered does not mean that
you were out of place for saying it. When you consider that the truth has
a way of putting people in their place, it is easy to understand why it is
often not accepted. None of which has anything to do with you!

You must be mindful, however, that we are talking here about *the
truth*. Not *your truth* or truth as you know it. The difference is that *the
truth* is always clear and spoken with a loving intent. *The truth* always
eliminates mental or emotional darkness and promotes healing. While
the truth can be shocking, it never diminishes or devalues a person. Only
when a person is unwilling to grow will they resist hearing and knowing
the truth. Should you happen to be the one to bring forth the truth to a
person who is not ready to hear it, have faith! When your heart is pure
and you bring forth the truth, know that it is heard. However, even
when it is heard, it is up to the listener to determine what to do with the
truthful insight you are offering.

Until today, you may have shied away from telling someone the
truth you know about them. Conversely, you may have told someone
the truth only to have them ignore it. Just for today, tell the truth without any expectation of what the response should be or will be.

*Today I am devoted to telling the truth and
allowing it to stand on its own!*

AUGUST 28

I am faith-filled and fear-free because . . .
I am a celebration of love.

Beneath all the pain, the disappointment, the resentment and fear that your life will never be as you want it to be, there is love. There is a memory of the touch, the feel, the excitement of love. There is a yearning to know and experience that expression of love. Go there! Be there! Rest there! Celebrate the love that you buried in your heart.

When you celebrate love, the unconditional love that lies beneath all the experiences you have witnessed and participated in, you find a degree of understanding that diminishes mental and emotional anguish. The love beneath the hurt and pain of your life will not allow you to blame anyone. It will stop you from judging yourself and others. The love beneath your pain and the fear of pain will help you to become aware of all the things that you told yourself about love that were just fantasies. Love will remind you not to be upset when the fantasy is revealed. It will remind you of the truth you knew in the first place. The love that lies beneath what happened, however it happened, will remind you that you haven't been rejected, abandoned, abused or defeated. You were simply being given an opportunity to remember that there is a place within you in which you can find everything you need or thought you lost or wished that you had more of. Go there now! Be there now! Rest there now! The only thing that you need to do to find the love in you is to remember, God's love has brought you this far.

Until today, you may have forgotten that beneath everything that you have experienced, there is God's love. Just for today, look for the love within and beneath every experience. Remember all of the love that you have given and received. Fill your heart and mind with thoughts of love. Then celebrate yourself for recognizing love.

Today I am devoted to remembering and celebrating love no matter what else is going on!

AUGUST 29

I am faith-filled and fear-free because . . .
I have been fire-proofed.

There is a simple procedure that you probably learned in kindergarten that will serve you well today. This procedure taught you what to do if your clothes caught on fire. It consists of three simple steps. Stop! Drop! Roll!

When there is a fire in your life, a problem that you have been unable to stop the spread of, do not try to fight it on your own. Don't run for the roofs! Don't try to fill a bucket or pry the extinguisher off the wall. STOP! Stop all movement! Stop all your attempts to fix it or make it better. Stop, and then DROP! Drop your defenses! Drop your excuses! *Drop all plans!* Drop the need to know anything! Drop the need to do anything! Stop and drop to your knees! On your knees, in prayer, is the position you must assume if you want the *Fire Marshall* to put the fire out. God is the fire marshal, and when you roll the situation over into God's hands, you can rest assured that help is on the way.

There are some fires in your life that you simply cannot put out. These are the Stop! Drop! and Roll over to God problems. These problems are like fires that will spread unless you do something quick! These are the problems that have been burning in your life for so long that you are about to lose everything. The heat of the problem is so intense, you are now on the verge of a melt-down. You can't think! You don't feel! You are afraid to move out! When a problem becomes this type of fire, you cannot stop to *gather memorabilia!* You cannot call friends and family to alert them! You were prepared for this a long time ago! You know what to do! Stop! Drop! Roll the problem over to God.

Until today, you may have been running around believing that you could put out the fires in your life. Just for today, go back to kindergarten. Stop! Drop! And Roll! Have faith that you will not get burned.

Today I am having a fire drill! I am practicing
how to stop, drop and roll!

AUGUST 30

I am faith-filled and fear-free because . . . I am being
transformed from the inside out.

Here is a prayer of faith.

I now call the activity of the Holy Spirit into every cell,
every tissue, every organ in my being. I invite the Holy
Spirit to lovingly transform every energy, every belief, every
idea, every understanding, every decision, every expectation, every judgment, every motivation and every behavior, bringing them into alignment with the *perfect will* of God, so that I may take the next step toward
the divine plan for my life.

I now call the activity of the Holy Spirit into every cell, every tissue,
every organ in my being. I invite the Holy Spirit to lovingly transform
every energy, every belief, every idea, every understanding, every decision, every expectation, every judgment, every motivation and every behavior, bringing them into alignment with the *perfect peace* of God, so
that I may take the next step toward the divine plan for my life.

I now call the activity of the Holy Spirit into every cell, every tissue,
every organ in my being. I invite the Holy Spirit to lovingly transform
every energy, every belief, every idea, every understanding, every decision, every expectation, every judgment, every motivation and every behavior, bringing them into alignment with the *perfect love* of God, so that
I may take the next step toward the divine plan for my life. For all I have
received and all that is yet to come, I am so very grateful! And So It Is!

Until today, you may not have known how to move your life to the
next level. Just for today, put faith and confidence into your prayers.

*Today I am devoted to allowing the Holy Spirit to guide
me into the next step of my personal growth
and spiritual development!*

AUGUST 31

I am faith-filled and fear-free because . . . I am learning
to swim through painful experiences.

If you have ever watched a child learning how to swim, you
have witnessed faith in action. It is obvious that the child,
standing before the pool or the ocean, is thinking, *"I'm not
going in there!"* With a little support, the child may eventually
stick his toes in the water. If the water is warm, he can be enticed to put
one whole foot in the water. That is enough for the first try. On the next
try, you might see the child stand in the water up to his knees. If he happens to feel particularly safe or confident, he might let his butt get wet.
That is quite enough. Step by step, day by day, with the right kind of support and encouragement, the avid nonswimmer will eventually immerse
his entire body in the water. The real test comes, however, when he is
knocked down by a wave or when a nearby swimmer splashes water in his
face. In that moment, the little swimmer must decide whether or not he
can conquer the challenge, the fear, of having water up the nose.

Those of us who are not living fully because we are afraid of the deep
waters of heartache are just like the child learning how to swim. We
must learn to do it step by step. Should we get knocked down or
splashed, we must decide in that very moment whether or not we will
continue swimming. Fortunately, faith is the *lifeguard* on duty. Faith can
pull you out of the water. Faith can help you dry off your face. Faith will
watch over you as you try again, step by step, until you learn how to
swim on your own.

Until today, you may have allowed difficult experiences and painful
memories to keep you out of the sometimes turbulent waters of life. Just
for today, stick one body part in the water. Do one thing you swore you
would never do again. Let faith hold you up as you swim through it.

*Today I am devoted to living by faith and opening myself to
a fuller experience of life!*

SEPTEMBER

TRUST

If there is something worth putting your <u>but</u> on the line for, you must put your <u>but</u> on the line.

If your <u>but</u> gets cut off, you must trust that you will be able to get along without it.

As long as you have a <u>but</u> to rest on, you will not trust yourself.

When you figure out how to get along without a <u>but</u>, you will know the meaning of trust.

SEPTEMBER 1

I experience and express the power of trust because . . .
I am learning to trust myself.

Trust is a simple process. Either you trust or you don't trust. You either trust yourself or you don't trust yourself. When you don't trust yourself, you will not trust other people. When you do not trust other people, you cannot trust the process of living or loving in which other people are involved. When you don't trust loving other people, you cannot live openly or fully. When you are not open to living fully, it means that you expect to be hurt. This expectation makes you constantly afraid that you can't handle the pain. When you don't believe you can handle something, it means you don't trust yourself. This is exactly where we started.

Until today, you may have believed that trust was something you learned to do in response to your experiences or that you have learned not to trust as a result of your experiences. Just for today, consider and reflect on the beliefs you hold and decisions you have made about trusting yourself.

*Today I am devoted to developing a deeper level
of self-trust!*

SEPTEMBER 2

I experience and express the power of trust because . . .
I understand the connection between trust and faith.

The concepts of trust and faith are so closely linked, it is often difficult to distinguish one from the other. You would be right if you said that without trust you cannot have faith. It is also safe to say it the other way around. Faith is the ability to see the invisible, to know that a thing exists before you see it. Trust is knowing that the invisible actually exists. Faith is the magnetic power of the heart to attract what it desires. Trust is the ability to have the desire. Faith is the substance, the sum total of what you believe to be real. Trust is knowing that what you believe in is real for you. Faith is the box that trust comes in. Trust is the substance that fills the box of faith. Faith is the cake. Trust is the butter you use to make the icing and the cake.

When you have faith in something, trust is what allows you to believe that your faith will bear fruit. When you have faith, you develop trust. When you trust, faith is not required. You already know.

Until today, you might have been confused about the slight differences between trust and faith. Just for today, allow your trust and faith to stand side by side. Put your faith in a heart's desire, then trust that your faith will bring it to pass.

Today I am devoted to faithfully trusting that I will experience the things I put my trust and faith in!

SEPTEMBER 3

I experience and express the power of trust because . . .
I always begin within.

Trust is never out there. The soul essence that we call trust resides within you. Trust is a decision. It is a reflection of what you have decided to believe.

Trust is not about being comfortable. It is about being willing to move beyond your comfort zone when there is absolutely no evidence that you will be supported. Trust is not about looking for evidence that you are doing things right every step of the way as you move toward the end result. Trust is about keeping the end results in mind no matter what steps you have to take to get there, or how bad you feel while you are stepping. Trust is not about the work you have to do in life being easy or having other people support you in getting through the work. It is about your ability to do the hard work without losing sight of why you are doing it, when other people try to convince you that you should be doing something else. Trust is not about getting something back for the work you do as a sign that you are doing the right thing. It is your ability to keep doing the work even when it looks like there is nothing coming back.

Think of it this way. Trust is based on your ability to stand your ground and rely on your own abilities, knowing that no matter what happens, you will be better off than you were at the beginning. Anything less than this is not trust. It is magical thinking that will take you on a carpet ride to nowhere.

Until today, you may not have been clear about what it means to trust or how you develop trust. Just for today, examine your beliefs about your ability to trust yourself and the process of life. Also explore why you trust some things and people more than others. Remember that self-trust is the foundation of your ability to trust.

Today I am devoted to understanding and embracing the
true value and meaning of trust!

I experience and express the power of trust because . . .
I am no longer willing to betray myself.

Let's say you put your trust in someone only to discover that they are untrustworthy. Now you are hurt. You are disappointed. You are also *mad as all get out!* The question is, are you angry with the person who betrayed your trust? Or are you angry with yourself for trusting them? If you are like most people, you will acknowledge that you are more angry with yourself.

When we open ourselves to another person, we expect them to behave. When they don't, we think we should have known better. There is, however, a flip side to this coin. Somewhere in the process of trusting them, *we forgot to trust ourselves!* When this happens, we feel, shall we say, *stupid.* Rather than admit this, we put the heat on the other person. It is easier to be mad at someone else than it is to sit around feeling stupid. There is always a lesson in betrayal. *Learn to trust yourself!*

There is a way to avoid being on the stupid end of being betrayed. Go back to the beginning of the experience and ask yourself a series of questions. Did you miss a sign? Did you ignore a signal? Did you see the potential of untrustworthiness and call it something else? If you did, that is why you feel stupid. The actions of the other person are simply reminding you *not to do that again!*

Until today, you may have been angry at someone who betrayed you when the truth may be that you betrayed yourself. Just for today, make a list of all the experiences in which you feel you have been betrayed. Include a brief synopsis of what occurred between you and the other person or people. After reviewing the list, ask yourself: *When did I first see the signs? Why did I ignore the signs? What was I really trying to accomplish?* Remember what you saw and felt. Next time, trust yourself!

Today I am devoted to understanding the difference between betrayal and self-betrayal!

SEPTEMBER 5

I experience and express the power of trust because . . .
I put my trust in the right things for the right reasons.

While many of us may think that we do not trust ourselves or others, we are always demonstrating some degree of trust. Trust is an essential element of our daily lives. We trust that when we go to sleep at night, we will wake up in the morning. When we are ill, we trust doctors and nurses to tell us how to get better. We trust banks with our money. We trust teachers with our children and mechanics with our cars. Still, for one reason or another, when it comes to our one-on-one relationships with other people, trust seems to be difficult. The truth is that we can and do trust. Unfortunately, we sometimes put our trust in the *wrong* things.

Once we are hurt by someone, we trust that we will be hurt again. We trust that the politicians who make up the government will lie to us. We trust that on any given day something horrible could happen to us. In preparation, we live behind alarms and fences, and we cross the street anytime we see some *dangerous* looking person coming in our direction. For many, the *issue is not* how do you learn to trust? The issue is *how do you learn to put your trust in the right things?*

There is a light of love and compassion in every human being. If each of us were to set an intention to be loving and compassionate at all times, our lights would begin to shine. As we learned to *see* the light in everyone and to *be* the light to everyone, we would learn to trust the light. Learning to trust your light does not mean that you will never face or experience difficulty. But you can trust your light to reveal even one untrustworthy person, and you can trust that your light will let you know how to handle it.

Until today, you may have believed that you had to learn how to trust. Just for today, examine the things that you put your trust in and ask yourself, *"Why?"*

*Today I am devoted to allowing the love and compassion
of my soul to shine through me in all situations!*

SEPTEMBER 6

I experience and express the power of trust because . . .
I am worthy of my own trust.

You don't have to *know* that you are doing the right thing. All you need to know is that you are doing what *feels* right for you. Trust what you feel! Do it!

You don't have to *know* that you are doing things in the *right* way. All you need to know is that you are doing the *very best* you can, based on what *feels* right for you. Trust what you feel! Do it!

You don't have to *know* how to do things perfectly the first time around. All you need to know is that your *intent* and your *actions* are *honorable and honest;* that you are doing the very best you can, based on what feels right for you. Trust what you feel! Do it!

You don't have to have the *approval* of your family, community or elected officials! All you need to know is that you are doing what feels right for you; with an honest and honorable intent, to the best of your ability. Trust what you feel! Do it!

When you learn to trust what you feel, the feelings become clearer and the trust grows.

Until today, you may have been waiting for the right time, the right way, and the approval of the right people before taking action. Just for today, trust what you feel! Take action!

Today I am devoted to trusting what I feel and taking the action that feels right for me!

SEPTEMBER 7

I experience and express the power of trust because . . .
I know how to stand up to the dark forces.

Can you remember a time when after pulling yourself up out of the muck and mire of *feeling bad* and *doing bad,* you have found the joy of doing good, only to have *someone bad* or *something bad* push you back down into the mud?

There is a dark force, an energy, which can enter your life at the most inconvenient times, in very disruptive ways. Some would call this force *Satan* or *the devil.* Others might say that it is *negative energy* or *bad vibes.* If or when this force enters your life, you might call it trouble, problems, a crisis, a challenge, difficulties or *issues.* Whatever you call it, be aware! When the dark force enters your life, it has only one intent: to whip your butt! That's right! The darkness is out to beat you down. If you are smart, you won't fight back. You will surrender, cover your face, pray and trust!

If you try to defend yourself against darkness with brute force, you are going to get beat up *very badly.* Your vision could be smashed. Your hopes and dreams could be shattered. In the realm of darkness, you better know how to protect yourself.

Don't try to fight the darkness alone! Darkness is not afraid of you! When you know that you are getting beat up by the dark forces, don't try to prove anything to anyone. *Lie down! Cover your face! Play dead!* Raise your voice in prayer, trust that your help is on the way and remember, *"God is my defense and my defender!"*

Until today, you may have thought that it was noble to try to fight off the dark forces when they entered your life. Just for today, stop trying to prove that you are stronger than the negative energies and dark forces around you. Protect yourself with prayer and trust.

*Today I am devoted to calling on the Great Defender
if I am confronted by forces of darkness!*

SEPTEMBER 8

I experience and express the power of trust because . . .
I have a clear understanding of what it takes
to make things happen!

People love to tell how life is unfair, unjust and inequitable. Here is the real story. *Life is a process of sowing and reaping!* The time, resources and effort you put forth is *your sowing.* What you get in return is *your reaping.* People will tell you stories designed to make you believe that you cannot trust the process of life to bring you your just rewards. In telling their stories, they often leave out the chapter that says *you must put forth a disciplined effort of sowing!* Perhaps they are just *confused.*

A focused, consistent, positively motivated and disciplined character is essential to making your life story have a happy ending. When you give your all, *you can trust* that all you have given will be returned! The day you doubt, your sowing is depleted. The day you voice fear, your energy is uprooted. This is where trust comes in. You must trust the process enough to be committed to sowing your energy in a disciplined way.

If you know that you have been ignoring details, avoiding difficulties and cutting corners, don't blame the process! Don't confuse the absence of discipline with the unreliability of trust. This is a process of life and living that you can always trust. The only time you cannot trust the process to have a happy ending is when your lip-service is greater than your disciplined effort.

Until today, you may have been making up a tale about what you want without doing what was required to make it happen. Just for today, till your mental soil with determination. Fertilize your emotional soil with positive words. Plant the seed of your heart's desire with your disciplined efforts.

Today I am devoted to being disciplined and trusting the
process of sowing and reaping!

SEPTEMBER 9

I experience and express the power of trust because . . .
I put my energy behind the things I put my trust in.

There are people who could be called *Godless*. For them, God
does not exist. In fact, if you ask them, they might tell you
that they are the only God they know or desire to know. You
might think of these people as *do-it-for-yourselfers*. In themselves they trust.

In spite of their lack of belief as far as God is concerned, these people
lead normal, healthy lives. You might even determine that many of them
are quite successful in the *worldly* sense. They are professionally stable
and financially secure. They have mates and are pretty decent parents.
They may even be loyal and trustworthy friends. Although some of us
would be horrified at the thought of trying to get by without some connection to God, so-called *Godless* people seem to make it through life
fairly well. In fact, some of them seem to make out a great deal better
than the *God-knowing, God-loving, God-fearing* folks.

Whatever you put your faith and the energy of your belief into will
work for you if you trust it to work. Trust, not what you trust, or what
you call what you trust, is the key ingredient. If you believe in yourself,
if you trust your judgment and back it up with your sincere energy and
effort, chances are you will hit the bull's-eye. It would probably take a little pressure off of you if you understood the concepts of grace, mercy
and the divine love of God. You might have a lot less stress if you could
lift your hands and voice every now and then just to say, "Thank you!"
for Divine order, Divine timing and Divine presence. But none of this is
necessary unless you believe it is necessary.

Until today, you may have believed that, "In God I Trust!" was a pre-
requisite to a successful life. Just for today, allow yourself and others the
freedom to choose the name of what they believe in. Examine how you
trust rather than the name you call what you trust.

*Today I am devoted to examining and exploring
the energy I give to the things I trust!*

SEPTEMBER 10

I experience and express the power of trust because . . .
I assume that what I do will be successful.

A successful life is the result of making the assumption that
you will be successful. Make the assumption that you *know
who you are*. Make the assumption that you know *what you
want to do*. When you are not sure, assume that you will figure it out. Make the assumption that you *will do* what you want to do. If
you put your trust into positive assumptions, they will undoubtedly
work on your behalf.

Many people assume an identity that is given to them based on the
assumptions other people make about them. You may try to live up to external assumptions. In some cases, you may have to live *down* to these assumptions. Under an *assumed identity*, you might make the assumption
that life for you will be hard. If you lay claim to a negative assumption, it
too will work on your behalf.

Then there are those who *assume drama* and terrorize themselves.
They assume that someone is out to get them. They assume that the difficulties they faced in the past are waiting for them in the future. They
assume that if they were to fall down, they will be unable to get up. They
assume that while they are down, someone will come along and kick
them. Of course if they get kicked in the face, they will incur hundreds
of thousands of dollars worth dental and plastic surgery bills. Has it ever
occurred to you why the unpleasant things you assume will happen
often do? Perhaps if you put your trust in some positive assumptions,
they too would take place.

Until today, you may not have realized the power of an assumption.
In fact, you may have been giving your power over to an assumed identity or a dramatically negative assumption. Just for today, begin to make
positive assumptions about yourself, your life and others in your life.

*Today I am devoted to assuming the best
about myself and my life!*

SEPTEMBER 11

I experience and express the power of trust because . . .
I am relying on the presence of the Divine Troops
to come to my assistance.

There is a powerful presence that surrounds you at all times. This presence is called the *God Squad*. The God Squad opens doors of opportunity and closes the portals of self-defeat. The God Squad nourishes your spirit and nurtures your mind. When you need to see something, the God Squad is your eyes. When you need to hear something, the God Squad whispers to you. Should you need to know something, the God Squad makes it plain, in a way that only you can understand.

Think of the God Squad as a legion or an army of super beings, whose mission it is to advance your intentions and efforts. These beings will lead you or follow you. They will guard you or expose you. Don't worry! The God Squad will never turn against you. It will keep your best interests in the forefront of your mind.

It is important that you become familiar with each member of the God Squad. The General of the squad is *truth*. Look for him all the time. He will be assisted by the Majors, *trust* and *faith*. They will always lead you back to the General. The Captain of the squad is *forgiveness*, whose First Lieutenant is *surrender*. These are the two who execute the battle plan. Reporting to the Master Sergeant, *perseverance*, is the Private First Class, *gratitude*. If you get into trouble with either of these two you will face a court martial in front of your *belief*.

Until today, you may have thought that you were marching through life on your own. Just for today, use the energy and ammunition of the *God Squad* for your protection and your defense.

*Today I am devoted to calling upon the power and
intelligence of the God Squad!*

SEPTEMBER 12

I experience and express the power of trust because . . .
I know I cannot take the easy way out.

There is always a better way! When your back is against the wall, do not be tempted to take the easy way out. Avoid taking the short cut. Never allow the pressure of the moment to force you to do something that is dishonest or dishonorable. Before you strike out in terror or anger, call for the strength, energy and presence of mind to do what is best for everyone involved. No matter what happens to you, you will be better off if you look for a better way of doing things. Trust that no matter what stands before you, you can handle it by taking the high road.

The high road is *any action* taken or *any word spoken* with the intention of restoring peace, invoking healing or advancing love. It can be difficult to keep your eye on the road when you feel like you are being dishonored or harmed in some way. Fear can also make you lose sight of the road—the fear of being abandoned, rejected *or discovered*. How you respond when you are faced with one of these fears is understandable. Unfortunately, in the universe, it may not be excusable.

When you are stressed, pressured or simply afraid, it is easy to be lured into being dishonest. If you are angry, it is understandable that you would want to strike out. Let's face it, in those situations when it seems that telling a lie will save you, chances are you will *consider* telling the lie. *Don't do it!* There is always a better way. When you deliberately trespass the boundaries of what is good, honest, loving and harmonious, there will be hell to pay. Don't be the one who has to pay it.

Until today, you may have allowed the pressures and stress of your life to make you sink down or act low down. Just for today, look for the high road. Refuse to say anything or do anything that will not create or support peace, healing and love.

Today I am devoted to choosing the mental, emotional and spiritual high road in all situations and experiences!

I experience and express the power of trust because . . .
I believe that who I am is enough.

When you secretly feel inadequate or believe that who you are is not enough for the world, you will do more and give more than is required in order to experience fulfillment. Try as you may, it never works. Rev. Michael Beckwith, author and publisher of *The 40-Day Mind-Fast Soul Feast* says, "You must enter every experience in life with a sense of *feel-full-ness!*"

Feel-full-ness means that when you walk into any situation, you know that you have what it takes to make a valuable contribution to the experience. This doesn't mean that you should act like you know everything or project that you can do everything. It means that you are full of yourself, within yourself, in a very loving and positive way.

Having a sense of feel-full-ness gives you the advantage of knowing that you have nothing to prove. You also know that there is nothing that anyone has or can do that you cannot have or do. You are not afraid to make a mistake. You are not shy about telling the truth. You establish and maintain clear boundaries and you honor the boundaries others have set for themselves. When you are not full, you have no boundaries. You step over other people. You also allow them to *step on* you.

Feel-full-ness is an affirmation that allows you to feel the fullness of divine energy as it moves within you. Feel full of God's love for you. If at any time you are besieged with feelings of inadequacy, accept one of the many invitations of feel-full-ness. Should you find that for some reason it does not seem to be working for you, don't give up! Fake it until you make it!

Until today, you may have denied, resisted or ignored the gnawing feelings of inadequacy that have motivated you to give more and do more than is required in any situation. Just for today, feel full of yourself! Trust that just as you are, you are more than enough.

*Today I am devoted to sharing the fullness of who
I am with the world!*

SEPTEMBER 14

I experience and express the power of trust because . . .
I am ready to have the things I want.

This is your lucky day! That's right! This is the day that you can have anything you want. Anything and everything you have ever thought of having or doing is yours for the asking. Go ahead! Ask for something. It doesn't matter how big or how small, just ask. No one is going to ask you for anything in return. You don't have to do anything beyond the asking. If you are willing to accept that life is on your side and wants for you exactly what you want for yourself, go ahead, ask for it. If you think you can handle having what you want, ask for it. If you believe that you are worthy of having what you want, ask for it. If you love yourself enough to have what you want without working hard or struggling to get it, ask for it. If your heart is open and free of hatred, anger, resentment or fear, ask for what you want. If you believe that you deserve it, ask for it. If you are not afraid of what people will say about you once you have everything you want, ask for it. What's the matter? Can't you think of anything you want bad enough to make yourself fit this criteria?

Until today, you may not have understood what it would take for you to have exactly what you want in life. Just for today, examine the criteria. Get yourself ready to have what you want.

Today I am devoted to doing what I need to do to prepare myself to have exactly what I want!

SEPTEMBER 15

I experience and express the power of trust because . . .
I realize I can never prove who I am with how much
I do or give.

There comes a point in time when you must know that everything you have already given or done is enough. This is not something anyone else can tell you. *You* must *know*. Also know, if you continue down the path of trying, you will reach the point of diminishing returns. This applies more specifically to relationships.

Remember, life is a process of giving and receiving. When you give with love or in joy, you must receive in equal measure. This does not mean that you should measure your giving. What this means is that your giving must be received with the same intensity with which it was given. In those relationships and situations where you give with no sense of satisfaction, either you are giving for the wrong reasons or what you give is not being received. It is being hoarded. It is being denied. It is being dishonored.

Once you cross the line of diminishing returns, if you continue to give, you run the risk of being depleted in ways that can be irreversible. To continue giving without receiving doesn't prove anything except that you know how to be taken advantage of. Give with love. Give in joy. Give of yourself for the joy and love of giving. Just be aware that when your giving is received and honored, you must be justly compensated.

Until today, you may have allowed yourself to stay in unbalanced, unhealthy relationships where you were required to give beyond the point where it was necessary or wise. Just for today, consider those experiences where you are experiencing a diminishing return on your mental, emotional, spiritual or physical investments.

Today I am devoted to analyzing the relationships
in which I am not being compensated for investments
I make!

SEPTEMBER 16

I experience and express the power of trust because . . .
I am willing to do the work I need to do to learn
more about myself.

When you find yourself in *another* relationship, with *another* person, doing the *same* things, feeling the *same* ways you did in other relationships, you are working on *unfinished business*. This means there is something you need to see about yourself or there is something you need to learn about yourself that has nothing to do with whom you are with. The things you are about to discover about yourself will help you rewrite your script.

The fact of the matter is that most people do not have *many relationships*. They have *one relationship* with *many people*. The same issues and challenges that you have in one relationship are the same issues and challenges you have in *all* relationships. The more relationships you are involved in, the deeper you go in terms of identifying your core issue, the issue that keeps attracting opportunities for you to get clear. Once the core issue is resolved, once you understand why you do what you do in relationships, you can choose to change. As you change your approach, your behavior changes. Once you change your behavior, you heal your wounds, fears, false expectations and judgments.

Should you find that you are arguing with your mate, your mother and your best friend, if you discover that you are in conflict with your co-workers and other shoppers in the supermarket, *take a hint!* There is something on the center stage of your life that requires attention.

Until today, you may have thought that every relationship in your life was different from the other relationships. Just for today, look for the common trouble spots and common experiences in all of your relationships. Then, examine yourself and your common complaints.

Today, I am devoted to examining the role I play in the difficulties of all of my relationships!

SEPTEMBER 17

I experience and express the power of trust because . . . I know I am divinely hooked up and spiritually hooked in.

From the story of Daniel, in the Holy Bible, we learn what it means to truly be spiritually connected. You can call it the *spiritual hook-up*. Daniel had the gift of spiritual vision and prophecy. He also had a very strong faith in and connection to the spirit of his Creator. Faithful, Daniel relied upon and trusted his spiritual hook-up for guidance, which enabled him to do and accomplish many things that others could not do. People were quite jealous because *they* thought *Daniel* thought he was *special*.

When you know, like Daniel, that you are *hooked up* with your spiritual source, pleasing people becomes almost insignificant. Even when jealousy turns people against you or causes them to attack you, somehow you know you will be just fine. The worst possible thing you can do when attacked by spiritually jealous people is jump off your spiritual hook in an attempt to please or appease other human beings. This was the lesson that Daniel had to learn.

When Daniel refused to do what the king and his jealous cohorts wanted him to do, the spiritually jealous people convinced the king to throw Daniel into a den of hungry lions. *Can you imagine?!!* It takes more than the average share of trust, faith and obedience to stand up against a pack of ravenous lions. You must be willing to lose everything to honor your spiritual hook-up. *Daniel passed the test!* He was so hooked up, he walked right into the lions' den without batting an eye. You know what happened? The lion had a terrible case of indigestion.

Until today, you may have believed that being hooked into people could and would sustain you in the tough times. Just for today, hook into Spirit for protection and divine guidance in dealing with jealous or disruptive people.

Today I am devoted to experiencing and strengthening my spiritual connection!

SEPTEMBER 18

I experience and express the power of trust because . . . if
I ask the right questions I will get the information I need.

If you ask the *wrong* question, you will not get the information you need. Nowhere is this more true than in our relationships. Rather than asking, *"Why doesn't he or she do this
or that?"* it may be more beneficial to ask, *"What is it that I
am to do?"*

Masculine energy represents mind. Men, do you trust your ideas?
Do you believe that the ideas you receive come from a divine source? Do
you know that once you receive an idea, everything you need to manifest
the idea is provided to you? Are you afraid to ask for what you need? Do
you trust yourself with your divinity?

Feminine energy represents the heart. Women, do you trust yourself
to be a loving and capable teacher? Are you aware that everyone who
comes into your life is your student? Do you know that as you teach
your students, you learn what you need to know? Do you know that you
are beautiful? Do you understand that beauty is a divine quality that you
possess? Do you trust yourself with your divinity?

Until we can answer these questions, we will not experience the
bounty of loving families, thriving communities and a peaceful world.
Our ability to ask ourselves these questions is an *act of faith*. Our ability
to know and act upon the answers is a function of trust.

Until today, you may have had distorted ideas about your purpose
and function in life and in relationships. Just for today, take the time to
consider some questions that you may not have asked yourself.

*Today I am devoted to asking the right questions
about myself and my purpose!*

SEPTEMBER 19

I experience and express the power of trust because . . .
I know I am not missing any steps I need to take.

You feel crazy! Everything around is in shambles. Anything that could go wrong has or is going wrong. The bottom has fallen out! The roof is caving in! The walls around you are collapsing! *What do you do?* You take one step at a time, in one direction, trusting that everything will be just fine. It won't be easy, but if you just trust that everything will be okay, it will be.

When things appear to be falling apart, a chattering imp will find its way into your head. This annoying little pest will whisper things to you. The imp will point out every little detail of everything that is apparently going wrong. If that's not enough to rattle your cage, the imp will give you a mental preview of how much worse things can get. The imp will bring to your mind things you never even considered, in an attempt to send you running off in ten directions at once. Unlike people you can walk away from, you cannot get away from the imp because it is in *your own mind.* If you listen to the imp, you will eventually be convinced that there is a fire-breathing dragon waiting at every turn to devour you. This is a manifestation of the *deceptive intelligence! What do you do?* You put one foot in front of the other. You take one step at a time, moving in one direction at a time, doing one thing at a time. More than this you cannot do. The imp and the dragon will simply have to realize that your life runs according to your schedule and your ability. You are only able to take one step at a time.

Until today, you may have allowed yourself to be pushed, pulled or frightened into trying to do too many things at one time. Just for today, choose one thing you know you must address. Focus on that one thing. Prioritize your steps. Take one step at a time.

Today I am devoted to moving slowly, carefully and consciously in one direction to do one thing at a time!

SEPTEMBER 20

I experience and express the power of trust because . . .
there is a divine place to put anything that challenges me.

Do you have a *God Jar?* If you don't, you should.

A God Jar is an actual jar, much like the old jars you have stashed away in the kitchen or basement. That's right! There is now a divine use for that old mayonnaise, pickle or jelly jar that you have been holding on to. That jar can be transformed into a divine healing tool. All you have to do is wash the jar, dry it out and find the lid for it. If you are so inclined, you can decorate the jar. It's up to you. Just know that with a God Jar, all of your worries will soon be over. Now here's how the God Jar works.

You must first prioritize all of the duties, responsibilities and desires you are working on or working through. Once you have your list, choose one that you are going to work on. Anything you are not working on goes into the God Jar. The way you put them into the God Jar is to write them down. Using as few words as possible, write each item on a separate sheet of paper. Avoid the temptation to tell God how you want the situation to unfold. Place the sheets of paper into the God Jar. Through the day and for days to come, should the situations come to mind, simply remind yourself, "God is taking care of it!"

If for some reason a God Jar situation remains unresolved or builds up pressure, write it down again. Be sure that once you put something in the God Jar, you do not try to fix it on your own. You will be guided and directed about what to do next.

Until today, you may not have had a way to deal with the mounting pressure of certain situations in your life. Just for today, make a God Jar for yourself. Use it as a way to surrender some of the things that you are unable to address in this moment.

Today I am devoted to realizing that when
I can't do something, God can!

SEPTEMBER 21

I experience and express the power of trust because . . .
I recognize the difference between fact and fiction.

Most of us live our lives based on facts. Some facts are based on actual knowledge and experience. Others are grounded in speculation. Truth always unfolds into a deeper understanding. Facts are often defended with statistics that support the position being promoted. Truth, which cannot be measured, needs no defense. In our day-to-day experience of living, we often fail to recognize or understand that there is a major difference between *a fact* and *the truth*.

A fact is a temporary condition or situation. The truth is a constant presence. A fact is subject to change or alteration. The truth is immutable. It never changes. A fact can represent the truth, or it can be based solely on speculation. The truth represents the power and the presence of Spirit. Facts stimulate the intellect. Truth opens the heart. A fact begins with a premise that requires more facts to prove a conclusion. The truth is the *conclusion,* the understanding of which colors or clouds facts. A fact can be ignored, resisted or denied. The truth must be reckoned with. You can never trust facts. You can always trust the truth.

The *fact* is that most of us live our lives *based on facts.* The truth is, until you understand that there is a truth about you of which you may be unaware, you will not be able to move beyond the influence of facts. Hopefully, this fact will change as you learn to trust that there is a deeper level of truth that exists and is available to you.

Until today, you may have accepted certain facts about yourself and life as the truth. Just for today, set an intention to know the truth about yourself. Ask that the power of the truth allows you to move beyond certain debilitating facts with grace and ease.

Today I am devoted to living the truth of my being!

SEPTEMBER 22

I experience and express the power of trust because . . .
I am ready and willing to walk through fear.

When it comes to moving forward, demonstrating your power, it is the same experience for everyone. When life calls upon you to step up your pace, to move into a higher level of being, to put your great potential to use, it will bring up every aspect of fear that is hidden in your consciousness. When this happens, unless you are willing to acknowledge and confront the fear head on, you will not be able to move. More important, if you do not trust that you will be able to walk through the fear, you will choose not to move.

We all have little fears we have not addressed. In fact, we may have some we don't know exist. These unknown fears can and do lie dormant until you are called upon by life to confront and overcome them. That is when the degree of trust you have in yourself will be tested. It doesn't matter how much potential you have or how many divine opportunities are laid before you, fear can zap your energy, stamina and ability to move. The fear of failure, rejection and success will rage in your brain the moment your potential is called upon. In moments like this, you must trust that you can feel bad and recover. That you can survive mistakes that might make you look stupid. How you respond to fear when it rises will determine how much you can trust yourself. The catch is, unless you trust yourself, you will not be able to confront the fear.

Until today, you may not have recognized that there were unacknowledged fears lying dormant in your consciousness. As a result, you may have given yourself many wonderful, and plausible reasons for not living up to your potential and taking full advantage of the many opportunities you have. Just for today, consider the fear vs. self-trust theory. It doesn't really matter if you know what you are afraid of. What matters is trusting yourself enough to confront it, walk through it and survive.

Today I am devoted to trusting myself enough to walk through known and unknown fear!

SEPTEMBER 23

I experience and express the power of trust because . . .
God knows what I am to do.

If you really want to work at learning how to trust, here's
what you have to do:

1. Have a good thought about yourself or for yourself.
2. Believe it is the right thought.
3. Develop a plan for following through on the thought.
4. Let God look at the plan and have a good laugh.
5. Surrender the plan to God for alterations.
6. Ask for direction and guidance in following through
   with the plan.
7. Give thanks that the guidance and directions you
   need are on the way.

If you are about to ask how you will know when you receive the
guidance and direction requested, go back to step one.

Until today, you may have been at a loss as to how you can develop a
deeper level of trust. Just for today, trust the process.

Today I am devoted to learning how to trust the process!

I experience and express the power of trust because . . .
I am willing to acknowledge different aspects of myself.

There is something that you really need to know about yourself. You have a split personality. We're talking about the
two very distinct and different aspects of yourself that are
usually in conflict and that can drive *you crazy!*

There is usually an aspect of yourself that truly believes that you can
do anything you set your mind to do. This is *Aspect A.* Then there's the
aspect of you that can always find a reason not to do what you know you
can do. This is *Aspect B.* The question you must ask yourself is, *"How can
I bring these two aspects of myself into alignment so that I can take the right
steps in my life."* There is a way.

When you find yourself in the midst of internal conflict, take a long
deep breath. Close your eyes. Pray this prayer.

> *Dear Holy Spirit:*
> *In this moment I cannot move. I do not know what to do. Please
> move through me, taking me in the direction that will serve your will
> for me. Fill my mind with the thoughts that will lead me in that di-
> rection. Shut my mouth. If I have to speak, speak through me. Shut
> my eyes. If I need to see anything, show me where to look. Close my
> ears. If there is something I must hear, please whisper it into my heart
> in a way that I can understand. If I stop, gently push me beyond fear
> and doubt. I am trusting you so that I may take the most appropriate
> action for my highest and greatest good. Thank you. And So It Is.*

Until today, you may have been embroiled in internal conflict,
which inhibited your ability to move forward. Just for today, bring all aspects of your being into alignment with the will of the Holy Spirit.

*Today I am depending on divine direction to lead me
where I need to go!*

SEPTEMBER 25

I experience and express the power of trust because . . .
I am living in the present moment.

Do not allow yesterday's garbage to influence your experience today. Do not allow your fears about tomorrow's garbage to steal the goodness that is available to you right now. Each time you fall into the past or jump into the future you miss what is going on right now. Right now you have the opportunity to create a fresh new start. The only things that come into your stream of thought are those things which you are ready to release or receive. Release the past! Receive your good now! Trust that when you reach tomorrow, there will be nothing but good waiting for you.

Until today, you may have been recycling garbage in your mind, creating and re-creating experiences that you no longer need to have. Just for today, stop collecting trash. Stop looking for it. Stop dragging it around.

Today I am devoted to releasing myself from past trash and fear of tomorrow!

SEPTEMBER 26

I experience and express the power of trust because . . .
I am always prepared to be tested.

Most of us think we have it all together. We believe that we know what we need to know and can call upon that information on a moment's notice. Much to our surprise, when we are unexpectedly confronted with a challenge, the brain is the first thing to go! Try as we may to find our way through the mental Jell-O that was once our brain, the information we need is simply not available at the moment we need it. It is usually in those critical moments, the moments of crisis and panic, that everything we trust and think we believe in will be tested. Unless we are really solid, really sure that we know what we know, we will find ourselves in the sinking sand of doubt and fear. Just to make sure that we know what we know and actually believe what we say we believe, life continues to test us.

If you really want to know how you are doing in the arena of trust, check out your responses to the pop quizzes God gives you. Do you trust that you know the answers, or do you call in sick? Do you put forth your best effort, or do you try to cheat? Do you admit that you don't know the answers and ask for help, or do you act like you know the answers and blame the teacher when it becomes evident that you don't? How you handle the little unexpected surprises that pop up in your life speaks volumes about where you are on the trust continuum.

Until today, you may have thought that you had it all together. Just for today, allow the little surprises of life to provide you with some more information that you need to know.

Today I am devoted to facing all tests and being honest about how well prepared I am!

SEPTEMBER 27

I experience and express the power of trust because . . .
everything I need always comes to me.

Very often we place demands on the universe to provide us with the things we want by saying that we need them. There is absolutely nothing wrong with having a want. However, when it is not satisfied, you must not be fooled into believing that the universe does not support you. Nor should you believe it is an indication that you cannot trust the universe to take care of you. The point is, do not confuse your needs and your wants. Here is an example of how that could happen.

Let's say you live 50 miles outside of town and you have no transportation. You might *think* that you *need* a car to get around. Granted, a car would make it more convenient for you to get around. It would make you feel a lot more comfortable knowing that if there was an emergency, you could get someplace fast. However, the truth of the matter is that you don't need a car, you want one. You have feet. There are bicycles. You probably have neighbors. Or perhaps you could be a bit more prudent about the situations you put yourself into and expect the universe to get you out of.

There are angels around you at all times. Their job is to protect you from harm and provide you with the essentials of life. These angels do not interfere with your choices. When you ask for help, the angels will respond. When you call out to the angels to help you with a *need* and they discover that it is actually a *want,* they really get *pissed!* So watch it! Once you send your angels on a wild goose chase, they will be a bit slower about responding to your next call.

Until today, you may not have realized that you were upsetting the angels who work on your behalf. Just for today, get clear about the difference between what you need and what you want. When you call upon your angels for help, be clear about what you are asking for.

*Today I am devoted to letting my angels know
exactly what I want!*

I experience and express the power of trust because . . .
all of my debts have been paid.

There are three very profound messages we can take away
from the crucifixion of the Christ. Once we understand
these three things, life takes on a completely different
meaning.

1. *I do this so that you don't have to do it.* I suffer so that you will not
have to suffer. You will never need to be afraid of people or circumstances. You will never need to be afraid of what people can do to you
or how you will survive what happens to you. You will never need to fear
ignorance, persecution or death. I do this so that you will never have to
do it.

2. *Father, forgive them for they know not what they do.* They know
not how they dishonor you with fear and doubt. They know not how it
saddens your heart when they do not trust you. They know not that they
dishonor you by dishonoring themselves. Father, forgive them for not
knowing how it disturbs the balance of the universe when they rely on
themselves rather than leaning on you.

3. *It is done.* All that could ever be required of you to move into your
rightful position as an heir of God is done. Trust me. It is done.

Until today, you may have thought that there was something you
needed to do to secure your future. Just for today, realize that it was done
a long time ago. The check was written and signed. All you have to do is
pick up the goods.

*Today I am devoted to claiming my inheritance
of good and goodness!*

SEPTEMBER 29

I experience and express the power of trust because . . .
I know I have nothing to worry about.

Why worry? If you have learned anything by now it is that worry serves no purpose. Yet you do it any way. Why? You sit around frantic. You run around frazzled. You make yourself sick. You have all but pulled your hair out, and for what? If your worrying could have made things better, you wouldn't have anything to worry about. What would you do with all that free time? How about trusting that all the things you have been worrying about will not change for all the *worry in the world*. How about dropping all the worry and picking up a little trust. Oh, no! There you go worrying about whether or not you have enough trust to trust. Get a grip!

Until today, worry might have been your favorite pastime. Just for today, use your time to develop a bit more trust.

Today I am devoted to freeing myself from
the bondage of worry!

SEPTEMBER 30

I experience and express the power of trust because . . .
I finally realize that I don't have to figure it out.

Why don't you just admit that you have absolutely no idea what is going on? The only thing required for your enlightenment, for your blessings to flow, is for you to figure out that you don't have to know what is going on. All you have to do is *trust*. Everything else is something that you make up in your own mind just to give yourself something to do or not do.

If you really want to give your mind something to do, think about the beauty that surrounds you. Think about the trees, flowers and all of the little animals that may not have dreams, visions and schedules, but seem to make it through each day just fine. Think about how much you have grown in your life. Think about how much you have learned in your life. Think how about how far you have come, even when you weren't quite sure of where you were headed or what you were going to do when you got to where you are. Think about all the *near misses* you have had. Then think about all the connections you have made. Think about all the *second chances* you have had. Then think about all the chances you did not take. If you just have to have something to think about, think about the glorious wonder that life is, has been and continues to be. Then ask yourself why you think that you should know, could know, are supposed to know what is going on? Think about all the *good stuff* that has happened to you that you didn't know was going to happen. Then ask yourself why you are so fixed on knowing when trusting seems to have paid off so well, so far?

Until today, you may have been preoccupied with trying to figure out what you don't know. Just for today, trust that whatever is going to happen will be better than what you know has already happened.

Today I am devoted to not thinking about my life.
I am trusting my life!

OCTOBER

WORTH

What you tell yourself you are, you will be.

*What you allow yourself to be reflects what
you have told yourself you are.*

OCTOBER 1

I will realize my own worth when I accept . . .
myself exactly as I am.

Self-Value means I know who I am!
  Self-Esteem means I am who I say I am!
  Self-Worth means I believe I am who I say I am!
    Until today, you may not have been aware of how your
knowledge of your own value affects your self-esteem or how your self-
esteem affects your sense of self-worth. Just for today, make sure that
what you know about yourself is reflected in what you say about yourself, because what you say about yourself influences what you believe
about yourself.

*Today I am devoted to knowing, saying and believing the
very best about myself!*

OCTOBER 2

I will realize my own worth when I accept . . .
conditions and circumstances cannot confine me
and do not define me.

Do not confuse the conditions in your life with the truth
about you. Conditions may be influential, but they are not
immutable. Conditions can and do change! Circumstances
may have an effect, but they are not the deciding factors in
your life. Do not allow what is going on around you to determine what
comes through you. Do not allow yourself to believe that what happens
to you can in any way alter the truth about you.

You are not what happens to you. You are *how you handle* what happens. You are not what is going on around you. You are *how you go through* all the things going on around you. You are not bound to or stopped by any condition or circumstance that may confront you. You are the boundless, unlimited, unstoppable power and energy of who you believe you are. Beyond that, nothing really matters unless you let it.

Until today, you may have believed that environment, conditions, circumstances or situations could alter, determine or change your identity. Just for today, examine what you believe about where you are in your life to see if what you believe is in fact coming true.

Today I am devoted to eliminating confining and limiting beliefs about myself and my life!

OCTOBER 3

I will realize my own worth when I accept . . .
certain conditions in my life are like shoes; at some point
they just don't fit me.

How long are you going to hold on to the things that are not working in your best interests? Things that are not fulfilling? Things that are no longer productive? How long are you going to deny yourself, your feelings and your power in order to meet the demands and expectations of others? How long are you going to overdo, overgive, overindulge, trying to convince yourself and others that you are worthy? Perhaps today is as good a day as another to let go of others and grab onto your *Self*. Perhaps today is the day that you will find the courage and the strength to start *being* worthy.

Life is not about holding on. Life is not about doing what will make others believe you are worthy. Nor is it about denying yourself to make others feel better. Isn't it obvious that life is moving on while you seem to be stuck in a holding pattern? Can you not see that you are carrying so much "stuff," perhaps so many people, that you can hardly move, let alone make any progress. In fact, doesn't it seem at times as if you are being left behind by the very ones you stayed behind to help?

Life is about moving through, moving on, growing up and growing through each and every experience. Life is about examination, elimination and re-creation. Perhaps today is the only day you have to examine your life, to make some adjustments and changes, so that you can take full advantage of the opportunities this day offers. Today sure seems like a good day!

Until today, you may not have realized that you can do in one day what you have avoided doing for so many other days. Just for today, take every opportunity you have to let go of thoughts, beliefs, behaviors, ideas and people standing in the way of your desire to stand squarely in your worthiness.

Today I am devoted to reclaiming my self-worth!

OCTOBER 4

I will realize my own worth when I accept . . .
what I believe either pushes me into a hole or
raises me toward the light.

The feeling of unworthiness is like a gaping hole in your heart. You never can seem to have or do enough to fill the hole. As a matter of fact, the more you *do get* and the more you *do* to try to fill the hole, the deeper, wider and more painful it seems to become. As it does, you set yourself up to do more things that seem to leave you *yearning* for more of something you can't quite name.

People who feel unworthy are always working on themselves. They always want to *be* better, *do* better, *know* more and *do* more. They believe that there is some *one thing* somewhere out there that will catapult them into a place of worth and value. In the quest to find it, they often dig themselves deeper into the hole because now they have a laundry list of things they have done and not completed, tried and been dissatisfied with. In the end, when those who *believe* they are unworthy run out of things to do to in an attempt to make themselves feel good, they will find someone else to work on. That's when the hole becomes a cave!

The only cure for a true sense of unworthiness is *belief*. Believe that you are more than anyone may have ever told you, and you will *be* more. Believe that you are miraculous, and the hole in your heart will be filled with the love and joy that you have for yourself. Seeking anything less than *a total belief in your worthiness* is akin to placing a sheet over a hole. If you are not careful, the sheet will give way and you will fall into the hole.

Until today, you may have been searching for something to make you feel worthy. Just for today, believe in your worthiness! Embrace your worthiness by simply being still and calling it forward in your heart.

Today I am devoted to climbing out of the hole of
unworthiness into the light of truth about myself!

OCTOBER 5

I will realize my own worth when I accept . . .
I am worthy of my own company.

You cannot stay in a relationship or any experience where you feel alone just to avoid being alone. To do so is to betray yourself. It is impossible to stay in a relationship where you are unsupported, unacknowledged or unappreciated without eventually being convinced that this is as good as it can get. Anytime you find yourself giving yourself a reason to stay in a relationship where *joy* is an illusion, *peace* refers only to cake or pie, happiness is just around the corner, love is just the way you sign off on letters, you are in the process of destroying your sense of worth.

It is often hard for us to realize, understand or accept that the way we treat ourselves sets the model for how we will be treated. Many of us allow ourselves to be treated the way we have *always been treated* because we don't know that we can be treated any other way. For some, being treated badly is better than being alone. This is the ultimate act of self-betrayal. Any experience of betrayal can diminish your sense of worth. There is nothing intrinsically wrong with staying to work things out or with working through the tough times with a clear vision of things getting better. There are times when staying takes more courage than leaving requires. However, when the only reason for being where you are is to avoid being by yourself, you are no longer a victim of abuse, betrayal or dishonor. *You are creating it!*

Until today, you may have believed that being alone would be worse than being in a relationship where you feel alone. Just for today, sit with yourself, by yourself, and ask yourself, *"Why is being alone so frightening to me?"* Write down your responses. Read them back to yourself and then ask yourself, *"Why am I choosing to believe this?"* When you get an answer, make another choice.

Today I am devoted to exploring some of the good reasons there are for spending time alone!

OCTOBER 6

I will realize my own worth when I accept . . .
the story I tell is the story I live.

Excuse me, but nobody wants to hear your story again! No one
wants to be rude, but you've been telling everyone and anyone who would listen why you did not, could not, have not,
moved beyond the situation you are in and *say* you no longer
want to be in. Quite frankly, no one wants to hear about it anymore.

It seems as if you have been trying to convince others and yourself
that something or someone other than you is responsible for all that you
have and *have not* done to move yourself beyond this predicament. *No
one is convinced by what you are saying!* Obviously, neither are you! Perhaps that's why you keep telling that sad story, the sob story, the ticky-
tacky dramatized version of your life. Enough!

Your villain is not bad enough to do all the things you say have been
done to you! Your central theme is missing! Your plots and subplots are
tangled! As a matter of fact, your story sounds more like one big, fat excuse than a reasonable explanation! It sounds like you are telling the
story you hope will excuse away your fear and your failure to take responsibility for making your life what you want it to be.

Credit must be given when credit is due. You tell a good story!
Action-packed! Full of adventure! Plenty of victims needing to be res-
cued! However, since only you can determine your own sense of worth,
here is a suggestion for you: *REWRITE YOUR STORY!* This time, please
don't start with "Once upon a time!"

Until today, you may have been telling the same old story about
yourself and your life. You may have been making excuses, trying to convince yourself that something or someone has been holding you back.
Just for today, be committed to telling yourself a new story. You can
begin by writing one that starts with the words *Today I am. . . .* Be creative and continue from there.

Today I am devoted to taking the time to
re-write my story!

OCTOBER 7

I will realize my own worth when I accept . . .
I am the most valuable thing that I have in life.

When something is important to you, you take care of it. You make sure it is protected, nurtured, and that those things required for its maintenance are provided. Whether it is your child, your home or your vehicle, if you consider the person or entity important, you will do your darndest to see that it is taken care of. In those cases where you have assigned a value to the thing you consider important, the stakes are even higher. Is it not true that there have been times when you have denied, jeopardized or put aside your own needs and well-being to provide for those you consider important and valuable? Most of us do it most of the time, and that is exactly why it seems perfectly normal.

The destruction of self-worth begins the moment we assign a value to something outside ourselves. The destruction continues when we accept the responsibility to care for and maintain something that has more value than we do. Being a parent or spouse is not more important than being a whole, healthy being. Being a diligent and responsible worker is not more important than being a peaceful, loving soul. Working hard to provide or take care of material possessions is not more important than taking care of your mind, your body or your spirit. Anytime you place a value on anything or anyone greater than the value you place on yourself, you are engaging in an unconscious form of suicide.

Until today, you may have considered someone or something more important than you. You may have pushed yourself to take care of people and things, believing they were valuable and important aspects of your life. Just for today, and again tomorrow, make yourself the most important and valuable aspect of your life. In other words, for the next two days, think of you, do for you, take care of you first.

*Today I am devoted to caring for the most important and
valuable part of my life—me!*

OCTOBER 8

I will realize my own worth when I accept . . .
the labels placed on me don't always fit.

Society, with its structures, expectations and divisions, has fostered certain ideas about women that are not at all flattering. There are many people who believe that strong women are not feminine and that assertive women cannot be trusted. My all-time favorite is that women who exhibit any degree of clarity about who they are and what they want are dangerous. Don't forget that a bossy woman is domineering and that makes her a b – – – –. We won't bother to mention the myths that women are not as smart as men or that they can't handle money as well. The point is, there are some people who believe these things about women, and some of them are women!

Labels define. Often, labels set up expectations. Labels prescribe how much, how little, how often and how long a thing can be used. Labels are descriptive. Labels are protective. Labels can be deceptive, and labels can be removed. It may just be that the time has come to take the labels off women. It's probably more accurate to say that it is time for women to take the labels off themselves.

In order for a woman to realize that she is more than a mother, more than a wife, more than what she earns or what she does to earn a living, she must know her own worth. It means she must test herself and her limits. A woman must learn to describe herself and establish her own expectations for herself. A woman must encourage herself. She must support and nurture herself. A woman must be willing to be disliked. She must be willing to violate the descriptions and confines placed upon her.

Until today, you may have placed defining, confining labels of unworthiness on women. Just for today, be aware that women are people. They are human beings. They are the divine energy of God. With that in mind, examine every thought you have ever had about women.

Today I am devoted to broadening my awareness of how I view women!

OCTOBER 9

I will realize my own worth when I accept . . . I have the power to convince myself that I am good!

How do you learn to believe in yourself if you haven't been taught that you are worth believing in? How do you find the words to say to yourself the things you have rarely, if ever, heard about yourself? How do you learn to do for yourself the things you have never been taught you are worthy of having done for you? How do you stop doing what hurts you when you haven't been taught how to do anything else? Well, *you just do it!* You do it until you *believe* it! You do it until you *feel* it! You do it until you can't stop doing it because you know that *you are worth the effort!*

In order to believe in and experience your own sense of worth, you make a decision that *you are worth believing in.* Then you tell yourself just that. You must find the words that capture all the things you need to hear and whisper them softly to yourself. You must ask yourself what needs to be done to make you feel stronger, better and brighter. Once you figure out what those things are, you do them for yourself. If by chance you discover along the way that what you are doing is not helping you to believe something better about yourself, stop! Do something else! Do something that makes you feel good and look good and brings you closer to realizing the truth that you are good.

Find the words to say what you need to hear. Find the way to do what you need to have done. Do it because you are worth it! Do it because you deserve it! Do it because you believe in yourself! Do it because you want to demonstrate that what you believe about yourself will attract others to you who will help you along.

Until today, you may have believed that you did not know how to do what you need to have done. Just for today, do things for yourself that will convince you that you deserve the best.

Today I am devoted to convincing myself that I am worth the effort that it takes to make myself feel good!

OCTOBER 10

I will realize my own worth when I accept . . . there is a
pure and right spirit within me.

It's all there. Everything you need to know. Why you are
here, what you are here to do and how you must go about
accomplishing every task. The answer to every question you
have ever asked yourself or asked of anyone else. Why you
are who you are. The cause of each and every experience you have endured or conquered and exactly what those experiences were designed to
teach you. It's all right there in your heart. Not the heart that beats to
keep you alive—a different kind of heart. The heart we are referring to is
the heart of your soul. Your heart of hearts. It is there that you will find the
voice of your Spirit. It is this heart that must be clean and peace-filled in
order for your mind, spirit and life to soar.

The Spirit's voice comes so softly into your heart that it will be difficult for you to hear it if you are angry. An angry heart is a hardened heart
that is closed to the spirit of healing. It will be equally difficult for you to
receive your heart's divine direction if you insist on blaming others for
what you are or are not. Your heart knows the truth—your true identity
and the true purpose of your life. If you are ready and willing to know
what your heart already knows, ask your heart to cleanse itself of all of
anger, resentment and fear. Ask that your heart be healed of all shame,
guilt, dishonesty and pain. With a clean and open heart, you can do anything you choose.

Until today, you may have believed that your heart was beyond re-
pair. Just for today, spend some time listening to your heart. Ask to be
guided away from what you no longer need or desire onto the path of all
that you deserve. Do it just this once, and you will never regret it.

*Today I am devoted to renewing my Spirit
by cleansing my heart.*

OCTOBER 11

I will realize my own worth when I accept . . . I already
know the answers to the questions I am afraid to ask.

Questions are wonderful. Questions open the mind and the
heart to new levels of awareness. Questions support our
steps toward growth, healing and evolution. They give us
something more to reach for and more things to consider as
we reach where we are going. Questions enliven our innocence. They
also solidify our wisdom. While we may think questions bring us answers, the truth is, the answer is always within the question.

How do you know when it is time to leave a place, an experience or
a situation? One sure sign is that you are asking the question. Chances
are that by the time you ask the question, you already know the answer.
If you are asking if you should leave, here are a few more questions you
may want to consider. How does being where you are make you feel?
What is it that you desire to feel? What is the experience you hope to
have if you stay? Is there another place in which you could have a better
experience? Does having a better experience depend on anyone else?
Why have you given someone else control of your power? Your joy? How
can you *give to yourself* what you are expecting from someone else? Why
haven't you done it up to now?

Very often the question we must ask ourselves is not *"Is it time for me
to leave?"* Rather, the question is *"How can I stay here and create a better
experience for myself?"* An even better question is "Is being where I am
worth the effort it takes to stay?"

Until today, you may have been waiting for someone to make something happen to make your experience better. Just for today be devoted
to uncovering any fear, resistance or unwillingness to making it happen
for yourself.

*Today I am devoted to asking questions of myself and
recognizing the answers that I already know!*

OCTOBER 12

I will realize my own worth when I accept . . .
my worthiness exactly as I am right now.

A truly healthy sense of self-worth is more than a head trip. Self-worth requires more than repeating flowery affirmations to convince yourself that you believe certain things about yourself. Self-worth is not a by-product of others' opinions about you and your abilities. Self-worth is an understanding on the intellectual level, trusting at the heart level, and accepting at the soul level that you are worthy just because you believe that you are.

Worth is a function of belief, trust, acceptance and understanding that there is nothing inherently imperfect or wrong with you. *You* are the sum total of your worth. In other words, your worthiness is proven by your existence. Your breathing. The beating of your heart. The expansion of your lungs. Your mere presence is all that is needed to establish your worth. What you believe about yourself simply confirms it.

When you *understand* what a gift it is to be alive, you will *know* that you are worthy. Once you *understand* that you can *trust* yourself to be a unique expression of life, you will *feel* worthy. Once you *feel worthy* and *accept* that you are not a mistake, that you have a right to be who you are, exactly as you are, you will *believe* that you are worthy. Once you *believe* that you are worthy of life and love and all sorts of other good things, you will come off the *head trip* of trying to prove your worth to others in order to convince yourself. Once you acknowledge and accept the presence of God's love in you and for you, there will never again be a question in your mind about whether or not you are worthy.

Until today, you may have thought that a healthy sense of self-worth was something you could create in your mind. Just for today, seek to understand why you are worthy, to trust that you are worthy and to accept your worthiness as your normal state of being.

Today I am devoted to understanding, trusting and accepting my own sense of worthiness!

OCTOBER 13

I will realize my own worth when I accept . . .
all aspects of who I am are important.

Could it be that you cannot see yourself as a valuable and
worthy person because you know how *mean, ugly and nasty
you can be*? Perhaps it is difficult to accept that you are worthy of love, honor and respect because you have seen your
dark side and know what you are capable of doing. If this is the case,
relax! Everybody has a dark side, and it has nothing to do with whether
or not you are worthy.

If you want to experience the truth of who you are and establish a
sense of self-worth, you must be willing to examine and explore your
dark side. You must acknowledge how bad you can be. You must accept
how horribly unlovingly you can behave. You must also admit that there
were times when the darkness got the best of you, causing you to act like
a real low-life. Dark thoughts, dark habits and dark tendencies push you
toward the light. As long as you are reaching for or searching for the
light, you stay above the darkness.

When you know how deep and dark your dark side is, it helps you
stand a little taller in the light. You know better than anyone *"from
whence you came!"* When you know how far down in the darkness you
have been or could be, the knowledge pushes you a little further, a little
faster. When you have seen the faces of your dark side, do not believe
that they make you unworthy. Acknowledge them. Learn from them.
Forgive them. When you can do that, you transform their energy into
more light.

Until today, you may have believed that having a dark side makes
you unworthy to seek the light or see the light. Just for today, remember
that only stars shine in the darkness. Transform the energy of your dark
side to enhance your star quality.

*Today I am devoted to forgiving and transforming
any darkness in my life!*

OCTOBER 14

I will realize my own worth when I accept . . .
I am nothing to be ashamed of.

Have you ever considered just being yourself? There is no
need for you to be some kind of super-being in order to
measure up to everyone else. Who you are is really quite
enough! You know enough and have enough to offer something valuable, whatever is going on. If you would simply show up, with
your smile, your way of doing things and your way of being exactly who
you are, you would recognize that *who you are is just fine!*

If you would, just for a moment, stop tearing yourself down because
of the mistakes you have made, you would feel like *who you are is enough.*
If you would choose to stop beating up on yourself for the things you
did not do to everyone else's satisfaction, you would understand that
who you are is enough. If you would decide to stop doubting and second
guessing yourself, you might realize that *who you are is enough.* If you
would allow yourself to be who you are without excuses or defenses, for
just a moment, you might have a very valuable experience.

If you were to let yourself know that you are enough for about thirty
seconds, do you think others might notice? Is it possible that you might
find a new vision of yourself and for yourself? What if you were to let
yourself know that you are enough by doing everything in your power to
believe it, trust it and demonstrate it, is it possible that those who find
you lacking might shut their mouths? It's all possible, but you will never
know until you take a chance on just being enough of yourself to make
yourself happy.

Until today, you may have been obsessed with fixing or changing
yourself in an effort to make who you are better. Just for today, try being
yourself and do what you do without pretense, defense or excuses.

*Today I am devoted to realizing that being myself is
enough to make me valuable!*

OCTOBER 15

I will realize my own worth when I accept . . . what I do for my own good will be good for everyone.

What you do for your highest good, for your own well being, is going to be good for everyone else. It will be a bit scary at first, but in the end, you will feel a lot better. You will be clear. You will have put everyone on notice. To their benefit, they will not be subjected to your anger and resentment when they try, and fail, to guess what you want. To your benefit, you will not have to waste time pretending that things are okay when they are not. It is for your own good to tell the truth.

It is for your own good that you must ask for what you need, up front. It may make you a little uncomfortable at first. In the end, it will save you a lot of grief. You will learn that your needs are important. You will learn how to let people support and assist you. You will learn that you don't have to muddle through without the things that are necessary. To do that makes you bitter, which doesn't benefit anyone.

It is for your own good and everyone's benefit for you to set clear boundaries for the people in your life. Let people know what you can and cannot do. Even if they try to persuade you to do something else, hold to your boundaries. Do not allow people to run amuck in your life. Nor should you run amuck in theirs. Know your place and stay in it! This will prevent arguments and hurt feelings. In the end, everyone benefits.

When you start doing what you know is best for you some people will be upset. They may be uncomfortable with the fact that you have the guts to be honest. They may challenge you or criticize you. You may question whether or not you are doing the right thing. It's all right! You will get over it! So will they! If they don't, perhaps it is just a sign that these are people who do not have your best interest at heart.

Until today, you may have been reluctant to do what is good for you. Just for today, stand up for your highest good.

Today I am devoted to honoring what I know is good and best for me!

OCTOBER 16

*I will realize my own worth when I accept . . . I have
permission to spend time with myself.*

Here's a pretty *risky* proposition that is not for the faint of
heart. If there is any fear, co-dependence or self-denial in
your being, you might as well *turn the page right now!* Although being afflicted by one of these aforementioned mal-
adies makes you a *prime candidate,* there is no way you could participate
in this awesome opportunity. Don't tempt yourself because *something
different* might happen. It would take courage, boldness, chutzpah that
you don't have yet. So go on, turn the page. This is for those daredevil
doers who are ready to blast into orbit. The whole plan will only take
twenty-four hours to accomplish. The proposition is as follows.

For the next twenty-four hours, you are to live totally for yourself.
You are to be *self-absorbed, self-obsessed and self-centered!* We are not talking about bragging about yourself or trying to impress other people. In
fact, you are not to talk to other people. For one entire day, talk to yourself! Compliment yourself! Encourage yourself! Correct yourself! Pump
yourself up with descriptive words and visions of grandeur! Focus only
on the things that you like and want. Suspend all duties, responsibilities
and obligations to everyone else. Take care of yourself.

For twenty-four hours, you are to nurture yourself. Soak your feet.
Wash your hair. Pour some warm oil on your body and rub yourself down.
Get dressed up. Take yourself out. Take a nap. What the heck! Take two.
Get naked with yourself. Write yourself a love letter. Pray about yourself.
Do whatever you want to do with you and for you for twenty-four hours.
It can be a phenomenally mind-blowing experience. There is, however,
one catch. It only works if you believe that you are worth the time.

Until today, you may have been totally absorbed by the people, duties, responsibilities and obligations of your life. Just for today, absorb
yourself in yourself.

*Today I am devoted to being self-absorbed,
self-obsessed and self-centered!*

OCTOBER 17

I will realize my own worth when I accept . . .
what I tell myself I am, I am.

Your self-worth and sense of worthiness begin with the belief and understanding that *you are not a victim!* When you know *who you are* and *whose you are,* you cannot be a victim. Sure, things happen to you. There are people who have dishonored you. You may have been born into circumstances that put you behind the so-called *eight ball.* You may have been rejected or molested. You may have been afflicted with mental, emotional or spiritual dysfunction. *None of it makes you a victim!* As long as you believe it does, *it will!*

In Yoruba culture, the story of Odi-Ejiogbe is a case against victimization. Odi-Ejiogbe's brothers lied to him and set him up to be murdered. Through prayer and meditation, Odi-Ejiogbe was warned. He left his homeland and, instead of being killed, found wealth and riches in another village. The Biblical story of Joseph is another case against victimization. Joseph's brothers threw him into a well and sold him into slavery. They also told their father, Isaac, that Joseph was dead. Joseph served as a slave and eventually became captain of the king's army. In that position, he was able to save his family, including his brothers, from starvation. Like Odi-Ejiogbe, Joseph knew he was not a victim. What he told his brothers is a mantra for all those who feel they have been victimized; *"You meant it for evil, but God meant it for good!"*

People have a propensity to do mean, mindless, irrational, irresponsible and unloving things. You know that! Rather than asking why, ask *"How can I use this for my own growth?"*

Until today, you may not have realized that you have the power to reshape and redefine any experience, no matter how devastating it seems. Just for today, take off the cloak of victimization. Look at your experience, and ask the Holy Spirit to show you how to use it for something good.

*Today I am opening my mind and heart
to the power of re-creation!*

OCTOBER 18

I will realize my own worth when I accept . . . I cannot
get away with inappropriate, unworthy behavior.

Life will let you get away with something for a while, but
sooner or later, you will pay the price! When you get the
bill, don't be shocked! Don't act like you don't understand!
Everything you do in life causes the effects that you experience. When you get the bill, be prepared to pay.

If you know that you are being dishonest, you must know that you
can only get away with being dishonest for a while. Eventually what you
do and say will come back to bite you. When it does, *don't cry over the
teeth marks!* Acknowledge what you have done. Forgive yourself. Ask for
forgiveness. Make amends or restitution if you can, and move on.

When you know that you are engaged in activities that dishonor
you, you know that you will eventually be *called on your stuff!* Only unworthy people can do unworthy things and get away with them. Since
you obviously are not in that category, *you can expect to get caught.* When
you do, don't act innocent! *Own your stuff!* Acknowledge your deeds.
Forgive yourself. Ask for forgiveness. Makes amends or restitution.
Move on! Now here comes the hard part.

When the moment of reckoning comes, you may feel as if you are unable to forgive yourself. You may be too proud to ask for forgiveness. There
may be no way you can make amends or restitution. In the worst case
scenario, you may be faced with all of these possibilities at once. Should
that happen, remember this: Life knows what you are capable of! The
only reason life has taken the time to point out your little shortcomings
and nasty habits is that life wants you to *act like you know* who you are.

Until today, you may have been trying to get away with doing something that is in conflict with the things life knows about you. Just for
today, stop doing things that are beneath you.

*Today I am devoted to stopping the things I do
that do not honor who I am!*

I will realize my own worth when I accept . . . I have the power and the ability to create my ideal life.

Some people have a way of acting as if their life is not their responsibility. They can give you chapter and verse of who did and didn't do whatever to make their life miserable. They can tell you point by point why they have been unable to do whatever because of whomever. They have no shame when it comes to letting you know what they don't have and can't do. Beneath it all there is someone else to blame. Their story may sound reasonable. It may even be plausible. You try to understand, to be sympathetic. Yet somewhere in the back of your mind, you know the truth. The *only reason* any person does not have the life they want is that somewhere in the back of their mind, *they don't believe they deserve it.*

For some people, this is a bitter pill to swallow. In fact, some people will spit the pill in your face! They will tell you about all of the attempts that have been thwarted by bad timing, bad people or people who had bad timing. They will tell you what they have had, what they have lost, what was stolen and who stole it. They will tell you about bad luck, bad breaks and all of the bad situations they have endured. Politely you will listen. Gently you may offer suggestions or avenues of hope. Much to your surprise, they don't want to hear it! People who are not willing to take responsibility for their lives would much rather hold on to their perceived limitations. Now you know the truth. The only reason a person does not have the life they want is that *somewhere in the back of their mind,* they don't believe they deserve it! They don't believe they are worthy of it! Which is why they will not take responsibility for making it happen.

Until today, you may have been trying to figure out how to turn your life around. Just for today, examine the reasons, excuses, limitations you may be holding on to. Take responsibility for getting rid of them.

Today I am devoted to taking responsibility for removing any self-imposed limitations!

OCTOBER 20

I will realize my own worth when I accept . . . God has
given me some things that nothing can change.

Your worth is not measured by what you do. Nor can you
calculate the degree of your worthiness by what you possess.
Your worth is a function of your *being*. Your being is color-
less, genderless and believe it or not, ageless. Your being is
worthy of honor, admiration and respect. It is a vessel of love and light.
It is a beacon of inspiration. Beneath all the things that your have told
yourself, been told about yourself, maybe even hold against yourself,
there is a *being* that you must learn to honor, value and embrace. It
doesn't take much to learn how to do it, and it is well worth the effort.
How you learn to "be" with yourself and how you honor the being that
you are will ultimately determine how worthy you feel.

Don't be harsh with your being. Don't waste your time regretting
things you have done or ways you have been. If you take a nice, long, slow,
deep breath, you will feel the truth of your being. Try it now. Take a nice,
long, slow deep breath. Slowly release that breath and take another one.
Sit in the stillness that is sure to fall over your being while you silently remind your being of its worth and value to the world. This simple practice
will put you in touch with all of the love, light, joy and inspiration you
need in the world. This practice allows you to embrace your being.

In learning to embrace your being, don't look at your mistakes. It is
a given that we will all make *some* mistakes in life. It is a given that you
will make inappropriate choices for inappropriate reasons. They will in
no way affect *your worth*. No matter what you say or what you do, nothing can minimize the worth of your being. Your worth is a gift from
God. Your worth is a gift of grace.

Until today, you may not have realized that God established the
worth of your being when you were given the gift of life. Just for today,
remain focused on the idea that your worth is not what you do or have.
Embrace the gift of your being.

*Today I am devoted to embracing my worthiness
as a divine gift!*

OCTOBER 21

I will realize my own worth when I accept . . . it is not
my job to make anyone else happy.

You cannot please other people. You cannot please your parents. You cannot please your friends or associates. You can
never please your children! If you are trying to please your
wife, husband, mate or lover, *forget about it!* As long as you try
to please one or all of these people, you will find yourself severely lacking.
You may even start to believe that you are inadequate. Eventually, you
may feel unworthy of the love, faith and trust they seem to place in you.

Have you ever considered that people don't want you to please
them? What they really want is for you to do what they think will make
them feel good. Often, they want you to do what they think is best for
you so that they will look good should you succeed. In an effort to spare
themselves the pain or shame of watching you fall flat on your face, they
will tell you what to do to satisfy and save their sensibilities. It has nothing to do with you! If you try to please these people without a clear understanding of their motivation, you will drive yourself crazy!

You may never be able to please anyone else, but there are a few
things that you can do. Do what you do, to the best of your ability, with
a loving intent, for the good of all involved. In doing this, you will be
true to yourself. You will be in alignment with the purpose of your life.
More important, you will be able to look at yourself in the mirror,
knowing you have done the best you know how to do. Be forewarned!
Anytime you try to do more than this, it can have a disastrous affect on
how you see yourself and how worthy you believe that you are.

Until today, you may have been caught in the trap of living your life
to please other people. They may have convinced you that it is your job
to make them happy or proud or feel better about you. Just for today,
live for yourself with a good intention for others.

*Today I am devoted to fulfilling my responsibility to do
what I am doing to be who I am!*

OCTOBER 22

I will realize my own worth when I accept . . . I cannot
fight my way to the top.

When you have an have an intact, healthy sense of worth,
you value other people. You realize that people are different.
You understand that people see things and interpret things
in different ways. You do not compare yourself to them, nor
do you feel the need to compete with them. You know who you are,
which means you can accept others as they are.

When you do not have a healthy or intact sense of worth, you feel
the need to win every argument. You feel the need to always prove your
point. You are threatened by differences. You need agreement with your
views, values and opinions in order to feel supported and acknowledged.
When you are not sure that who you are is good enough, you will do
your darndest to prove that you are better than someone else. Since you
do not have enough of your own worth to draw upon, you will set out to
destroy the worth of those who you believe are opposing you.

Should you ever find yourself on the attack, realize that you are experiencing a sense of *less than* or *not as good as*. When you find yourself
tearing someone else down in order to prove your point, realize that you
have lost your grounding. You are not centered in yourself. *Disagreement
is not the same as an attack!* When you call someone out, when you criticize their physical being, their talents, gifts or efforts, believing that their
inability to agree with you somehow *makes you wrong,* realize that *you
have lost it!* You have lost your sense of worth.

Until today, you may not have realized that you attack, criticize or
tear people down when they do not agree with you. Just for today, draw
on the strength of who you are. Stand in the strength of what you know.
Should you be faced with a different point of view, allow yourself and
others to simply be different.

*Today I am devoted to embracing the understanding
that my differences do not make me wrong!*

OCTOBER 23

I will realize my own worth when I accept . . .
life does not have to be hard.

When we are not clear that we are worthy, worthwhile and valuable beings, we believe that life must be hard. This belief will bring into your experience difficult situations that you will have to fight your way through. On the other end of the fight, you can sit back and marvel at what you have done. You have bragging rights about what you have *been through* and *come through. You are a fighter!* It may be difficult for you to understand that you are *creating* these situations to support the subconscious belief that you do not deserve to live a joy-filled or peaceful life.

Just because you can take a punch does not mean you must make yourself a punching bag! When we learn how to duck and dodge the punches life sends our way, this process of living can become an exhausting habit! There are people who are in the habit of living hard lives. When you expect to be punched, and you are always looking for the fist, it comes, again and again. Eventually, you become punch drunk—waiting to be knocked down so that you can prove that you can't be or won't be knocked out.

Life does not have to be hard! There is no good reason for you to be beaten up by the conditions in your life. If this is happening to you check out your expectations. Check to make sure that you are not waiting for the next disaster to strike, just to prove that you can take it.

Until today, you may not have been aware of the role your thoughts, words and expectations play in the creation of your life experiences. You may be creating pain in your life as a reflection of the belief that you are not worthy of anything else. Just for today, refuse to fight your way through life! Open your mind and your heart, asking that they be filled with a vision and an expectation of a joy-filled and peaceful future.

Today I am devoted to expecting and experiencing a peaceful, nonviolent way of living and being!

OCTOBER 24

I will realize my own worth when I accept . . .
there is something good within me waiting
to be released and realized.

If you look too good on the outside, people will not like you.
They will talk about you, making nasty accusations about
who you think you are or what you are doing to get what
you have. If you rise too high, people will be upset with you
for moving beyond what they think about you. If you are not clear about
who you are, you will fall prey to these people. In response, you will do
your best to stay where they want you, in a place where they are comfortable. This may not be the place you need or want to be; however,
when you depend on others to validate and acknowledge your experience, you can only be *what they think* you are worth being. You will only
allow yourself to be what someone else thinks about you.

It is not healthy, nor is it a worthwhile endeavor, to hold yourself
back to make other people comfortable. There is something great and
powerful within you that is waiting to be expressed. Other people may
not be able to see it. For that matter, *you may not be able to see it!* This
does not mean that it is not there. Quite often, you can be talked out of
your greatness by people who get uncomfortable when you start to rise.
Your rising demonstrates what they have chosen to believe is not true. If
you rise, you will prove that they are wrong. *Who wants to be wrong in
public?* When folks like this start talking to you, reach for the stars! Get a
grip on your greatness! Step into your bigness! And never look back!

Until today, you may have allowed what other people think you cannot do to become what you do not try to do. Just for today, move beyond
the expectations of others. Dare to be bigger, better, bolder than anyone
ever imagined. Surprise yourself! Do one thing that someone has encouraged you not to do. Just make sure it is something that is good for you.

*Today I am devoted to living bigger and better than
anyone ever imagined I would!*

OCTOBER 25

I will realize my own worth when I accept . . . I have access to a Divine source of information.

There is a divine and universal information bank that is readily available to you anytime and anywhere. It has been designed to meet your needs. It can be printed on your mind or your heart. It can be retrieved by anyone who holds the basic knowledge that *God is the software! You are the hard drive!* Whenever there is something you need to know, push your *faith button*. God will do the rest. If there is something you need to do or accomplish, push the *trust button* and *voilà!* God will do it through you! If you have been wracking your brain trying to remember something, let God program you to *receive grace*. In an instant, what you need will be downloaded into your thoughts. If you need restoration or reconciliation in a relationship, simply enter *forgiveness*. Mercy will generate a new program. If you are faced with an illness or disease of any kind, put a power, strength or wholeness disk in the zip drive of your mind. Program a new diet, a new thought pattern, a better connection to your source. Enter a prayer. Ask that your thoughts be formatted for a new design. Just you wait and see what comes forth!

As a human computer with divine programming, you have all the information you need. Every button you need to push is in your heart. All of the connecting cords are in your mind. The information package with directions is in your actions. Best of all, you have a *lifetime guarantee* that there can never be an irreparable breakdown when *God is your software!* And, if anything ever goes wrong with your hard drive, it can be fixed.

Until today, you may have had no idea that you were a divine instrument, full of useful and valuable information. Just for today, make sure that you are connected to your Source. Ask to have whatever you need to do or know downloaded from the Divine.

Today I am devoted to being a walking, talking human computer!

OCTOBER 26

I will realize my own worth when I accept . . . my life is a
worthwhile expression of a divine energy and purpose.

According to noted karmic astrologer Dora Jones, *"Each of
us comes into life with a promise, a gift, a passion and a deep
heartfelt desire."* As you become aware of what each of these
elements represents for you, your life becomes a quest to
bring yourself into alignment with the experiences that will ultimately
lead to self-realization.

The promise is what you have come to life to master. You have made a
promise to yourself to overcome, resolve or heal some aspect of your consciousness. As you face your life's experiences, you are given the opportunity to fulfill this promise. Your responses to your experiences determine
whether you fulfill or break the promise you have made to yourself.

The gift is what you have come to give to life. It is the cornerstone of
self-determination and self-actualization. The gift constitutes your talents and abilities—the special things you do as only you can do them.
The gift is enhanced or diminished by *how* you do *what* you do and how
you share with others those things that you do naturally or well.

*The passion represents those things that you pursue for the sheer joy of
it*—those things that you do that make you feel alive and meaningful,
valuable and worthy. Most of us are *frightened away from* or *talked out of*
our passion. We are made to feel it is inappropriate or useless.

The heartfelt desire is the thing you most want to experience in life.
Some want love. Others want acceptance. Most of us want both. The
difficulty we face is not losing our *identity* or *integrity* in the pursuit of
the heartfelt desire.

Until today, you may not have been aware of the true meaning and
purpose of your life. Just for today, ask the Holy Spirit, your guardians,
angels or guides to reveal to you how each of these elements is repre-
sented in your life.

*Today I am devoted to pursuing a deeper meaning and
a more divine expression in my life!*

OCTOBER 27

I will realize my own worth when I accept . . . what I do
says a lot about who I believe I am.

You have probably heard this statement before. This time,
really hear it. Take it into every fiber of your being with the
desire to really understand what it means. *"Your life is a testimony of who you are."* Your response to every experience in
your life is a witness to your character. Do you react defensively? In
anger? Or, do you respond lovingly? How you treat yourself and others
will convict you or exonerate you. Do you care about yourself? Do you
provide good, loving care for yourself? How you present yourself to the
world shows how you judge your character. Are you a hangman? An ex-
ecutioner? Or are you a caring, compassionate comforter? What you do
and how you do it is your jury. Are you biased or balanced? Are you open
or judgmental? The conditions and circumstances in which you live are
your courtroom. Are you free? Or are you mentally, emotionally or spiritually imprisoned?

As you review and examine the testimony your life is making to the
world, you gather the evidence of who you really believe you are. *You are
the only one who can testify for you or against you!* The evidence you present builds a case either for your worthiness or against it. What you believe about your own worthiness determines *how* the evidence is
presented. The amount of freedom you experience as well as the length
and degree of your mental, emotional or spiritual imprisonment is determined by the evidence you present. Perhaps it is time to overturn
some of your decisions.

Until today, you may not have been aware of how the conditions in
your life and how you live your life demonstrate what you believe about
yourself. Just for today, review the evidence and bring in a verdict. Are
you worthy? Are you not worthy?

*Today I am devoted to supporting the evidence for me and
changing the evidence against me that is me!*

OCTOBER 28

I will realize my own worth when I accept . . . how I take care of myself is important.

You may be in the process of trying to figure out why you don't do the things you say you want to do for yourself. Why don't I have a better diet? Why don't I get more rest? Why don't I spend more time doing the things that make me feel good? Why don't I exercise more? Why don't I work less? Why do I keep doing the things I say I am not going to do? Why do I wait until the last minute to do certain things? Why do I create so much stress and pressure for myself? Why do I say yes when I want to say no? Why do I act like the things that really matter to me don't matter at all? Why do I stay in situations where I am dishonored or devalued? Why don't I take time or make time for myself? Why don't I express what I feel when I feel it? Why don't I speak up for myself when I feel the need to do so? Why do I doubt myself? Why do I sabotage my dreams? Why do I abuse myself? Why do I feel taken advantage of? Why am I not earning what I believe I am worth? Why don't I save more money? Why do I waste and squander so much money? Why do I put others before myself? Why am I constantly faced with these questions?

If you are asking yourself one or more of these questions, there is something you are probably not aware of that you may want to consider. Perhaps you do not believe that taking care of yourself is important. In other words, maybe you don't believe that you are worth the effort.

Until today, you may not have understood how a belief of unworthiness can be manifested as a behavior. Just for today, adopt one behavior that will demonstrate your belief that you are important and worthy of the best of care.

Today I am devoted to behavior that will enhance my sense of worthiness!

OCTOBER 29

I will realize my own worth when I accept . . . everything
I set out to do begins within me.

In order to accomplish anything in life, you must have cooperation among all of the forces involved. The mind must
cooperate with the body. The body must cooperate with the
heart. The heart must cooperate with the desire. The desire
must cooperate with the vision. The vision must cooperate with will
power. The will power must cooperate with the ability. The ability must
cooperate with the opportunity. The opportunity must cooperate with
the timing. The timing must cooperate with the order. Order must cooperate with the outcome. The outcome must cooperate with the mind.

The point is, you must have *inner* as well as *outer* cooperation in
order to accomplish anything in life. The level of inner cooperation is
determined by your sense of worth. This means that what you think you
can do, you believe you will do. When you undertake any endeavor harboring a conscious or unconscious belief that you are not worthy of
doing it, you will find that you are unable to move forward.

The desire to do anything is Divine. The ideas you receive are *God's
ideas for you.* Until you believe that you, with all of your faults, can still
receive Divine inspiration, it will be difficult to get your head, your heart
and your body to move in one direction together.

Until today, you may not have been able to get the various aspects of
your being to cooperate with your desire. Just for today, examine resistance. What are you telling yourself? This is mental resistance. What are
you feeling? This is emotional resistance. What steps are you taking toward manifesting your dreams and goals? This is physical resistance.
Once each is identified, ask the Holy Spirit for support in bringing each
of these aspects into cooperation with the others.

*Today I am devoted to learning how
to cooperate with myself!*

OCTOBER 30

I will realize my own worth when I accept . . .
miracles happen every day.

Do you feel worthy of a miracle? Do you believe that for no
reason other than your being who you are, the good forces
of life will bring you something good or do something good
for you? Do you believe that you can experience divine
change, divine healing, divine inspiration simply by asking? It would be
a miracle if you could open your heart to receive a miracle. If you can *believe* it can happen to you, it just might happen. Miracles happen all the
time, but they only happen to those who believe they are worthy of
them.

When you first start to do something new, it is quite normal to
doubt or question your ability. You may feel unsure of yourself. You may
feel self-conscious because people are watching you. After a while, you
begin to get the hang of it. Your confidence is building. You feel more
comfortable within yourself, less doubtful about what you are doing.
This same concept can be applied to asking for and experiencing miracles in your life.

When you first ask for a miracle, all the reasons why your miracle
cannot or will not come true may come to mind. That's okay! Ask again.
The second time you ask, you may be experiencing disappointment that
your miracle did not manifest itself the first time you asked. That is fine!
Ask again. The third time you ask for a miracle, the miracle will have occurred. You will have opened your heart and moved beyond the belief
that you, for whatever reason, could not ask for a miracle.

Until today, you may have been reluctant to opening your heart and
asking the universe for something you really need or desire. Just for
today, believe in miracles. Ask for one, believing that you are worthy of
receiving it.

*Today I am devoted to being miracle-minded
and miraculously blessed!*

OCTOBER 31

I will realize my own worth when I accept . . .
I am worthy of divine blessings.

For those who experience feelings and bouts of unworthiness, the Beatitudes, Jesus' teaching presented in the Holy Bible, offer hope. If they were to be rewritten to address this very common human experience, they might be explained this way:

Blessed are those who have done all they know how to do.

When they stop, God starts.

Blessed are those who doubt their importance to God.

God will never give up on them.

Blessed are those who resist the urge to prove themselves.

They are the owners of true wealth.

Blessed are those who understand that life is a process of growth and
    healing.

They will grow, and their minds will be healed.

Blessed are those who don't beat themselves up for making mistakes.

They will live a peace-filled life.

Blessed are those who realize they are doing the best they can.

They go within themselves to find a better way.

Blessed are those who hold no against-ness.

They will be open to new ideas and insights.

Blessed are those who keep working toward a better understanding
    of the truth of who they are.

They will ultimately find the truth.

Until today, you may not have understood the simple things you can do to eradicate, eliminate and erase any beliefs that support unworthiness in your mind. Just for today, remember the divine words and divine love of a Divine Being who knows the truth about you.

Today I am devoted to remembering and experiencing the
blessings I have been given!

NOVEMBER

SERVICE

Once you know the truth,

you cannot go back to not knowing.

Living the truth that you know

is the greatest service you can offer the world.

NOVEMBER 1

*The greatest service I can offer is . . . no expectation
of recognition or reward.*

Service is not about fixing, changing or helping anyone. Service is about you. Service is about giving what you have to offer without expecting recognition or reward. It is about doing what needs to be done, as you are asked. It means giving 100 percent of your attention to what you are doing as long as you are able to do so without causing yourself harm. Anything more than this is an attempt to gain control. Anything less than this is a *disservice*.

When you go into a restaurant, it is the server's job to bring you whatever you order. Let's say you order a grilled chicken breast. It is not the server's job to *slaughter the chicken!* In most cases, the server is not the one who cooks the chicken. Hopefully, the server will not add hot sauce, bar-b-que sauce, gravy or ketchup to your chicken breast unless that is what you ordered. Nor would your server be likely to tell you about the cholesterol content of the chicken skin. It would not be appropriate for the server to take your order and then go get a haircut. Once your meal is prepared and presented, it is unlikely that the server would cut or chew the chicken for you. Nor would he tell you how big to cut the chicken pieces or how long to chew them. Once you have received the meal you ordered, if the server has done exactly what you asked and expected, you might leave a tip in appreciation. If the server expects the tip, he has not done his job. He has not served you.

Give what you have to offer without expectation. Do what you are asked to do—nothing more. Give 100 percent of your attention without causing yourself harm. Give with love. Give in joy. More you cannot do. Less you must not do, if it is your intention to be of service.

Until today, you may not have been aware of the elements and aspects of true service. Just for today, put forth the effort to serve, rather than trying to help someone.

*Today I am devoted to being a divine servant
and a servant of the Divine!*

NOVEMBER 2

The greatest service I can offer is . . . a blessing.

Bless difficult people! Those people who truly get on your nerves. Those who seem to be totally unaware that what they do has an impact on others. The people who have no qualms about demonstrating in word or deed that they do not want to be where they are, doing what they are doing. People who pout or mope while they are working. People who speak harshly, roll their eyes, suck their teeth or show up late without an explanation. Be willing to see difficult people in a new way. Don't be so quick to believe that their behavior has anything to do with you. Don't be impatient. Don't give them a hard time. Take the high road. *Bless them!*

When you bless difficult people, do it silently. Do it in your heart. Do it because you know the truth: Every living being is a divine creation. Some people forget their divinity. Others never know it because no one has told them they have it. Others will cleverly disguise their divinity with nasty dispositions, bad attitudes or indifference to those around them. The greatest service you can offer to God, yourself and the energy of the universe is a blessing. For all you know, your blessing may be exactly what a difficult person needs to open their heart and renew their faith in who they are and encourage them in what they are doing. Bless difficult people because there may come a day when you are having a difficult time and will need to be blessed by someone else.

Until today, you may have been sucked into letting difficult people create difficulty for you. Just for today, open your heart to difficult people. Bless them! Don't expect them to change. Instead, change your perspective about who they are and how you can save them.

Today I am devoted to encouraging and uplifting difficult people with a silent blessing!

NOVEMBER 3

The greatest service I can offer is . . .
a clear and loving message.

People do not have to hear your message. That is not their responsibility. When you are given a message, an insight, a revelation, your only responsibility is to deliver what you have been given. What happens once the message is delivered is not, IS NOT, your responsibility. If you judge the correctness, accuracy or power of your message based on how it is received, you will miss the point. Once you, the messenger, miss the point, the message is lost.

Most of us are well aware that God uses people do to Her/His most sacred work. Often, we are not sure exactly what it is that God is doing, and we become confused. We think that it is our idea and that we are doing the work. We assume the responsibility for getting God's work done right. We exhaust our time, energy and attention trying to make people understand or accept what we are saying or doing. If we do not get support and agreement from the right people, or the right number of people, we doubt ourselves. We begin to doubt the effectiveness of the message. Ultimately, we may begin to question God's authority.

It is important not to lose sight of the fact that we are God's messengers. The purpose of the message or the work we do belongs to God. Once you try to determine who should get the message, how they should receive it and what the response should be, the purpose, power and efficacy of the message can be lost.

Until today, you may have judged the importance of what you were saying about life or doing in life in response to the number of people who agreed with and supported you. Just for today, be the messenger. Let your life be the proof that the messages you receive are real.

*Today I am devoted to being a faithful
and obedient messenger!*

*The greatest service I can offer is . . . to remember that
my heart is strong.*

Your heart is a very strong muscle. What you think your
heart cannot withstand, it can. When you believe that your
heart doesn't know something, it usually knows. You do not
have to learn how to fix or mend the heart once it has been
broken or bruised. Instead, you must learn how to take care of the heart
so that you do not waste its energy and strength.

Someone once put it this way, "Your heart will not break, even when
you feel its pain." It is quite normal to avoid people and situations that
you believe will hurt you. It is natural to take precautions to protect
yourself from grief. However, what we really do is *test* people. We *try* situations. Testing and trying will not spare us heartache. In fact, these are
the very actions that weaken the capacity of the heart.

You know at the beginning of an endeavor whether or not it will be
fruitful. Make the choice to be involved or not involved at that time. In
doing so, you preserve the strength of your heart. Believe what people
show you about who they are! Make no attempt to *fix them!* Believe what
you see and choose whether or not you will be involved with them. This
preserves the strength of your heart.

On those blessed occasions when what you know is changing, when
what you believe proves not to be true or worthy, when what you expected does not manifest itself, do not tax your heart with fear, anger,
disappointment or resentment. Use a little faith and forgiveness to build
your heart's strength. Embrace any little shred of goodness you have received. This is the only way to build your heart's capacity to sustain you.

Until today, you may been operating under the false notion that
your heart can be broken. Just for today, remember that your heart is a
muscle that grows stronger as you move through experiences. Preserve
the strength of your heart by following its guidance.

*Today I am devoted to utilizing and building
the capacity of my heart!*

NOVEMBER 5

*The greatest service I can offer is . . . elimination
of my own self-doubt.*

You have a right to believe whatever you believe. It is also
quite normal to want to be supported in what you believe.
When, however, your attempts to gain support cause you to
get angry with others, there is something else going on. You
are asking someone else to say, *"You are okay in what you do or believe"*
because your confidence in yourself is not strong enough. In attempting
to draw your strength from others, you do yourself a grave disservice.

When you know something, know it! When you believe in something, believe it! If your experiences have led you to understand certain
things in a particular way, stand firm on what your experiences have
taught you. As you move forward, more experiences will bring you
greater clarity. As your experiences bring you greater clarity, your vision
will be enhanced. Enhanced vision will guide you in the right direction.
As you move from experience to experience, draw on your own inner
strength. Avoid the temptation to doubt yourself when other people
can't see or don't understand what you are saying or feeling. The key is to
be willing to go for what you know, when you know it, with or without
the company of others.

Until today, you may have sought the support of those who simply
cannot or do not know what you know. Or those who do not agree with
what you believe. Just for today, know and accept what you know without trying to gain support or validation from others.

*Today I am devoted to validating myself
and supporting what I know!*

NOVEMBER 6

The greatest service I can offer is . . . open, honest,
caring communication.

When two or more souls are blessed to be in the presence of
each other, the greatest service they can offer each other is
communication. Communication is more than *just talking!*
Communication is interaction between souls that serves a
higher purpose. Communication is a process of ingesting, digesting, as-
similating and utilizing the light, love and wisdom of the souls surrounding you. It is a process through which we learn to be authentic and
to trust the wisdom of our own hearts. Communication is also a process
in which we learn to trust as we learn that we can be trusted.

Honest, open, heartfelt communication is one of the greatest gifts we
can offer ourselves. It is a means of learning to *hear others* while we experience *being heard.* When you are in true communication with another
being, you have an opportunity to get clear about your own needs, desires
and intentions. You also become clear about the expectations others may
have of you. In the process, you gain clarity about the judgments and decisions you have made, the fears by which you are challenged, the changes
you may need to make, the forgiveness you may need for yourself and the
forgiveness you may need to offer. Open, honest communication allows
you to get your *perceptions and predispositions in check!*

Communication is the ultimate process of sharing your truth, learning the truth and experiencing the impact of truth. True communication is so much more than *just talking.* Talking to impress someone.
Talking to make a point. Talking to pass the time. True communication
rises to the level of interaction between minds and hearts and is a great
service toward the healing and evolution of the soul.

Until today, you may not have realized the value and importance of
communication. Just for today, set an intention to communicate each
time you open your mouth or your ears.

*Today I am devoted to healing myself and evolving with
others through the process of communication!*

NOVEMBER 7

The greatest service I can offer is . . . to step aside
and let God into someone's life.

When you decide for someone what they can or cannot do,
what they should or should not do, what they need or do
not need, you are standing between them and God. This
does not serve you, God, or the other person. When you decide what is right for someone, what is best for them, or how they should
go about doing what you feel is right and best in their life, you are getting between that person and what God has in store for that person. God
never sleeps! S/He knows exactly what each one of us needs and S/He
knows how to go about delivering it to us in a way that we can understand. When human beings learn to get out of God's way, they grow the
way they need to grow. They are able to do the things they need to do.
They move at a pace and in the direction that best serves them. The reason God gave us each a life is so that we could take care of it. If someone
needs your insight, wait until they ask for it. Once they do, ask their
Creator what you should do or say. As teacher and writer Marianne
Williamson would say, it may be as simple as asking,

Dear Lord:
What would you have me do? What would you have me say?

Until today, you may have allowed your love or concern for another
person to lead you to believe that you know what is best for them. Just
for today, take care of your own life. In other words, mind your own
business!

*Today I am loving and supporting others without
interfering in their lives!*

NOVEMBER 8

The greatest service I can offer is . . . making up
my own mind.

Do not allow others to make decisions for you unless you believe in your heart that you can live up to them. Few things will destroy your self-worth more completely than doing something simply because someone else wants you to do it. When you convince yourself that it is okay for someone to decide who you are, what you can do or how you should proceed in your life, you open the floodgates to powerlessness and worthlessness. If you feel either of these two things long enough, you will eventually believe that they are true.

There is a big difference between cooperation and coercion. When you cooperate you are commingling your thoughts, choices, needs and desires with others. You are standing fully in the truth of who you are and what you desire to experience. Cooperation is *being* along. Coercion is *going* along. When you are being coerced, you go *along* to avoid confrontation. You *go along* in fear of retaliation. You *go along* to keep the peace. You *go along* rather than take responsibility for your own choices or the fulfillment of your own needs. Coercion only leads to believing that someone else knows *more about you than you do!*

In order to serve your own best interests and escape the trap of coercion, you must know that what you believe about yourself is valuable to you. You must believe that what you feel can be trusted. Even when you are not sure of what you know or what you feel, be willing to take a risk. When you believe in yourself enough to take a risk, you can avoid allowing others to make decisions for you.

Until today, you may have gone along with the plans other people have for your life. Just for today, make a decision to run your own life. Once you do it, let everyone know.

Today I am devoted to taking a risk and making some
decisions about how my life will be!

The greatest service I can offer is . . . open up to learning
more, doing more and being more.

In the midst of a difficult or challenging situation, don't shut
down, *open up!* Just when you think you can't take any more,
do any more, be any more, do not give up! *Open up!* When it
feels like you are about to fall off a cliff, *jump!* When it looks
like everything is falling apart, start rebuilding from the rubbish and
remnants of what is left. The only way to get to the next level is to *go there.*

There are times when we do not recognize that it is time for us to move
forward. Other times we recognize the need to move, but are not sure of
how to take action. Then there are those times when we keep putting off
what we know we need to do, hoping where we are will be just fine. Perhaps we are waiting for the right opportunity to come along. In any event,
when life is ready for us to move and we resist, life will move us *by any
means necessary!* What may feel like a disaster is actually a graduation.

When something goes *thud* in your life, remain open. Do not resist
the need to move when your life tells you that it is time to move. Resistance closes your mind and heart. When your mind and heart are closed
by resistance, what you need will have no way to enter your consciousness. Remain open to being taught what to do next. Remain open to
healing your feelings about who and what you may be leaving behind.
Remain open to knowing things that you don't already know. Remain
open to testing what you already know. Remain open to being guided,
supported and protected by the universe. For all you know, what you are
challenged by may be the very thing you have been waiting for.

Until today, you may have allowed difficulties and challenges, hard
times and bad times, breakups and breakdowns to close your mind to
the possible breakthroughs. Just for today, open your mind and your
heart to life. If you are being forced to move out of a familiar situation,
remain open to being told and taught what to do next.

*Today I am devoted to dusting off my wings
and flying!*

NOVEMBER 10

The greatest service I can offer is . . .
being a light on the path.

At night, the ocean can be a huge, dark and scary place. When riding on the seas, you can never know for sure if the water will be calm or turbulent. You never know if you will drift off course or run aground. That is why there are lighthouses. When ships lose their way, they are guided by the lighthouse. When there is trouble or danger at sea, you can seek refuge by the light of the lighthouse. In the midst of a storm the lighthouse will always guide the ships safely to shore. Best of all, there is always someone in the lighthouse.

Be a lighthouse. Let your life be a shining symbol for others. Let everything you do be in service to someone. Stand tall in the knowledge of who you are. Stand proudly in the midst of difficult times. Be aware that who you are and what you have to offer can be a beacon to some lost soul.

Be a lighthouse keeper. Be on the lookout for lost souls. Be alert to those who may be in need and have nowhere to go or no way to get there. Be a lighthouse to a child. Guide a child. Protect a child. You don't have to say much. Just let the child know that you are there should a need arise. Be a lighthouse to an elder, someone who has traveled the sea of life but now needs a little warmth and comfort—perhaps a cup of tea or some interesting conversation. Be a lighthouse to a young man or woman who has lost their footing or may be losing their direction in life. Remember, no matter what condition a wind-blown sailor reaches the lighthouse in, the keeper is always welcoming. The keeper always encourages. The keeper always has something on hand or knows what to do to get you up and sailing again.

Until today, you may have been wondering how you can be of greater service to your family, your community or the world. Just for today, be the keeper of a lighthouse.

Today I am devoted to shining the light of compassionate support and service on those who may be in need!

NOVEMBER 11

The greatest service I can offer is . . . to revive my heart, my mind and my life.

Have you ever been to a revival? I am talking about a foot-stomping, hand-clapping, song-singing, soul-stirring revival. If you have never been to one, you just might need to convene one today. Stop everything you are doing! Cancel your appointments! Turn off the telephone and the television! Lock your doors! Pull down the shades! Kick off your shoes and have a spirit-filled revival in your life! Here's what you have to do.

Call forth all of the things that are testing you, challenging you, pushing and pulling you, knocking you off center, causing you to feel unsettled. Call them by name. Call them by details. Call them into the center of your life. Stomp your feet and say, NO MORE! When a person in a revival gets to stomping their feet, every ungodly thing is going to flee. Then call into being all of the things you long for, the things you believe will lift you up or propel you forward. Call them into your life. When you feel as if these things are real in your mind and your heart, clap your hands, giving thanks for them. Then cast out the things you are ready to release. Drop to your knees and ask for guidance. While you are down there, you might as well offer someone forgiveness. When you are done, jump up. Ask for protection from *inner* and *outer* adversaries. While you are jumping, shake off bad habits, bad feelings, bad attitudes, and don't forget people who may be a bad influence. When you are finished jumping, you may be tired. So lie down! Lie down and surrender! Surrender your will to Divine Will. Surrender your mind to Divine Mind. Surrender your life to the Divine plan for your life, and stay down until you know in your heart that you have been revived in the spirit.

Until today, you may have been searching for a way to get your life cleaned up and cleared out. Just for today, have a revival. Revive your faith. Revive your strength. Revive you head, heart and spirit.

Today I am devoted to creating a revived and renewed energy in my life!

NOVEMBER 12

*The greatest service I can offer is . . . being a star
with a good and supportive cast.*

Lights! Cameras! Action! Your life is on center stage, and you are the star. You have been practicing for the opening of your show all of your life. You set the stage with what you believe. You chose the cast for every role with what you chose to think about yourself. You wrote the script with every word you have ever spoken and every action you have ever taken. The question is, what part will you play in your own show? Will you be a victim or a victor? A lover or a loser? Will you be a hero? A villain? It is *your show,* which means you get to choose what role you will play in your life.

Many people believe that the way their lives play out has more to do with the characters in their lives than how they direct themselves. Others believe it is the *producer* who hires people to do them harm and fires people who are good to them. It is this same producer who some believe has written the script for their lives, casting them in a role for which they are unprepared. Few of us understand that what we believe about who we are determines the role we play in life.

You can act helpless or be powerful. You can act victimized or be vigilant. You can act up each time you do not get your way, or you can act out your greatest dreams. You can act like a star and live like a star, or you can be an underpaid understudy. Whatever the scene or circumstance, you will always act out the role you have been practicing in your mind. You will live the script you believe you are worthy to live. You will have an entire cast of characters who either support you or turn on you, based on what you believe.

Until today, you may have been waiting for a producer to discover you and cast you in a life role that would make you a star. Just for today, decide whether the script you are acting in now serves you or is doing you a disservice. Remember that you are directing the entire show.

*Today I am devoted to being a skilled director and
producing a better life experience!*

NOVEMBER 13

The greatest service I can offer is . . . accepting the value
and importance of who I am and where I am in life.

You are exactly who you are because who you are is important. Everything you are is valuable and important. You are important to yourself and to everyone else. If you were not exactly who you are, somebody very important would be missing from the experience of life.

You are exactly where you are because all that you have to give and receive is right where you are now. Where you are is valuable and important. Everything you know is needed right where you are. Everything you can do is *do-able* right where you are. If you were over there or over here, there would be a big void right where you are now.

You have gone through all that you have been through because of who you are. Because of what you needed to know. Everything you have done and been through is valuable and important. In order to be who you are, to know what you know, to be where you are in this moment, you needed to go through what you went through.

Who you are, where you are, what you know gives you value. It either makes your life important or discounts the importance of your life. How much you believe in who you are, serve where you are and use what you know can make a very big difference in who you become, where you go and what you do when you get to the next place.

Until today, you may have resisted, ignored, denied or underestimated the importance and value of who you are, where you are and what you know. Just for today, don't do that!

*Today I am devoted to accepting the value and importance
of every aspect of my life as it is now!*

NOVEMBER 14

The greatest service I can offer is . . .
doing what needs to be done.

Of course you deserve to have the things you want in life. Of course you are worthy of having them. These are givens. The question is, are you willing to do the work required to get what you want? I am not talking about physical work. Oh no! Most of the time, we are all ready and willing to *kill ourselves working* to get the things we want. If that is all it takes, everyone's success would be assured. It is the mental, emotional and spiritual work that we usually overlook. When there is something that you really want, there is one thing you must really do—FOCUS! Focus your thoughts. Focus your energy. When you really want to focus on something, there is something you must develop and maintain—DISCIPLINE! You must be disciplined about what you think. You must do everything in a disciplined way. When you are working to master the art of discipline, there is something you must be—OBEDIENT! Obediently follow your *first focused* thought. Obediently follow through on the disciplined actions you take. When you are really obedient, there is one thing you will undoubtedly develop—FOCUS! With focus, discipline and obedience, you will reach any goal successfully.

Until today, you may have believed that you could physically work your way to success. Just for today, focus your energy and attention on the mental, emotional and spiritual work that will serve you as you reach for your highest and greatest good.

Today I am devoted to being obediently disciplined about the things I am focused on being and doing!

The greatest service I can offer is . . . learning to recognize the root of the problem.

Television evangelist Rev. Creflo Dollar once said, "When you get to the root, you will grow fruit." He was in essence saying, the *root of a problem* is the *cause of the problem*. The root feeds and nurtures the entire plant. The same is true with a recurring problem that you may face in life. You cannot solve a problem by pruning the stem. You have to get to the root of a problem in order to *uproot it*. When you get to the root, you find the core issue, the foundation on which the problem has been built.

A core issue is a belief that is imprinted on the consciousness. Let us say, for example, that you believe life has to be difficult. Try as you may to make your life easy, peaceful or joy-filled, you will attract experiences and situations that support the core belief. What you may not realize is that you have *root rot!* There is a rotten belief in your thought system.

All core beliefs manifest themselves as experiences. When something unpleasant happens in your life, call for the core belief. Get still. Take a few deep breaths and ask yourself, "What is at the core of this experience?" In other words, what is it that I think, say or do that supports the existence of this problem. Undoubtedly, your first instinct will be to say that you had nothing to do with what is going on. *It's them! It's not my fault!* This is the very thinking that will allow your root rot to spread. Remember, you are responsible for every experience in your life. Experiences come to show you what you really believe. Pull up the root, and it will die.

Until today, you may have been pinching off little pieces of a problem just because you did not understand that you must pull the sucker up from the roots. Just for today, closely examine any and all challenges in your life. Ask the Holy Spirit to bring to your awareness the root, the cause of the problem. Then ask for guidance about how to plant a new belief that serves a greater good in your consciousness.

Today I am devoted to eliminating root rot and rotten roots from my own consciousness!

NOVEMBER 16

The greatest service I can offer is . . .
living my life in grace.

Have you ever had the experience of doing something you really love for an extended period of time, only to discover that you no longer want to do what you are doing? For no reason, you are suddenly unhappy being where you are or doing what you are doing. Yet for some reason, there is a gnawing feeling in the pit of your stomach that where you are no longer serves you. You may even feel bad because you have no *logical explanation* for it. However, the reason may be that the grace and the blessing have been lifted.

When God's grace and blessing have been lifted from a situation, you will no longer be able to stay there. Once you have fulfilled the purpose, once you have grown, learned and *gifted* all that is required of you, according to God's purpose, grace is then lifted. When you are in a good situation, the lifting of grace may make you feel guilty. You may want to stay because you don't have a *good reason* to leave. Here's a good one: to stay once God has let go of a situation may take you *out of grace with God.*

There are many ways to know when the grace has been lifted from a situation. The excitement, enthusiasm and fulfillment you once received may have vanished. Perhaps your energy and effort are no longer yielding fruit, or you are achieving a *diminishing return* for the energy you are expanding. Grace makes your way easy. Grace opens closed doors. Grace will also close doors when God's purpose has been served.

Until today, you may have thought you needed a good reason to leave a good situation even when you don't feel good about being there. Just for today, get still and ask the Holy Spirit to tell you whether or not God's grace has been lifted from where you are. You may not like the answer you get, but it can only serve your best interests to consider it.

*Today I am devoted to confirming where I must be and
what I must do to be covered by grace!*

NOVEMBER 17

The greatest service I can offer is . . . following the light
of the Holy Spirit.

The *Holy Spirit* is the activity of God. It is the light of God that shines in your life, guiding you into experiences that are loving, joyful, peaceful. The light of the Holy Spirit brings you ideas, dreams and visions of what your life could be. There are times when what you think is good for you and what the Holy Spirit knows is good for you are two different things. What you *think* is usually based on what you know and what you can see. What the Holy Spirit *knows* is always based on God's plan and purpose for your life. The question is, *are you willing and available to follow the light of the Holy Spirit?*

Everything you have ever desired for yourself already exists in the realm of the Holy Spirit. At just the right time, in just the right way, the Holy Spirit will shine its light into your life to show you where to go and what to do. You may see it and not believe it. You may feel it and find the feeling uncomfortable. When this happens, you become resistant. You talk yourself out of the very thing the Holy Spirit is pushing you into. *Your knowledge is never a match for the Holy Spirit's knowledge!* You will never have a *vision* until God has allocated the *provision* for the manifestation of the dream.

The provisions for the manifestation of your dreams and visions exist right now. They are being incubated in the light of the Holy Spirit. The only thing that is required of you is an open heart and a willing spirit. If you have done all you can do to prepare yourself in the physical realm, the light of the Holy Spirit will do the rest.

Until today, you may not have been aware that the Holy Spirit knows more about you than you do. You may have believed that you were not ready to live the manifestation of your dreams and deepest desires. Just for today, look for the light of the Holy Spirit in your life. Ask the light to shine on the path you must follow toward the realization of a dream.

*Today I am devoted to looking for and following the light
of the Holy Spirit!*

NOVEMBER 18

The greatest service I can offer is . . . willingness to do things in a new way.

Some of us are given the awesome task of breaking our family's pattern of poverty, pain, suffering, ignorance and fear. Some of us come into life for the sheer purpose of guiding our family into a new way of thinking, living and being. For this reason, your family may think you are *weird* or different. They may accuse you of doing things that are not *right*. They may even tell you that what you are doing is *wrong*. You may feel that you *are* wrong. If everyone is content *going right,* who are you *to go left?* If everyone in your immediate family has made it through life in a cold-water flat, *who are you* to want a town house? Should you find yourself in this predicament, stop trying to convince them, *show them!*

We are living in a new age, a new time, when things must be different. You cannot continue to do what has always been done. *Something or someone must change!* It might as well be you! You have the visions. You have the opportunity. The only thing you need is the strength and courage to recognize that you have been chosen for the awesome task of implementing change. If you follow your own inner guidance, your progress will be the only evidence you need. Your life will provide a new direction for the generations that will follow you. Your job is to bring about change in a loving, gentle and harmonious way. You may have to leave some people behind. Should that be the case, bless them and keep on moving.

Until today, you may have been so loyal to your family patterns that you would not step beyond what you have been taught to believe. Just for today, dare to be different! Dare to introduce a new way of living and being. Dare to climb out of the family tree.

Today I am devoted to recognizing that the patterns of my family tree may be a noose around my neck!

NOVEMBER 19

The greatest service I can offer is . . . allowing myself
to be used to serve a greater good.

Are you available to be used by the Holy Spirit? Do you
make yourself available for the good things in life? From
your perspective, you always endeavor to do the best possible thing, for the good of all concerned under most circumstances. No matter what you may tell yourself or others, making and
keeping yourself available *to do good and be good is a full time job!*

Have you ever been led to give someone a compliment? Yet when the
opportunity presented itself, you decided that the other person didn't
deserve it or that you didn't know how to say it the right way. Holding
back the good that you are led to share means that you are not available
to do good. How many times have you been inspired to be silent, to hold
back your comments and opinions, to let the comments or behaviors of
another person go unchallenged by you? Your first thought may be, *"I'm
not going to say a word."* Yet for some reason you cannot hold your peace.
You make some comment that leads to an argument or disagreement.
Speaking when you are led not to speak means that you are not available
for peace. Have you ever been led to apologize but let your self-
righteousness or ego get in the way? If you have engaged in these behaviors, you were not available to be used by the Holy Spirit.

Here is a theory that may help you the next time you fail to make
yourself available to do something good: *Stealing is not only taking. It is
also refusing to give.*

Until today, you may have considered yourself to be a good person
who is always available to do good things. Just for today, consider all of
the good things that you *have not* done, and consider the reasons why.
Set your intentions to always be aware of an opportunity to do something good and to be in service to the Holy Spirit.

*Today I am devoted to being a good servant
of the Holy Spirit!*

NOVEMBER 20

The greatest service I can offer is . . . not engaging in crimes against myself.

You cannot be useful to yourself, others or God if you run yourself ragged. Many of us believe that in order to be useful, helpful or in service, we must give our all to all, all of the time. We become *yes* people. We say *yes* when we are tired. *Yes* when we are busy doing other things. We say *yes* when we know there is *no way* we can take on anything else. You may believe that in order to be worthy of the love, admiration or respect of others, you must always say *yes*. What you may not understand is that there are times when saying *yes* causes you to make unnecessary sacrifices.

There is a passage in *A Course in Miracles* that says, "Giving of yourself to the point of sacrifice makes the other person a thief!" When you allow others to take what you need, what you have earned, what you deserve, you are making a sacrifice. When you sacrifice, you are not giving freely. Nor are you serving others when you give to your detriment. In addition, when you give to your own detriment, you become resentful. You resent yourself and you resent the one who has received. Resentment is a clear-cut path to anger and unworthiness.

In order to serve others, support others, give to others, you must first be able to serve, support and give to yourself. You must be willing to share your overflow, not your necessities. This is called *self-support, self-care* and *self-love*.

Until today, you may not have realized that you have allowed others to be involved in a crime against you. You may have allowed them to support you in sacrificing yourself and believing that you were helping or serving them. Just for today, don't be a yes person! Take care of yourself. Don't give what you don't have or what you need. Be self-supportive and self-loving enough to say *no*.

Today I am devoted to not making unnecessary sacrifices!
Today I am willing to say no!

NOVEMBER 21

The greatest service I can offer is . . . acknowledging
all that I am aware of in my life.

Here are a few things you may want to explore and consider on your path of personal growth:

1. Know everything you can know about you! Know what makes you tick. Know what makes you laugh. What makes you cry. Know what opens your heart. Know what happens when your heart is open. Share what you discover with as many people as possible.

2. Know what life is all about! What is important in life. Know what is sacred and holy in life. Know what life is and what life is not. Know where life comes from and why. Know what makes you want to be alive. Share what you discover with as many people as possible.

3. Know why you are alive! Know that you are essential. Know that you are valuable. Know that every experience is an important step toward helping you figure out your purpose. Share what you discover with as many people as possible.

The more you learn about life, the more you learn about yourself. The more you learn about yourself, the greater is the purpose you serve in life. Some people live their entire lives never sharing what they discover about themselves or about life. Others never explore these questions and never experience what the answers can uncover. Don't be one of them!

Until today, you may have been wondering how to go about developing a greater perspective of yourself and your life. Just for today, spend some time pondering and reflecting on these three simple points and sharing your discoveries with others.

Today I am devoted to sharing my discoveries
about self-discovery!

NOVEMBER 22

The greatest service I can offer is . . . courageous
investigation of everything I see, know and believe.

Go deep enough to get under a thing to discover what is
holding it up.
Rise high enough above a thing to see it from a new
perspective.
Until you get to the core of a thing, or
see it from a new place,
you will not be able to determine how or if the experiences
of your life
serve your highest and greatest good.

Until today, you may have been walking through the middle of an
experience, trying to figure out what it is. Just for today, courageously
investigate every possible angle of the situation. More important, be
willing to acknowledge how *you* have been keeping it in place.

Today I am devoted to digging deep and flying high!

NOVEMBER 23

The greatest service I can offer is . . .
to always be observant.

Take a long, slow look around your life. *Don't leave anything out!* Look at every experience. Next, look at every person. Look at the role they play in your life. Look at the size and shape of your body. Look at the state of your health. Next, turn within. Examine every thought. Examine every feeling. Examine every belief that you currently call a reality in your life. Once you have finished looking, ask yourself, *"What monuments have I built to the belief that I am unworthy? Unlovable? Unimportant? Insignificant?"*

Think of it this way: In the political world, if you want to harness public opinion or gather evidence about a particular belief, you look for statistics. Statistics and opinion polls prove what you want to know and demonstrate what is believed. The same principle holds true in your life, with one *slight twist.* In your life, you must *first* believe it. Then you attract or create, consciously and unconsciously, the evidence that proves you are right.

If you believe you are unlovable, you will build relationships to memorialize that belief. If you believe you are a failure, you will attract or create experiences that will statistically prove that which you already believe. If you believe that you are not important, somehow, someway, it will be evidenced in your life by the people and experiences that surround you. The only way to create or attract new experiences is to look at the very clear evidence of what you now believe.

Until today, you may have been unaware of the monuments you have built and evidence you have gathered to support your conscious and unconscious beliefs. Just for today, take a look around. Ask yourself whether or not you are proud of what you have built in your life. If you are not proud, re-read yesterday's message.

Today I am devoted to observing and examining the monuments that are standing in my life!

NOVEMBER 24

The greatest service I can offer is . . . being the best of who I am.

Do you go the extra mile? Do you do more than is expected? Or do you do just enough to get by? Do you expect the best? These questions pertain not only to your relationship with the world, they also pertain to *how you* treat yourself. Do you go the extra mile when it comes to you, or do you think that the least is enough for you?

There are people who believe that struggle, servitude and sacrifice are the best they can hope for in this life. They look for ways and reasons to be *okay* with the things they believe *are not okay* in their lives. Other people believe they must always be on the giving end. These are the people who give until it hurts. In fact, they may not know *how to receive.* These are the people who have not learned how to go the extra mile in exploring what may be possible in their lives.

Going the extra mile means taking what you have and looking for ways to expand it—you believe in your ability to make it happen. Going the extra mile means doing just a little more than is expected, being just a little more than is expected, having just a little more than even you expected. It means moving beyond limiting beliefs, restrictive behaviors and being willing to have more than you do right now. Going the extra mile does not mean that you have prideful ambitions. It means that you want to feel better about yourself. You want to know that you can surpass your own expectations. You want to push your mind to the limits. It can be quite a rewarding experience!

Until today, you may have been doing just enough to keep yourself alive and going. You may have been expecting just enough to keep yourself from being unhappy. Just for today, go the extra mile. Stretch your mind. Expand your vision. Elevate your expectations as far as you can imagine is possible for you.

Today I am devoted to allowing myself to explore the best of all possibilities for myself!

NOVEMBER 25

The greatest service I can offer is . . . being gentle with myself as I change.

Changing your life does not always mean that you *stop doing* certain things. It may mean that you *start doing* certain other things. It may mean moving your time, energy and focus away from all the things you *should not* be doing and placing them on the things you *should be* doing. Rather than beating yourself up for what you are *not doing,* appreciate and celebrate the things that you *are doing.* When you shift your focus away from what you do not want, you can create a vision for what you do.

Changing your life means *learning* a new way to be. Learning occurs in a loving and supportive environment. When you are hostile toward yourself, frustrated or angry with yourself, it will be difficult for you to learn. You will set expectations for yourself that you cannot live up to. *How can you be for yourself if you are against yourself?* Learning occurs best when there is an attitude and an environment of acceptance. When you judge the mistakes you make as "bad," you will be resistant to learning the lesson. If you were to be completely honest, you would admit that *you don't want to be wrong!* Being wrong makes you feel ashamed of yourself.

What you really want to do is nurture the attitude that you are open to learning more about yourself. Accepting more about yourself. This is the information that will inspire you to do something new. Rather than creating an internally hostile environment by focusing on what you must stop doing, focus on what you want to do. Choose a new course of action that will change the way you experience yourself.

Until today, you may not have recognized the things you do to yourself that make it hard for you to do anything different. Just for today, lighten up! Don't fight with yourself! Focus on what you do, can do, choose to do, are ready to do.

Today I am making a shift in the way I focus on my activities!

NOVEMBER 26

The greatest service I can offer is . . . standing confidently in my power.

It does not serve you or the world for you to behave as if you are powerless. It is an insult to the Creator of your life, in whose image and likeness you were created, for you to bow or bend down to conditions and situations that are beneath you. It is arrogant of you to assume that you are incapable *because you don't believe* you are capable.

You have gifts. You have the gift of intellect. You can think yourself into and out of any situation with which you are confronted. You have the ability to speak for yourself. You can defend yourself! Promote yourself! Encourage yourself! Teach yourself! Correct yourself! That is power. You have a heart. Through it you can experience love, grief, compassion, empathy, joy, peace and an entire realm of emotions that let you know that you are alive. While you are alive, you can create, destroy and rebuild something as insignificant as a Lego house or something as significant as the capital city of a state. You can create another life! Through that life you have the opportunity to share words of compassion, to express feeling of love, to know the joys of sharing and to experience the wonderment of seeing a life grow before you eyes. That is powerful! You are powerful! Now, why don't you try acting like it?

Until today, you may have believed that money is power, education is power, or that the things that you can do make you more or less powerful. Just for today, know that you are powerful. Stand up in your power! Embrace your power! Serve the world by bringing your power into your life. Start by being grateful for the power you have been given and are using free of charge!

Today I am devoted to experiencing myself as a powerful being!

NOVEMBER 27

*The greatest service I can offer is . . . freeing myself
to live freely.*

Have you ever watched small children playing alone in a
room? They will talk to themselves, and they will answer.
They will dress themselves up. They sing and dance. A
small child in a room all alone can have a marvelous time en-
tertaining himself. Children can do this not only because they have an
innocence that helps them to rise above the cares of the world; they don't
mind being alone with their thoughts and their dreams. They don't
mind acting out their fantasies. They can live their lives beyond the expectations of others. In a room all alone, children have no inhibitions.
They have nothing to prove and no one to satisfy but themselves. *They
feel free!* They are unencumbered by opinions and directives. It happens
because *nobody is watching them.*

Live your life like nobody is watching you. Live beyond expectations.
Live beyond what you have been told is right, wrong, good or bad. Just
for one day, live like you are totally free to be anything and do anything
you choose for yourself. Live from your innocence. Live from a sense of
total satisfaction with who you are and what you have available to you.
Let yourself dream like nobody can stop you. Let yourself sing like nobody is listening. Let yourself dance like nobody is watching. Play dress
up! Talk to yourself! Tell yourself something that you would never repeat
aloud. Let yourself be exactly who you are and live like it is okay—because it really is.

Until today, you may have been living your life under the impression
that your every move is being watched. You may have felt like there are
certain things you *could not* and *should not* do. Just for today, allow yourself the childlike freedom of talking to yourself, dreaming for yourself,
dancing with yourself and living your life like nobody else in the world
cares or is watching what you are doing.

*Today I am going to live my life like nobody is
watching me!*

NOVEMBER 28

The greatest service I can offer is . . . being willing
to live through the pain I experience.

There are several ways to commit *suicide*. Some people actually do something to end their lives. Others take pieces of
their lives and pieces of themselves and tuck them away.
They live only a part of a life, with only a part of themselves,
allowing the other parts to die off. Still others live in a state of numbness.
They shield and protect themselves from feeling anything, believing
that they can avoid the onslaught of pain. All of these people are the
walking dead! They try their best to act alive. They are not alive because
they have yet to discover the blessings of pain.

To experience mental or emotional pain is actually a gift of life. At
the core of your pain is an answer, possibly the very answer you have
been seeking. We mistakenly believe that the path to a good life or a better life is to eliminate pain. *Suicide is not the way out of pain!* In fact, the
most loving, alive and self-supporting thing we can do is to embrace our
pain. Often this requires a skill we have not been taught. It requires that
we remain present in the midst of a painful experience.

All forms of pain come to teach you. To strengthen you. To reveal
some deeper understanding of your true identity. Moving through pain,
you may find your true purpose. Often pain comes into your life to wake
up the parts and pieces of you that are numb. Those parts that are *fear-
fully* dead. *Doubtfully* immobilized. You begin to pick up pieces and
parts that you have tucked away. Staying present in the pain can often
remind you that you really do want to live in a more loving, more honest, more fulfilling way. What a gift! What a blessing!

Until today, you may not have been aware of the benefits of painful
experiences. Just for today, open your heart to be present in your own
pain. When it seems as if the pain or the memory of the pain is more
than you can handle, ask for it to present you with its gift.

*Today I am devoted to remaining fully present and
alive to my every thought and feeling!*

NOVEMBER 29

The greatest service I can offer is . . . resisting the
tendency to be resistant.

There is a process of living that few of us know much about
but many of us practice. It is a way of living and being that
creates hostility and bad feelings. This process has even led
to war! It is a process that pits your good against the good of
someone else. In order to engage in the process, one must believe in right
vs. wrong. Good vs. bad. My way vs. your way. In the midst of the
process, people are hurt. Sometimes lives are lost, and for all the arguing
or fighting that goes on, nothing is ever proven conclusively. The process
is *against-ness.*

To be against something is to deem it unworthy of consideration or
bad at the very least. At worst, *against-ness* poses a threat to who you are,
what you believe in and what you want in life. *Against-ness* is the belief
that if someone gets what they are after, you *will not* get what you are
after. If you believe that you have the right way to the good thing, it
stands to reason that everyone else is wrong. You are constantly on the
lookout to ensure that the thing you are against is not coming near. Unfortunately, the harder you look for it, the more of it you will see.

The way to live without against-ness is to live from a place of *for-ness.*
Rather than working *against* something, simply be *for* something else. In-
vest your time, energy and attention in working to bring about the things
that you desire to experience. When you are confronted by something
that challenges what you are working toward, do not be against it! Allow
other things to exist. Simply choose to put your attention elsewhere.

Until today, you may have been expending so much energy working
against certain things that you have not been working for anything else.
Just for today, drop all against-ness. Focus your attention and energy on
the things that you can stand up for.

*Today I am devoted to allowing everything the right
to exist and choosing what I am for!*

NOVEMBER 30

The greatest service I can offer is . . . prayer.

Here is a prayer for you today.

Blessed and Divine Holy Spirit:
I thank you right now for the manifestation of every good intention I have ever had. I thank you that my good intentions manifest so that I may experience a deeper sense of self-love and self-appreciation. I thank you for the light and energy of your love that support my intention to know, experience and express the truth of who I am. I thank you for the grace and mercy of your love that support my intention to become a light of inspiration to others in my life and to the world. I thank you for your wisdom that supports my intention to be more loving and accepting of others. Thank you for reminding me that it is not loving to hold on to hurt or to withhold forgiveness from myself and others. I thank you for allowing my life to reflect back to me those things about myself that I have been unable to see, unwilling to acknowledge and unable to heal. Thank you for demonstrating to me that I can experience joy and happiness without pain and that the greatest joy of all is being able to accept and embrace myself exactly as I am, right where I am. Thank you, Holy Spirit, for holding my intention to be a living example of all that you are. For this I am so grateful!

Until today, you may not have realized the power of an affirmative prayer. It is the power you possess to call a thing a reality when it may not yet be. Just for today, affirm your intentions for yourself and your life in the form of a prayer.

Today I am devoted to praying for a higher experience and expression of the intentions I set for myself!

DECEMBER

PEACE

You have survived life-threatening, life-altering crisis and challenge to prove only one point: that you can and have survived!

Be at peace with the way you proved the point.

DECEMBER 1

I will be at peace when . . . I choose to be at peace,
no matter what is going on.

 ## PLEASE
EXCUSE
ALL
CRAZY
EXPERIENCES!

It is just life's way of letting you know that things can, will and do get
better.

Until today, you may have thought is was necessary to eliminate
all craziness from your life. You may have believed that the craziness in
the world is a bad thing. Just for today, see beyond the craziness. Use
your mind to find the presence of peace and to shift the energy that surrounds you.

*Today I am devoted to bringing peace into all
situations and experiences!*

DECEMBER 2

I will know peace when . . .
I learn to focus on one thing at a time.

There is a place in your mind where various aspects and responsibilities of your life all blend together. In this place, there are various thoughts vying for your attention. Like chattering mynah birds, all the things you need to do, want to do and are expected to do will start talking to you at once, creating a chorus in your head that says: Everything needs to be done *now!* Everything is important and needs your attention right *now!* Everything is your responsibility! Do it *now! Right now!* At the first sign of anything going wrong, the chatter in your head gets louder. If you respond to the chatter, you will be stressed out or get burned out.

When the chatter of urgency invades your mind, you will feel like you cannot tread water fast enough to stay afloat. Feelings of fear, inadequacy, unworthiness and, often, desperation will intensify the urgency you are already experiencing. In these moments, it will serve you well to remember that *you can only do one thing at a time!* The key is to prioritize.

Make a list of all the things that must be done. Make sure that you *eliminate* from your list all the things you have taken the responsibility for doing because no one else wants to do them. Make a plan for your approach. Not *attack*. Approach. Once you are clear about what you are going to do, give everything else to God. When you feel overwhelmed, remember the scripture which says, "The Lord will perfect that which concerns me." If you do what you can, God will take care of the rest.

Until today, you may have been trying to cope with feeling overwhelmed by trying to do everything in order to get everything done. Just for today, share your load with the perfecting presence of God.

*Today I am devoted to living my life in order
of priority with God's help!*

DECEMBER 3

I will know peace when . . . I stop finding excuses for
what I am not doing.

You can fool some people some time but you can never fool
yourself. You can tell yourself almost anything to excuse
away your fear. The bad news is, you will actually believe it
for a while. The good news is, there will come a time when
the excuse will not be strong enough or big enough to camouflage your
fear. Eventually what you tell yourself will begin to sound so *weak,* so
lame, so *utterly ridiculous* that you will have a hard time convincing
yourself or anyone else that it is true. When that time comes, don't be
defensive. Be willing to face the thing you fear.

As long as there is something you fear lurking in the back of your
mind, you cannot, will not have peace of mind. When you defend yourself for taking or not taking a particular action, you are denying the
foundation upon which peace is built. *Truth!* When, however, you wait
or prepare to the point of avoiding what you say you really want to do,
when you know you are afraid but refuse to admit it, there is no way you
can have peace of mind. In fact, if you *insist on defending* the excuse, you
may lose your mind.

Until today, you may have found yourself making excuses for not
confronting the things you fear. You may have had a great excuse for remaining in a relationship, work environment or living arrangement that
is not fulfilling. Just for today, lay down all of your excuses. Ask yourself,
"What am I afraid of that makes me stay here?" Make a list of the responses
that come to mind. Prayerfully offer the list to the Holy Spirit, asking it
to show you the way out. Repeat the process as often as necessary until
all excuses vanish.

*Today I am devoted to eliminating all excuses that
camouflage fear!*

DECEMBER 4

I will know peace when . . . I become teachable.

There is a very simple way to create a space for peace to exist in your mind. The way is to admit *what you don't know.* Many of us reach the age, usually around thirty, when we realize that there are things we need to know that we don't know. The common first response to this realization is fear. Fear is usually followed by embarrassment and shame. When pressed to demonstrate your knowledge on an issue you have no knowledge of, you will probably lie! You will lie because you are afraid, ashamed or embarrassed to admit that you don't know what others think you should know. Let's face it, some of us missed some *basic living fundamentals!*

It is perfectly okay to not know something. What you don't know won't hurt you unless you try to cover up the fact that you don't know. When you do that, the lie used as cover will *eat you alive!* No one will think poorly of you when you don't know, unless you try to convince them that you do know what you don't know. When you do that, there will be hell to pay. The hell is in your mind. It is the hell of living with the fear that you will be *found out.* You can survive the fear, shame or embarrassment of not knowing by simply acknowledging that you don't know. If you do so with a willingness to learn, people will probably have a great deal of respect for your courage.

Until today, you may have been afraid to acknowledge, admit or accept that there are some things about life and living that you simply don't know. You may not have realized that the only way not knowing can hurt you or be used against you is when you try to hide it. Just for today, be willing to admit to yourself what you don't know. That simple act will open your heart and mind so that you can learn what you need to know.

Today I am devoted to opening my mind to learn what I need to know!

DECEMBER 5

I will know peace when . . .
I learn to forgive myself.

It can be challenging to forgive someone. The hardest person to forgive may be *you*. Considering what you know about yourself and what you are capable of, there are times when you cannot forgive things you have done. At times, it is hard to believe that you can forgive yourself, that you deserve to be forgiven or that you are worthy of forgiveness. For some reason, you mistakenly believe that to forgive means to *allow* or to say it is okay. Most of us will never *allow* ourselves to make a mistake without *being punished*.

It is cruel and unnecessary to punish yourself for being human. As human beings, our growth, learning and healing are always at stake. Forgiveness fosters all three. Each of your actions is motivated either by something you are ready to receive or something you are ready to release. Detrimental or dishonorable actions usually mean that you are ready to release something. Some false, limiting or unloving belief. Some unreasonable fear. Your actions will demonstrate how and why the belief or fear no longer serves you. Your actions will demonstrate where you need to grow; what you are ready to learn or what you are ready to heal. When you forgive yourself for believing you deserve to be punished, growth occurs, learning takes place and healing is the result. Punishment rarely fosters learning. In fact, it is the precursor to control. When you forgive yourself, you release fear, eliminating the possibility that fear will continue to control your behavior.

Until today, you may have found that it was very difficult to forgive yourself for certain behaviors you have engaged in or certain actions you have taken. Just for today, be willing to grow, learn and heal yourself. Prepare yourself to release the fear that controls your mind. Forgive yourself.

Today I am devoted to creating a divine growing, learning and healing opportunity with self-forgiveness!

DECEMBER 6

I will know peace when . . . I accept and acknowledge the truth.

Some people sleep around with many other people regardless of the physical and emotional risks involved. Others drink alcohol or ingest chemical substances to their own detriment. There are people who are *very fond* of taking things that do not belong to them. Some people lie just for the fun of it, others because they cannot seem to stop themselves. People do any number of things that are harmful, mean or self-destructive. Usually we do these things when we forget the truth of who we are.

The truth is that we are all *messiahs* of one sort or another. According to Webster, a messiah is: *The leader of some hope or cause.* When you are living the truth, you offer others hope. When you are living the truth, you cause other people to realize the truth about themselves. When people see the glory, the grace, the peace of your life, they are inspired.

There is nothing that you can ever do to erase the truth about who you are. One day when you least expect it or when you ask for it, one kernel of living truth buried somewhere in your being will be awakened. On that day, which could be today, all of your false beliefs and harsh judgments will vanish! All reluctance will disappear, and your greatest detriment will become the divine core of your life's ministry. Let today be that day!

Until today, you may have been engaged in self-destructive behavior to support the reluctance you feel about being a *chosen one.* Just for today, activate the truth in your consciousness. Accept the fact that you are important. Acknowledge the fact that you have been chosen to lead others out of a fear-based, unproductive lifestyle. Let your life and your determination inspire others to live the truth of their being.

Today I am devoted to living my life as a ministry to inspire others!

DECEMBER 7

I will know peace when . . . I reclaim all
the pieces of myself.

If you can't seem to get it together, it may be that you have given too much of yourself away. It may be that you have compromised, over-compensated, given in and given over so much of yourself that you no longer know where all of the pieces have been scattered. Perhaps the things you thought you needed to do to get love, to experience yourself as loveable, to be acknowledged, to be accepted, to increase your value and to establish your worth have left you splintered, shattered and broken into so many pieces you feel like you will never be able to pull yourself together. Don't worry! You have simply experienced an invasion of *body snatchers!*

A *body-snatchers* invasion will distort the truth about you. It will make you forget your true identity. It will make you feel guilty about your desire to take care of yourself and honor yourself. It will point out the wrongness of your choices, the dangers of your decisions, the impossibility of your visions and the fallacy of your beliefs. A little nip here. A little peck there.

There is a way to pull yourself back together when you have been accosted by body snatchers. You must examine all the times you gave others the right to make your decisions, when you expected others to do for you what only you had the power to do, when you gave others the right to decide your destiny and when you dishonored yourself in order to please others. When you remember what you have done, *forgive yourself!* Most important, you must say, *"Never again!"*

Until today, you may not have realized that you had been invaded by body snatchers who have dismembered pieces and parts of your identity. Just for today, protect yourself! Be aware of the things you do that diminish and distort your sense of wholeness, worthiness and your ability to make your own choices and decisions.

*Today I am devoted to reclaiming and protecting all of the
pieces of myself that are important!*

DECEMBER 8

I will know peace when . . . I organize my mind and my
life according to the truth.

 How is the truth organized in your mind? Are there cate-
gories of truth? Are there pieces of truth that you use when
it is convenient? Are there parts of the truth that you have
not been able to accept? Is there:

Real truth?
Some truth?
Big truth?
Your truth?
Their truth?
World truth?
Religious truth?
Spiritual truth?
Social truth?
Economic truth?
Part truth?
Foreign truth?

The truth is, there is only *one* truth. God is truth! Love is truth! You
are the embodiment of God's love, on a quest to recognize this truth
about yourself and everyone else. Anything else that is cleverly disguised
as the truth is a manifestation of what you must grow through in order
to realize the truth.

Until today, you may have lost sight of the one truth that will give
you peace of mind and the strength you need to move through life
peacefully. Just for today, remember the truth about who you are. Remember the truth about your life. Remember that only when you know
the truth will you be free to live in its glory, covered by its grace.

*Today I am devoted to living the one and only truth
about myself and my life!*

DECEMBER 9

I will know peace when . . . I make
spiritual wealth a priority.

Many people struggle or work hard to attain material wealth.
Once you achieve it, you must struggle and work hard to
maintain and protect what you have attained. In the midst
of the struggle and hard work, it is easy to lose sight of the
fact that material wealth can only serve you in this lifetime.

How much material wealth do you think Harriet Tubman left for
her heirs? How many stock options did Denmark Vesey pass on to his
children? They discovered that freedom of the mind, body and spirit was
of the utmost importance. They realized that you need not own a great
deal to do a great deed. They left legacies that were created by the way in
which they lived their lives.

So very often, the things we struggle and work to achieve enslave us.
Our desires hold us captive. A philosopher once said, "Success is not
having much but wanting little." Our desires and accomplishments in
the material realm have no meaning whatsoever in the spiritual realm. In
fact, the struggle to accomplish often creates mental and emotional discord. While there is nothing inherently wrong with the pursuit of physical comfort, material wealth or power, it is important to remember that
there are some things equally as important, fulfilling and more lasting.
Pursuit of these things often brings us an experience of peace and worthiness that money cannot buy.

Until today, you may have sacrificed your peace of mind and spiritual balance to pursue material wealth. Just for today, examine whether
or not your quest is a blessing or a curse. Ask yourself what it is that you
can leave behind aside from wealth.

*Today I am devoted to living a spirit-filled, peace-filled
life and leaving a legacy that is more valuable than money!*

DECEMBER 10

I will know peace when . . . I allow myself
to trust my vulnerabilities.

Driving a car places you in a vulnerable position. Even when
you are alert to the actions of other drivers, you are vulnerable, and you *trust* that you will make it to your destination
safely. When you are vulnerable, you trust that as you stand
defenseless, you will be protected.

Most people squirm when they hear the word *vulnerability.* They expect to be harmed when they are vulnerable. These are the same people
who go in and out of all kinds of relationships, placing themselves in po-
sitions in which they can be hurt, abandoned, rejected or violated in any
number of ways. These are people who do not trust themselves and who
cannot trust other people. Yet, when you think about it, vulnerability is
not something you can avoid. It is our natural condition, and we must
learn to trust it.

When you allow yourself to be vulnerable, it means that you are
standing in the power of your authentic self, which has no defenses and
holds on to no pretenses. Your authentic self is the foundation of your
power. It allows you to be innocent while being strong. It allows you to
be strong while being compassionate. Your authentic self is the part of
you that has the courage, strength and fortitude to survive your fears.
Your authentic self is the part of you that knows no matter what happens
to you, you will survive. Consequently your authentic self trusts your
vulnerability. It trusts the process of life, and it trusts the resiliency of
your spirit.

Until today, you may have believed that if you were vulnerable you
would be hurt or harmed in some way. Just for today, acknowledge that
the presence and power of your authentic self protectes you in all of the
vulnerable situations you face each day.

*Today I am devoted to embracing the power and presence
of my authentic self!*

DECEMBER 11

I will know peace when . . . I heal my need for
external acceptance and recognition.

There is a need that many people struggle with for a good
portion of their lives. It is the need to receive or experience
the acknowledgment and acceptance of others. Even when
we are not aware that this is what we are doing, we equate
these two things with being loved. To be loved is a basic human need. Beneath the need for acceptance and acknowledgment is the cry for self-
love. Sometimes having someone else acknowledge you is far more
satisfying than simply loving yourself. Perhaps it is because you really
don't trust yourself or your own love. When you know in your heart of
hearts that you are withholding love or forgiveness from someone else,
your love will not be enough to satisfy you.

The principle at work in this experience is, "What you withhold
from others will be withheld from you!" When you withhold your love
from someone in response to their actions, you are withholding acceptance. When you withhold acceptance, you will be driven to receive it.

Every living being, regardless of their actions, deserves your love.
Your love is an acknowledgment that regardless of their behavior, you
recognize them to be a divine creation of God. The Spirit of life knows
when you are withholding acceptance. It also knows that you can never
experience what you will not offer. You will never experience the external acceptance you desire until you internally acknowledge your acceptance of another.

Until today, you may have been seeking the acceptance that you
have been withholding from someone else. Just for today, open your
heart to someone you have shut out. It doesn't mean that they were
right. It means that you are willing to heal.

*Today I am devoted to opening my heart, to acknowledging
and accepting that I have enough love to sustain
myself and to offer to others!*

DECEMBER 12

I will know peace when . . . I seek consolation
from the right Source.

There are some things that you need only discuss with God.
It is not necessary for you to let *everyone* know *everything*
about you. In fact, it is probably wise that you don't. There
are some things that do not need to be exposed to the views
and opinions of other people. There are some things that people cannot
help you figure out or resolve. There are some aspects of your personality that you should not reveal to people, not because you want to hide
them, but because they need healing. *People cannot heal you!* Only God
can do that. There are some places in your life that are such a mess that
you cannot risk someone stepping in and making things any more difficult than they already are. There are things about you and about your
life for which you do not need counseling. These are things about which
you need *Divine Counsel,* and you know exactly what they are. Take
these things into the sanctuary of your heart and ask God to show you
what to do.

Until today, you may have been telling other people things about
yourself and your life that you need only share with God. Just for today,
go into your sanctuary for Divine counsel.

*Today I am devoted to receiving counseling from the
Divine about certain areas of my life!*

DECEMBER 13

I will know peace when . . . I examine what I feel
beneath what I am feeling.

It can be frightening to experience and express anger. Even
more frightening is the hurt that caused the anger in the
first place. When you get hurt, you get angry. You believe
that the anger is directed outward, toward the person who
hurt you. The truth is, anger as a response to hurt is always directed inward. You are angry that you *trusted someone* who turned out to be the
wrong person to trust. You are angry that you *loved* too much. *Cared* too
much. Because it is hard to admit these things to yourself, about yourself, you point the finger *out there, at them!* The challenge is to recognize
that it is much easier to be angry at someone than it is to say, "You hurt
me." When you are angry, you are in control. Control is what you believe you must have to avoid being hurt.

Being hurt is a sign that there is something in you that requires your
attention. Being hurt is a sign that you have been engaging in a pattern
of behavior that no longer serves who you are. When you get hurt, it
means that you have a *tender spot* you have been resisting the need to address. Along comes some unsuspecting soul, doing what they do, in the
way they do it, and they stick their finger in the tender spot.

It makes you angry that you didn't see it coming. You are angry because you believe you *should have* known better. Anger in response to a
hurt is a clear sign that you were hurt to begin with. You need to stop
being angry long enough to examine your own heart and mind.

Until today, you may have believed that someone you trusted or
loved has done something to make you angry. Just for today, lay your
anger aside. Look beneath the anger to find the hurt that you have
buried to avoid dealing with it.

*Today I am digging up old hurts and
putting them to rest!*

DECEMBER 14

I will know peace when . . .
I start doing God's work.

If you were to be perfectly honest with yourself, you would probably admit that there are quite a number of things you are angry about. You might also admit that your anger is directed toward God. You may feel that it is not nice to be angry with God. In fact, it is probably pretty darn frightening to admit it and to feel it. After all, God could get you! When however, you have had enough, seen enough, heard enough, taken enough, you might just be mad enough to let God know what you really feel.

Think about war and drugs and rape and mass murderers. If God is so powerful, where is the power of God when all of that stuff is going on? Where is God when fathers walk away from their children? Where is God when mothers abuse themselves with drugs or alcohol, resulting in the abuse and neglect of their children? Where is God when hurricanes kill people and destroy the homes of others? Does it seem that God doesn't do the things God needs to do? Doesn't that make you mad?

Well, if you really want to know the truth, God is always right where God has always been. In your heart. Perhaps if you stop being mad at God, you would know it. You would feel it. You would begin to live from that place, doing whatever you can do to spread a little more God around the world. In case you have forgotten, God works through people. That's how S/He gets the real work done. Perhaps you were too mad to realize it.

Until today, you may have been mad at God for all the things God seems to be doing and not doing. Just for today, be God on earth. Love somebody. Help somebody. Touch somebody. Guide somebody. Feed somebody. Support somebody. Forgive somebody.

*Today I am devoted to being an embodiment
of God in action!*

DECEMBER 15

I will know peace when . . .
I stop stewing in anger.

Have you ever been so angry with someone that you shut them down? Not only do you stop speaking to them, you refuse to acknowledge them by thinking about them or speaking their name. After a while, trying to convince yourself and the other person that you intend to be angry with them forever can become very tiring.

When you become so angry with a person that you want to shut them out of your life, you need to know that there is something going on with *you* that has nothing to do with *them*. At this level, anger is a response to your own judgments, the failed satisfaction of your own expectations, your failed attempts to gain control or your subconscious response to fear.

Rarely is it just *one* thing that creates anger in a relationship. It is usually the *flavor* of everything that has been going on. *You too have seasoned the pot!* If you added too much of this or not enough of that, the final product is going to leave a bad taste in *your* mouth! If you want to establish and maintain peaceful relationships with other people, surrender all judgments of who they are and who they are not. If you want your relationships with other people to be healthy and fulfilling, surrender your expectations and set clear boundaries. When you let people know what you need and want, they can decide if they want to be involved. If it is your intention to establish and maintain loving relationships with other people, you *absolutely must* surrender the need to be in control.

Until today you may have thought that you were justified in your anger toward another person. Just for today, open the doors of your heart. Take a look at your role in how things happened. Take an honest look at what happened so that you can walk away with valuable information.

*Today I am devoted to taking the heat off
an angry situation!*

DECEMBER 16

I will know peace when . . . I am clear about what
I am doing and feeling.

There is a major distinction between a conscious level of detachment and an unhealthy indifference. Detachment is a
choice. Indifference is a *reaction*. When you are indifferent,
you say that *you don't care*. Even when you love and care
about a person, it is possible for you to intrude into their life. When
your energy and efforts do not yield the results you expected, your ego
goes into shock! Fear, anger, guilt set in and lead to indifference. *You
can't handle caring any more!*

Detachment is a totally different experience. When you exercise
conscious detachment, you care, but you don't intrude. You honor people and their process even when it looks dysfunctional by your standards. You allow people to learn, grow and unfold at their pace. You
trust and respect people enough to let them live their own lives. You
hold no expectations or judgments about what *their process* must look
like or how long it must take to unfold. You ask them what direction
they are choosing for themselves. You trust that divine order will guide
them. You remember how your learning, growing, healing process must
have looked to others, and you offer the compassion you did not receive.

There are some things and people about which you may believe you
are indifferent. Rather than allowing indifference to close your heart and
mind to situations and people, learn how to be detached. In this way,
you will be available to offer what you can, when you can.

Until today, you may have allowed overinvolvement to turn into indifference. Just for today, practice detachment. Trust that people can
make it on their own. Trust that you will know what to do in every situation. Be available at those times and to those people you can support or
assist without any attachment to what the process must look like.

*Today I am devoted to moving through difficult situations
with a healthy level of detachment!*

DECEMBER 17

I will know peace when . . .
I learn to let go.

When a thing has served its purpose, it will go away. Sometimes it will break. At other times, it will simply die off.
Then there are those times when for no reason, it will simply fall apart. There will be tiny pieces that are missing, making it impossible to put the thing back together. When a thing no longer
has any purpose in your life, it will go sour. Or it may run away. Or it
may pack and leave very abruptly. When a thing has served its divine
purpose in your life, there is no explanation. There is no excuse. It cannot, will not, must not stay in your presence. If you try to hold on to
something that has already fulfilled its purpose in your life, you are
going to hurt yourself. If holding on is disturbing your peace of mind, it
makes sense to let go.

Until today, you may have been holding on to something or someone, not realizing that its purpose in your life has been served. Just for
today, surrender all attachments to people and things that you have been
struggling to hold on to.

*Today I am devoted to releasing everyone and everything
that does not serve a divine purpose in my life!*

DECEMBER 18

I will know peace when . . . my learning
is reflected in my doing.

Your learning and growing in life is not measured by the
pace. It does not matter how fast you do it. Your progress,
the level of your understanding and the ultimate rate at
which you grow can only be measured by what you do. You
may know how to do many things. You may feel like you understand
even more. You may have made vigilant attempts to gather as much
knowledge and information as is available about yourself and your life.
However, learning, growth and understanding can only be measured by
doing. As you learn, your behavior changes. As you change your behavior, what you do and the results you get solidify what you have learned.
If you think you have learned something but you are still unable to execute it, then your learning and growing have not been completed. Give
yourself time. It is sure to happen.

Until today, you may have believed that all you needed to do was
learn a thing. Just for today, examine how your learning has affected
your doing. If one is not reflecting the other, know that there are more
lessons in store for you.

Today I am devoted to examining how I do what I know!

DECEMBER 19

I will know peace when . . . I acknowledge that
I have buttons that can be pushed.

Isn't it amazing that you can be kind and loving to one person and within moments, bite someone else's head off? Of course you tell yourself it was their fault. You allow yourself to believe that it was the way they *spoke* to you or *looked* at you. It may seem to be true that while you can be on your best behavior with some people, other people seem to bring out the worst in you. Some people really know how to push your buttons! That's right! *Your* buttons. How you respond has nothing to do with anyone else. It's all about you.

Your greatest adversary is also your greatest teacher. Like it or not, it is the job of certain people to bring out the worst in you. What they trigger is already in you. They have come to teach you what you are capable of doing when you get triggered, when your back goes up, when your claws come out. They have come to give you an opportunity to heal. These people *love you so much* that they have taken time out of *their lives* to come into *your life* to ruffle your feathers so that you can go within and heal. It may not feel like a wonderful experience, but just knowing that someone can get on your last nerve, can shake your foundation, can look in your kitchen and see your mess means that you have something that needs to be healed. The way they make you feel needs to be healed. What you think about them needs to be healed. Don't waste your time being mad at *them*. Be about the business of healing yourself!

Until today, you may have believed that it was perfectly fine to be nice sometimes and wicked at others. Just for today, thank everyone and anyone who can push your buttons. Realize that they are providing you with a wonderful and divine opportunity for healing.

*Today I am devoted to healing the sore, tender, wounded
places in my heart and mind!*

DECEMBER 20

I will know peace when . . . I accept that things
are the way things need to be.

Stop trying to be perfect! *Stop it right now!* Stop trying to fix
yourself. Change yourself. Perfect yourself. Stop trying to
do everything *just so.* Stop trying to improve every little
thing so that everything about you will be perfect. Stop trying to impress people with just *how perfect* you are. Stop making up stories about how perfect your life is. Stop looking for little imperfections
so that you can perfect them. Stop making excuses for the things you
think are imperfect. The quest for perfection is a waste of time and energy. It is a quest that closes your mind and your heart to the beauty that
is all around you. You can be so preoccupied perfecting the cracks in you
that you fail to realize that *light comes through the cracks.* Remember the
words of the famous author Ernest Hemingway, who said, "Not everything that appears to be broken needs to be fixed. In fact, some of us are
strong at the broken places!" In other words, everything need not be perfect in order to be divine. This includes you!

Until today, you may have held perfection as the standard that you
needed to live up to or achieve. Just for today, accept that you are perfect
just as you are. Embrace the cracks in your life and breaks in your heart
as places into which divine light can shine.

*Today I am devoted to releasing the quest to be
any more perfect that I am!*

DECEMBER 21

I will know peace when . . . fear no longer determines
what I do not do.

How long have you been living with the fear of being hurt? Being abandoned? Or being rejected? What have these fears motivated you to do? More important, what have they motivated you *not to do?* When you live with the fear of being hurt, it is difficult to experience peace. When you hold back in fear of being abandoned, you will not find peace. When you move through life with the fear of being rejected, you also avoid the peace of love.

The average human being will go to any lengths to avoid the experience of being hurt, being abandoned or being rejected. Hurt takes on a totally different perspective when you are afraid of it. In order to protect themselves, there are people who will not indulge in personal contact or closeness. Some of them will go so far as to strike first, hurting others before they can be hurt. When you are afraid to be hurt, you can spend a better part of your lifetime on the lookout for hurt, expecting to be hurt. There is something you must remember. What you *expect* you usually get!

You cannot experience the fullness of your authentic self or life when you live to avoid hurt. You will never know the joy of love or the peaceful satisfaction of being loved if you hide from hurt. When hurt is the focus, the heart closes. When your heart is closed, your mind fills with every idea about hurt, every belief in hurt, what hurt can do to you and how hurt happens. *Get out of your head!* It is your fear of hurt that is destroying your peace of mind and your chance to be loved.

Until today, you may have believed that if you could avoid being hurt, you would live a peaceful life. Just for today, consider all of the life, love and peace you are missing out on in your attempt to avoid being hurt.

*Today I am opening my heart to the fullness of life and love
with no expectation of being hurt!*

DECEMBER 22

I will know peace when . . . I take the time to experience
the blessings of closure.

All great events cast a shadow before them, and so many of us
get caught up in the shadow. How? We move on to something new without closure. We jump into something new
before we understand the old. We think that we can start a
new relationship when we are still angry about the old relationship. We
think we can find a new, better-paying job when we are still upset about
how we were treated on the old job. You cannot move forward into
something bigger, better, brighter than what you had until you clear
your feeling about what the old thing was, what you learned and what
you are taking with you. Without closure, the bad stuff you had before is
going to follow you.

A shadow is cast by a coming event. The shadow is not the event itself. Some shadows are dark. They may frighten you. They also obscure
your vision. Other shadows are bright, so bright in fact that they blind
you to what is really going on. A bright shadow may lead you out of the
darkness but may not provide you with a clear vision of where you are
headed. When you attempt to leave where you are without closure, you
will undoubtedly get lost in some kind of shadow. A shadow in your
mind. A shadow on your heart. The only way to ensure that you are
standing squarely in a new event and not the shadow is to make the effort to understand what you are leaving, why you are leaving, what you
have learned and how you plan to make the next event different.

Until today, you may have been compelled to move on without fore-
thought or closure. Just for today, be still! Make no decisions. Give yourself some down time. When you feel ready to move forward, ask the
Holy Spirit to show you where and how to move into an eventful new
beginning.

*Today I am devoted to bringing closure to those
experiences that could propel me into a shadow!*

DECEMBER 23

I will know peace when . . . I am fully present in love in order to experience the full benefits of love.

There are many ways to exit a relationship. You can exit mentally by demonstrating that you are preoccupied by *more important* thoughts. You can exit emotionally by finding somewhere else to express and experience your passion. You can exit physically by finding ways and excuses for not being present. Or you can leave spiritually by removing your trust, your respect, your love, your compassion from what you do and what you say.

Sometimes we exit a relationship because of unresolved feelings of anger or betrayal stemming from past experiences. More often than not we exit a relationship because we feel we are not getting the love we need. Unfortunately, we often blame the other person when our desires are not met. In reality, we haven't asked for what we want or need.

How often have you honestly expressed to your partner exactly what you want or why you want it? When was the last time you shared with your partner how you will feel when you get the thing you need? How can you expect to get what you want if you don't ask for it? How can you expect to receive the things you say you want if you are not physically, mentally, emotionally or spiritually present to receive them?

There are some cases when we know without a doubt that the time has come to leave a relationship. This is not the kind of exit we are examining here. We are talking about taking your mind, your body, your heart or your soul out of where you are being loved because you are not getting what you have not asked for. This type of exit is not only self-destructive, it is a surefire way to ensure that you never get the very thing you say you want. Could it be that you really don't believe you deserve it?

Until today, you may have remained in a relationship that you exited a long time ago. Just for today, be present enough to ask for what you want, and remain present long enough to receive it.

Today I am devoted to being fully present, open and willing to receive the things I say I want in a relationship!

DECEMBER 24

I will know peace when . . .
I realize I am never alone.

When you really move into the presence of God, you are
going to feel lonely. In fact, you may find yourself alone.
When God takes you in and prepares you to change, S/He
will strip away everything and everyone around you in order
to build a fortress within you. If you continue to focus on the outside
world, you will think you are alone. You will feel abandoned. You will
conclude that there is no one standing with you or for you. When you
are moving into the presence of God, you will be surrounded by angels.
You will be protected by *wise men, prophets* and sages. You will be held
up. Propped up. Pulled up and opened up. When you are in the presence
of God, you will be cleaned up so that nothing that happens outside of
you will have the power to hurt or harm you. In the presence of God,
everything you need will come to you and through you.

Until today, you may have thought you were all alone. Just for today,
submit yourself to the presence of God. Ask to be fortified with God's
love and grace.

*Today I am devoted to experiencing the presence
of God in my life!*

DECEMBER 25

I will know peace when . . . I acknowledge
all that God is, I am.

 Your mind is the fertile ground in which love resides.
God is in your mind.
God is love.
God cannot be a hazy or passing thought.
Do all things with God.
Do all things in love.
Make up your mind to:
Be present with God.
To be present in love.
Follow God.
Seek God first.
Follow your first thought because
it is your first and natural instinct to love.
Until today, you may have thought that God resided in some far-off
place that you could not reach from where you are. Just for today, re-
member that God is your first thought. Your natural thought.

*Today I am devoted to being God minded and
re-minded with God!*

DECEMBER 26

I will know peace when . . .
I can laugh at myself.

It is easy to see something as somebody else's lesson. When it is *their stuff*, you don't have to address it. When it has nothing to do with you, you don't have to deal with it. If somebody has a problem that *just happens* to be spilling over into your life, it has absolutely nothing to do with you right? Ha! Ha! Ha! Ha! Ha! Ha! Ha! Ha! Ha! Oh, boy! Who are you kidding! Ha! Ha! Ha! Ha! Ha! Ha! Ha! You're kidding me, right? Ha! Ha! Ha! Ha! Ha! Ha! Ha! Ha! Ha! Ha! It's a joke! You're telling me a joke! Ha! Ha! Ha! Ha! Ha! Ha! Ha! Ha! Ha! Ha! You can't be serious! Ha! Ha! Ha! Ha! Ha! Ha! Ha! Ha! Ha! Ha! You don't believe that, do you? Ha! Ha! Ha! Ha! Ha! Ha! Ha! I'm sorry! I don't mean to laugh at you, but I can't help it! Ha! Ha! Ha! Ha! Ha! Ha! Ha! Ha! Ha! Ha! Ha! Ha! Ha! Ha! I'm hysterical! Ha! Ha! Ha! Ha! Ha! Ha! Ha! Ha! Ha! Ha! I can't believe that you would believe that! Ha! Ha! Ha! Ha! Ha! You can't believe that! Ha! Ha! Ha! Ha! Ha! Ha! Ha! Ha! Ha! I'm so sorry! Please forgive me! I had no idea that you were trying to be serious!

Until today, you may have thought that the problems that show up in your life have nothing to do with you. Just for today, make sure you really believe what you are saying.

Today I am devoted to understanding why certain experiences are a part of my life!

DECEMBER 27

I will know peace when . . .
I am willing to be peaceful.

Fighting to have your way does not increase your peace. Fighting others about their ways does not increase your peace. Refusing to acknowledge when you have made a mistake does not increase your peace. Going to extraordinary lengths to avoid making a mistake does not increase your peace. Refusing to acknowledge and embrace your shortcomings does not increase your peace. Pointing out the short comings of others does not increase your peace. Trying to fix other people does not increase your peace. Constantly telling yourself there is something wrong with you does not increase your peace. Not asking for what you want does not increase your peace. Accepting less than you want does not increase your peace. Trying to prove your worth and value does not increase your peace. Refusing to accept that others are worthy or valuable does not increase your peace. Failing to take responsibility for yourself does not increase your peace. Taking on the responsibility for the lives of others does not increase your peace. Avoiding unpleasant things does not increase your peace. Trusting that you are always doing the very best you can will and does increase your peace.

Until today, you may have been engaged in behaviors and activities that disturbed your peace of mind. Just for today, increase your peace. Engage in self-loving, self-nurturing, self-supporting behaviors and activities.

Today I am devoted to increasing the peaceful experiences in my life!

DECEMBER 28

I will know peace when . . .
I understand that love and peace work hand in hand.

Love is the only experience that replaces fear.
Peace is the result.
Love is the experience of taking in the breath of life,
without fear.
Peace is the result.
When you know that you can handle all things in love,
Peace is the result.
When you love yourself through every experience,
without any fear about where you are going,
Peace is the result.
Peace is the helpmate of love.
When you commit yourself to loving all and
doing all in love,
Peace takes care of everything else.
Until today, you may not have realized the divine relationship that
exists between love and peace. Just for today, be a part of the divine rela-
tionship that can bring miracles into your life.

*Today I am devoted to loving myself and all others
in a peaceful way!*

DECEMBER 29

I will know peace when . . . I understand
divine profits and losses.

Few of us understand why we are here. We have some vague
ideas but are not really sure why we are on the planet at this
time. We know that something is going on but we may not
be sure exactly what it is. For those who are seeking enlightenment about the plan and their purpose in the plan, here are a few tips.
You are here:

To gain character as you lose ego
To gain integrity as you lose dishonesty
To gain strength as you lose fear
To gain compassion as you lose disappointment
To gain discipline as you lose willfulness
To gain equality as you lose separation
To gain appreciation as you lose resentment
To gain enthusiasm as you lose hostility
To gain tenderness as you lose rigidity
To gain boldness as you lose bitterness
To gain generosity as you lose selfishness
To gain optimism as you lose inadequacy
To gain excitement as you lose embarrassment
To gain gratitude as you lose greed
To gain love as you lose ignorance

Until today, you may not have been aware that as you surrender one
thing, you gain something to replace it. Just for today, live life like it is a
spiritual stock market. Cut your losses and celebrate your gains.

*Today I am devoted to investing in the development
of my spiritual nature!*

DECEMBER 30

I will know peace when . . . I align myself with
the way the universe works.

Peace cannot exist in disorder. When things are out of order,
there will be chaos and confusion. When there is chaos and
confusion, things cannot be clear. When you are clear, you
are peaceful. The universe of life is so benevolent and merciful, it has provided us with a recipe for peace. The recipe is called the
Law of Universal Order. The law states: God first! Then you. Next come
family and friends. Finally, there is work. *It is not the other way around!*
This in no way means that you should neglect your duties and responsibilities. Oh, heavens no! It only means that you address them in order of
priority. The order is: God first! Next there is you. After you come family and friends. Bringing up the rear is your work. *Got it?* Now, if you do
your very best to follow the law to the letter, you will experience so much
peace, you will hardly be able to stand it. You will have a *peace that surpasses all understanding. Peace that the world cannot take away.* Peace in
your mind. Peace in your heart. Peace with yourself, and peace with others. Peace that is perfect. If you are not living in peace, it could mean that
your life is *out of order!*

Until today, you may not have realized what you needed to do to experience more peace in your life. Just for today, follow the letter of the
law. Order your life!

Today I am devoted to the pursuit of peace!

DECEMBER 31

I will know peace when . . . I put my confidence
in my prayers.

Here is a prayer for you today.

God, my Father. God, my Mother. God, my All in All.
Remind me that your pre-sent presence is present wherever I
am. Open my eyes that I may see you. Open my ears that I may hear you.
Open my soul that I may feel your presence in a way that enlivens the truth
of who I am. Open my heart so that I may feel, know and express your love
in every situation and under all circumstances. Open my life and read me
like a book. If there is a chapter, a page or a verse in my life that does not serve
you or your purpose for my life, erase it!

God, I give myself to you as a loving offering. May I always recognize the
ways in which you are loving me. May I always be an expression of your love.
May I always be an expression of your truth. May I always act upon your
wisdom. May I always bring the energy of your Spirit into every situation so
that you can touch the hearts and minds of all people.

God, I open myself to you. May I be filled with the light of your presence.
May I be filled with the power of your truth. May I live up to the faith you
have in me. May I fulfill the purpose you have etched into me. May I learn
to depend upon, rely upon and trust you in every aspect of the life you have
entrusted to me. May my life be a shining example of your wisdom and glory.
May I dignify your presence in me and in my life by living the principle of
your love.

Thank you God! For I know that as I ask, you answer. For all I have re-
ceived and all that is yet to come, I am so very grateful.

Until today, you may have been unaware that God always says *yes* to
your prayers. Just for today, pray with confidence knowing that it is
God's pleasure to respond promptly to your heartfelt requests.

Today I am devoted to putting my full confidence
in my prayers!

And So It Is!

INDEX OF ENTRIES

JANUARY: LIFE

Life Will Work for Me When I Realize . . .

1   I must put first things first!
2   I must make myself available to life.
3   I have the power to walk right! The power to talk right! And the power to live right!
4   Trying to prove something to someone is never a valid reason for doing anything.
5   Every decision I make is based on every other decision I have made, which is based on everything that has ever happened in my life.
6   I will continue feeling bad until my attitude improves!
7   Within me is the essence of everything I am!
8   The "right now" problem could be a "happened long ago" story.
9   The only walls, locked doors and prisons in my life are the ones that I have built.
10   The experience of my faith keeps my faith alive.
11   I have everything I need within me to create everything I want out there!
12   When I've done all I can do, I cannot regret what I did not do!
13   I cannot fail in life!
14   The only problem I have is the belief that I am not doing the right thing.
15   When I tell myself the truth, I can trust myself!
16   I must be open to receive and willing to accept the goodness of life!
17   I cannot break through until I have a breakdown!
18   I am the light of the world!
19   There is more to life than meets the eye!
20   I can take my own advice!
21   I can always re-create what I believe!

22 I am loved by life!
23 I am in a different part of the same boat as everyone else.
24 Life is always accommodating my requests!
25 I must learn how to wait!
26 Goodness and mercy do follow me.
27 I am totally, completely and fully responsible for what goes on in my life!
28 I cannot change what I believe as long as I believe it!
29 I have a Father who has always loved and will always love me!
30 I must know the elements of success if I plan to be successful!
31 Trouble comes to pass, not to stay.

FEBRUARY: LOVE

I Will Know Love When I Realize . . .

1   Love is not what I say. Love is who I am and what I do.
2   I have the power to call a thing that is *not* as if it *is* so that it *will be!*
3   God wants to love me!
4   There are times when I allow fear to stand between me and those I love.
5   I can love people even when I believe they are not nice!
6   The only way I can challenge fear is to do the very thing I am afraid to do in the moment that I feel afraid.
7   The world as I know it begins and ends with love!
8   My life is the sacred and holy ground of love!
9   There are times when the right road takes a wrong turn!
10 I am a sexual being, and I am okay!
11 People will come into my life for a reason, a season or a lifetime!
12 I cannot hide what I think, what I feel or who I am!
13 Relationships never die. They change!
14 If I am hurting, I am not loving!
15 The goodness of love is its presence!
16 Truth is a powerful and meaningful expression of love!
17 Love equally given and equally received is love equally shared.
18 I have to see the love that is present right now!
19 I must open my heart if I want to feel love!
20 I cannot do unloving things for the sake of love.

21 There are places in me that only love can heal!
22 There is nothing in my heart that God doesn't know, love or understand.
23 There is nothing I have done that God cannot forgive or understand.
24 The fibers of a relationship are constructed from the fibers of my heart.
25 It doesn't have to be easy to be good!
26 People do not change just because I want them to change!
27 Loving myself helps to resolve the things that make me feel bad.
28 Love may embrace some of the stuff I do not want to see!
29 Love offers me many things that I may not always see.

MARCH: AWARENESS

I Open My Heart and Mind to Be Aware . . .

1 That I am the matter that matters!
2 I must make a decision about how my day is going to be.
3 I cannot judge my clarity based on someone else's response!
4 I cannot sit in judgment of anyone else!
5 Everyone who grows up does not become an adult.
6 Pain is a warning that something is out of order!
7 God can only do for me what God can do through me!
8 I am constantly setting the standards for how others will see me and treat me.
9 There are some things about me that nothing can change.
10 If I walk in the footsteps of the Master I will master my true Self.
11 The energy I give to what I do determines if my actions are healthy or unhealthy.
12 That I can be led into believing things that are not true!
13 That I may not always be aware of exactly what I am seeing!
14 That I have the power to take what appears to be bad until it becomes something better!
15 The power to change leads to a powerful change!
16 There is a difference between constructive criticism and destructive criticism.
17 Only my inner authority can give me outer authority.

18 I have allowed what others believe about me to become what I believe about myself.

19 Without death there can be no change.

20 When I am listening to myself, I cannot hear other people.

21 Trust in the foundation I must build my life upon.

22 There is no need for me to be guilty about what I cannot or could not do.

23 The things I see in others could be the very things they see in me.

24 People can see things about me that I cannot see about myself.

25 I cannot hurt for someone else more than they hurt for themselves.

26 I have to establish inner cooperation in order to have outer results.

27 There are no points in the game of life. How I play determines if I win.

28 I must believe that whatever it is, I can handle it.

29 When I do not open up, I set myself up to blow up.

30 As long as I am holding on to what I have, what I desire cannot get in.

31 How my ABCs will lift my spirit.

APRIL: ACKNOWLEDGMENT

I Am Willing to Acknowledge . . .

1 There are things in my life that I have left undone!

2 I must pay more attention to the messages I receive from my life.

3 The information that I need is readily available to me.

4 Everyone is completely capable and equipped to take care of themselves and handle their own problems!

5 A good word supports and encourages good work!

6 In some battles, victory is won with the element of surprise.

7 It is safe for me to acknowledge and honor my feelings!

8 What I know, when I know it!

9 There are things in my life that do not smell quite right.

10 I am at the point of no return.

11 There are some things I could be addicted to experiencing.

12 If I am not giving my all to myself, I am not giving my all, at all.

13 There are certain realities I must face about my life.

14 There are certain things about me I'd rather others did not know.

15 In some areas of my life, I have been less than honest.
16 There may be some parts of my story that I have left out or changed.
17 It is not my place to tell other people what to do.
18 It may be difficult to pick through my experiences to find the things that will nourish me.
19 All little boys need guidance and direction from the Father.
20 A little girl needs a Father to help her grow into a woman.
21 The fear of fear leads to a struggle for control.
22 There are times when I need to be alone.
23 A mistake is a lesson in humility and a powerful healing opportunity.
24 I am powerful! I am brilliant! I am the lover of my life!
25 The truth must be told in a way it can be heard.
26 There doesn't need to be anything wrong in order for me to be all right.
27 What I choose for myself is very important to me.
28 I Am!
29 The ups and downs of life need not get me down.
30 There is a part of God in me that requires time, attention and care.

MAY: ACCEPTANCE

I Am Now Receptive to the Idea That . . .

1 There are some things that I can live without!
2 When I get there, everyone will not be there.
3 I can make things more difficult than they need to be.
4 I must learn to doubt my doubt and to negate my own negativity.
5 No matter what it looks like, I did the best I could.
6 I am capable of doing everything better next time!
7 God is on my side!
8 In God, there is no time or space beyond now.
9 Everything I am seeking is on its way to me.
10 I am the only one who can determine how people see me and remember me.
11 It is time for me to stop whispering and to start living out loud.
12 If I don't ask for what I need, the need will keep getting bigger!

13 Sometimes people do things that have nothing to do with what I have done!

14 When I am afraid to hear the truth, I make up the truth the way I think it should be.

15 I may be blocking myself from receiving more that I am holding on to.

16 Whenever I see a hole, I am to move around it.

17 If people really know who I am, they will probably like me anyhow.

18 I always have a choice about how I respond to experiences in my life.

19 God's inner vision of me can be the outer vision I create for myself.

20 A spiritual master is a master of self.

21 What I did not do cannot stop me from doing something else.

22 Parents can see the hidden parts of themselves in their children.

23 There comes a time when a parent must stop parenting.

24 What I see in others represents the fears I have about myself.

25 The need to be liked is a reflection of what needs to be healed.

26 The purpose of living is to honor life, honor God and honor myself.

27 A spiritual path is a heart-centered path that cannot be found in a book.

28 Nobody can really love me until I really love me.

29 It is possible that I have been following the wrong directions.

30 Some things never grow old. They just get better and go deeper.

31 I am the body that is the body of God.

JUNE: FORGIVENESS

I Am Now Willing to Forgive Myself . . .

1 Because I am not always aware of what I am doing to cause myself harm.

2 For remaining loyal to inaccurate information about myself.

3 For believing my worth is established by what others have told me or believe about me.

4 For forgetting that I am not in charge—Spirit is!

5 For the judgments I have held about myself and against myself.

6 For believing I am not worthy of love.

7 For believing there is something wrong with being wrong about some things!

8   For believing there was something wrong about needing correction.
9   For engaging in actions and behaviors I now believe are unforgiv-
    able.
10 For not being willing to risk proving that someone may be wrong
    about me.
11 For all of the time I have refused to follow Divine Orders.
12 For being critical of my mother.
13 For the judgments I have held about and against my father.
14 For allowing the shadows of my past to eat away at me.
15 For holding on to grievances and grudges.
16 For acting like nothing when the truth is I am everything.
17 For my inability to accept people exactly as they are.
18 For taking on more than is necessary or required for me to take on.
19 When I stumble.
20 For being hard, rigid, unable to bend or give.
21 For holding on to the need to be right.
22 For believing that people who do not agree with me are wrong.
23 For believing I could offer something to others before I have of-
    fered it to myself.
24 For believing that telling the truth can hurt me.
25 For not being willing to acknowledge my own anger at myself.
26 For believing that I have the power to create victims.
27 For not taking time to deal with certain unpleasant memories.
28 For refusing to acknowledge what my life is showing me about my-
    self.
29 For making life harder than it is meant to be.
30 For holding myself hostage to things God has forgiven me for.

JULY: UNDERSTANDING

I Will Gain More Understanding When I Realize . . .

1   Each person has an experience of the experience they are having.
2   I must open my heart to others if I want to stop hurting.
3   I cannot forget my pain or bury what is unpleasant.
4   That when I withhold the truth of who I am, I cannot receive the
    truth of what I want.
5   Exactly where I am is exactly where I need to be.

6   As long as I have an emotional attachment to a goal, I am attached to the fear of not achieving the goal.
7   Divine action is always working on my behalf.
8   I must feed my spirit if I want to stay alive.
9   Spiritual malnutrition is a condition that can be cured.
10 Little creatures can teach me big lessons.
11 Who I am is Divine.
12 I must maintain a power line into the power source.
13 I am an important part of the wholeness of life.
14 There is an *i* in me that longs to become the *I* of Spirit.
15 I am always in touch with all forms of life and those who have lived.
16 I must not allow the spirit of grief to take over my life.
17 Until I handle my unfinished childhood business, I will behave like a child.
18 There are some things I need to heal before I can forget them.
19 I have been a captive audience for the reruns of my life.
20 Discipline is the one magical power I must develop and use.
21 A teacher is not one with many students but one who creates many teachers.
22 There is no light more brilliant than the light I am.
23 To be on pause is a good thing.
24 When I expect to experience pain, I experience things painfully.
25 How I interpret what comes at me is a reflection of what is in me.
26 I have an ongoing relationship with things I cannot see but can feel.
27 I cannot force others to see that what I feel is real.
28 Loving in unloving ways is not love at all.
29 Trying to hide what I feel does not work.
30 There is a place called home where I am always welcome.
31 There is a divine purpose for my living and my being.

AUGUST: FAITH

I Am Faith-Filled and Fear-Free Because . . .

1 I have more than enough of what it takes to make it through the rough times and tight places.
2 God is always on duty!
3 The law is on my side.
4 This day belongs to God!
5 I know that every experience opens my heart to a greater and grander experience.
6 I know what time it is!
7 I am diligent! I am patient! I am built for the victory!
8 God is still God after all of these years!
9 I know what to do without doing anything at all.
10 I am willing to test what I know.
11 I can see in the dark.
12 I cannot lose when I play life by the rules!
13 I know exactly who I am.
14 I am aware that fear of failure leads to failure.
15 God always delivers what God has promised to deliver.
16 I am never alone.
17 I know that my greatest challenge will strengthen me.
18 I know what I have to do.
19 I have something to do and someone to be.
20 I know that I don't have to know.
21 I am not afraid to look at my life.
22 I am on a search-and-recovery mission, led by a divine rescue squad.
23 My heart always knows what I need to know.
24 I have a wonderful imagination that imagines wonderful things for my life.
25 Every concern I have is a concern of God's.
26 Having one grain of what is true will eradicate a million grains of what is not true.
27 I know the power of truth.
28 I am a celebration of love.
29 I have been fire-proofed.
30 I am being transformed from the inside out.
31 I am learning to swim through painful experiences.

SEPTEMBER: TRUST

I Experience and Express the Power
of Trust Because . . .

1   I am learning to trust myself.
2   I understand the connection between trust and faith.
3   I always begin within.
4   I am no longer willing to betray myself.
5   I put my trust in the right things for the right reasons.
6   I am worthy of my own trust.
7   I know how to stand up to the dark forces.
8   I have a clear understanding of what it takes to make things happen!
9   I put my energy behind the things I put my trust in.
10 I assume that what I do will be successful.
11 I am relying on the presence of the Divine Troops to come to my assistance.
12 I know I cannot take the easy way out.
13 I believe that who I am is enough.
14 I am ready to have the things I want.
15 I realize I can never prove who I am with how much I do or give.
16 I am willing to do the work I need to do to learn more about myself.
17 I know I am divinely hooked up and spiritually hooked in.
18 If I ask the right questions I will get the right information I need.
19 I know I am not missing any steps I need to take.
20 There is a divine place to put anything that challenges me.
21 I recognize the difference between fact and fiction.
22 I am ready and willing to walk through fear.
23 God knows what I am to do.
24 I am willing to acknowledge different aspects of myself.
25 I am living in the present moment.
26 I am always prepared to be tested.
27 Everything I need always comes to me.
28 All of my debts have been paid.
29 I know I have nothing to worry about.
30 I finally realize that I don't have to figure it out.

OCTOBER: WORTH

I Will Realize My Own Worth When I Accept . . .

1   Myself exactly as I am.
2   Conditions and circumstances cannot confine me and do not define me.
3   Certain conditions in my life are like shoes; at some point they just don't fit me.
4   What I believe either pushes me into a hole or raises me toward the light.
5   I am worthy of my own company.
6   The story I tell is the story I live.
7   I am the most valuable thing that I have in life.
8   The labels placed on me don't always fit.
9   I have the power to convince myself that I am good!
10 There is a pure and right spirit within me.
11 I already know the answers to the questions I am afraid to ask.
12 My worthiness exactly as I am right now.
13 All aspects of who I am are important.
14 I am nothing to be ashamed of.
15 What I do for my own good will be good for everyone.
16 I have permission to spend time with myself.
17 What I tell myself I am, I am.
18 I cannot get away with inappropriate, unworthy behavior.
19 I have the power and the ability to create my ideal life.
20 God has given me some things that nothing can change.
21 It is not my job to make anyone else happy.
22 I cannot fight my way to the top.
23 Life does not have to be hard.
24 There is something good within me waiting to be released and realized.
25 I have access to a Divine source of information.
26 My life is a worthwhile expression of a divine energy and purpose.
27 What I do says a lot about who I believe I am.
28 How I take care of myself is important.
29 Everything I set out to do begins within me.
30 Miracles happen every day.
31 I am worthy of divine blessings.

NOVEMBER: SERVICE

The Greatest Service I Can Offer Is . . .

1   No expectation of recognition or reward.
2   A blessing.
3   A clear and loving message.
4   To remember that my heart is strong.
5   Elimination of my own self-doubt.
6   Open, honest, caring communication.
7   To step aside and let God in to someone's life.
8   Making up my own mind.
9   Open up to learning more, doing more and being more.
10 Being a light on the path.
11 To revive my heart, my mind and my life.
12 Being a star with a good and supportive cast.
13 Accepting the value and importance of who I am and where I am in life.
14 Doing what needs to be done.
15 Learning to recognize the root of the problem.
16 Living my life in grace.
17 Following the light of the Holy Spirit.
18 Willingness to do things in a new way.
19 Allowing myself to be used to serve a greater good.
20 Not engaging in crimes against myself.
21 Acknowledging all that I am aware of in my life.
22 Courageous investigation of everything I see, know and believe.
23 To always be observant.
24 Being the best of who I am.
25 Being gentle with myself as I change.
26 Standing confidently in my power.
27 Freeing myself to live freely.
28 Being willing to live through the pain I experience.
29 Resisting the tendency to be resistant.
30 Prayer.

DECEMBER: PEACE

I Will Be at Peace When . . .

1   I choose to be at peace, no matter what is going on.
2   I learn to focus on one thing at a time.
3   I stop finding excuses for what I am not doing.
4   I become teachable.
5   I learn to forgive myself.
6   I accept and acknowledge the truth.
7   I reclaim all the pieces of myself.
8   I organize my mind and my life according to the truth.
9   I make spiritual wealth a priority.
10 I allow myself to trust my vulnerabilities.
11 I heal my need for external acceptance and recognition.
12 I seek consolation in the right Source.
13 I examine what I feel beneath what I am feeling.
14 I start doing God's work.
15 I stop stewing in anger.
16 I am clear about what I am doing and feeling.
17 I learn to let go.
18 My learning is reflected in my doing.
19 I acknowledge that I have buttons that can be pushed.
20 I accept that things are the way things need to be.
21 Fear no longer determines what I do not do.
22 I take the time to experience the blessings of closure.
23 I am fully present in love in order to experience the full benefits of love.
24 I realize I am never alone.
25 I acknowledge all that God is, I am.
26 I can laugh at myself.
27 I am willing to be peaceful
28 I understand that love and peace work hand in hand.
29 I understand divine profits and losses.
30 I align myself with the way the universe works.
31 I put my confidence in my prayers.

INNER VISIONS WORLDWIDE NETWORK, INC.
926 Philadelphia Avenue
Silver Spring, MD 20910
Phone: 301.608.8750 Fax: 301.608.3813
http://Innervisionworldwide.com

Inner Visions Worldwide Network was founded by bestselling author, motivational speaker and empowerment specialist, Iyanla Vanzant. Iyanla began Inner Visions as a way of reaching out to and serving her many readers and supporters.

Inner Visions is a multi-cultural, multi-ethnic network of spiritual and holistic practitioners who embrace various spiritual philosophies. We believe that all individuals must be empowered. We believe that empowerment is a function of knowing who you are, why you are on the planet and the role you play in the divine order of life.

EMPOWERMENT BEGINS WITH HEALING!

We invite you to become a member of the Inner Visions Spiritual Life Maintenance Network and/or a student at the Inner Visions Institute for Spiritual Development (IVISD).

As a Network member you will . . .

- Learn how to consciously apply spiritual principles to your life
- Learn how to use affirmative prayer to create a shift in your life
- Receive a bi-monthly newsletter and Soulwork Assignment

Annual Membership Dues for UK $51.00 (Newsletter Only)

Name _____

Address _____

City _____ State _____ Zip _____

Phone (Day) _____ (Eve) _____

EMail _____

Payment: ❏ Check/MO ❏ Visa ❏ MasterCard ❏ AmerExp ❏ Discover

Account Number _____ Exp. _____

Card Holders Name _____

Card Holders signature _____